October 7,

LaCristal —

Thank you very much for your support. Keep the faith!

Sincerely,

A.P. Miller

Preach My Sister Preach

A Biblical Defense for Women in the Gospel Ministry

Alvin E. Miller, Sr., D. Min.

Copyright © 2015 Alvin E. Miller, Sr., D. Min.

All rights reserved. No part of this book may be used or reproduced by any means, graphic, electronic, or mechanical, including photocopying, recording, taping or by any information storage retrieval system without the written permission of the publisher except in the case of brief quotations embodied in critical articles and reviews.

Scripture taken from the King James Version of the Bible.

Front and back covers designed by Alvin E. Miller Jr. and are reproductions of *The Coronation of the Virgin*, originally painted by El Greco in 1591 CE (public domain). Picture is from Free Clip Art (totallyhistory.com/art-history).

WestBow Press books may be ordered through booksellers or by contacting:

WestBow Press
A Division of Thomas Nelson & Zondervan
1663 Liberty Drive
Bloomington, IN 47403
www.westbowpress.com
1 (866) 928-1240

Because of the dynamic nature of the Internet, any web addresses or links contained in this book may have changed since publication and may no longer be valid. The views expressed in this work are solely those of the author and do not necessarily reflect the views of the publisher, and the publisher hereby disclaims any responsibility for them.

Any people depicted in stock imagery provided by Thinkstock are models, and such images are being used for illustrative purposes only.
Certain stock imagery © Thinkstock.

ISBN: 978-1-4908-7239-1 (sc)
ISBN: 978-1-4908-7240-7 (hc)
ISBN: 978-1-4908-7238-4 (e)

Library of Congress Control Number: 2015903568

Print information available on the last page.

WestBow Press rev. date: 7/8/2015

Contents

Preface ix

Introduction xiii

1. Women Preaching the Kingdom of God 1
2. Women Called to the Gospel Ministry 29
3. God Has the Power to Break Down Walls 70
4. Women in the Ministry 99
5. The Separation of Church and State 124
6. The Deadly Force of Religious Legalism 141
7. God Promotes Women in Ministry 163
8. Jesus Endorses Women in Ministry 182
9. The Holy Spirit Empowers Women in Ministry 190

To my loving and supportive wife,
Lady Dominique Haywood Miller

Some people you meet are friends in passing,
But some people you meet are your family for life.
—Alvin E. Miller, Sr.

Preface

Preach, My Sister, Preach is a treasure chest that expounds on the Holy Scriptures and lays a clear and practical foundation for women to preach the gospel of Jesus Christ. It encourages women ministers to stand boldly and preach God's gospel with genuine conviction and without shame, guilt, or fear from anyone or any force that is contrary to God's calling. *Preach, My Sister, Preach* gives Christian women biblical evidence to support their divine calling, so they can stand boldly on the mandates of God's words without any reservation, intimidation, or fear.

Preach, My Sister, Preach is biblically sound and offers a safe haven for women ministers to process their calling seriously despite negative environments, denominational rules, and religious affiliations that are anti-female in relation to women serving in the Christian ministry as ministers and preachers of the gospel of Jesus Christ. When it comes to allowing women to exercise their God-given gifts of proclaiming the good news about Jesus through the preaching of the gospel, no human should attempt to stand in the way of such a gigantic and life-sustaining task and calling from God. If a judge summons you to court to testify, no one can stand in your way and say you do not have to make the court appearance without negative retribution, such as being charged with contempt of court. If God called you to testify on His behalf in court and give your testimony about what He has done for you, do not allow anyone or anything to hinder you from the world's largest courtroom. Always remember in God's court of justice, truth and righteousness always prevail.

I am appalled that men and women would try to deny the power of God in a person's life once God has deputized the person. I am even more concerned that bounty hunters in pulpits across America feel as though some of them have been commissioned by God to hunt down women ministers and bring them to justice. These 'so-called' deputies are encouraging women to acknowledge they have only been called to serve as missionaries, but not as preachers of the gospel.

This scavenger hunt process reminds me so much of how Saul, in the book of Acts, thought it was his job to be the champion bounty hunter for God and his religious sect. He later discovered he was wrong in his overzealous ambition to set things in order for God. Saul thought he was on target for God, but to God, Saul was totally out of his lane and a destructive influence for the initial expansion of God's kingdom on the earth. Saul thought he was doing God a favor by abolishing the threat of the newly formed Christian movement, which was on the rise in Israel. Even Saul learned he could not fight against the hand of God and win.

Since the job of beating and killing converts from this newly formed Christian religious sect was too dirty for Sanhedrin religious leaders, they commissioned a devoted Pharisee by the name Saul to do their dirty work for them. At the time, Saul felt it was part of his national and religious duty to prevent the spread of Christianity throughout the nation of Israel. This goes to show us sometimes a person's heart and commitment can end up in the wrong place when he or she does not fully undstand the plan of God. The person could mean well with all sincerity, but fights against the plan of God.

No one has the right to hinder another person from God. No man or woman has the right to interfere with another's journey of peace and goodwill toward humanity. No individual has the right to become a stumbling block in a man's or woman's life when God has paved the road for the person. No one has the authority to deny what God has approved just because he or she does not believe it or agree with it.

No man or woman has the right to speak against what God has ordained for the life of His creation. No person should have the freedom to dictate the vocational calling or occupational venture of another person and still feel good about himself or herself as a respectable human being. The man or woman of compassion and humility will strive to help others. He or she will become a reflection of the dreams and desires embedded in the heart of the sojourner as he or she travels the earth in search of justice, freedom, compassion, and equality for all God's people.

This manual challenges the chauvinistic doctrine and bigoted attitudes and spirit that have suppressed the gifts, talents, and creativity of women ministers for years, even centuries. I pray to God Almighty that a genuine change will occur in the hearts of men and women about how women in the ministry are viewed and hindered in a mostly male-dominated clergy world. It is my most sincere prayer that my brothers and sisters in the land where the gospel of Jesus rules supreme offer an olive branch and open their hearts and minds to accepting female ministers as co-laborers in the building of God's earthly kingdom as they attempt to obey their humble calling from God.

Introduction

Every Christian woman in ministry needs this book because it uses Scriptures from the Holy Bible to give them a biblical road map for understanding and validating their call to Christian ministry. It provides extensive biblical research, so women ministers can stand strong and demand their stake in God's kingdom as a servant and messenger, proclaiming the gospel of Jesus through the preaching ministry. Christian women must look to Holy Scriptures concerning their call to the ministry.

Female ministers should not allow the theological opinions of others or the philosophical advice from pundits hinder their calling to fulfill a mission from God. It is God who ordains one in ministry. Also, it is God who wills His Ministry, and it is God who has the final report card when the assigned mission succeeds or fails. God renders the final verdict concerning whatever accolades or punishments we will receive at the end of our journeys in this life. At the end of the day, it is all about what God has to say about a matter or issue and not about how we feel about it.

It is my desire that this book challenges people to consult the Word of God before formulating an opinion on political, social, ethical, and theological matters. We must keep in mind just because something may seem right, or look or feel right, does not make it right in the eyes of God. Christians need to be very careful about accepting the traditions of humanity for guidance and direction concerning the call of women into God's preaching ministry.

It is easy for parishioners or worshippers to get thrown off course or become misguided by people who withhold critical biblical evidence while presenting their reasons why they are against women preachers or ministers. It is a greater danger when religious leaders fail to tell the whole truth and nothing but the truth when arguing why they feel or believe women should not preach God's gospel. Do not ever forget Jesus Christ is the Holy One who saves men and women from their sins by the grace of the Father.

Once a person knows he or she has been called by God to feed and nurture His starving sheep, why is there a need to get the approval from someone else by asking, "Should I go and feed?" When a person is truly called by God into the gospel ministry, God will make clear his or her mission and purpose in the kingdom of God and life. When God has called you, the message is so powerful and clear you do not need to ask anyone if it is the right thing to do. God gives such simple instructions about His business that you will know without a shadow of doubt that you are the one who has been called for the greatest purpose in life!

Yes, you are the one who has been identified and chosen from a lineup by the Holy Spirit, even with others standing by your side. Only you have been selected by the "One and Only I Am," who never makes mistakes. The God we serve is perfect, omnipotent, and knows the future, even before it was printed on the calendar of history and the ages. The God we serve is so right that it is impossible for Him to go wrong or make a mistake. So, why would you allow anyone to make you question or doubt the decision God has selected you to serve in His army? God is the greatest recruiter in the world and knows the kind of soldier He needs to stand tall and fight for Him.

Whenever and whatever God calls, it is always the right response to accept His invitation without controversy or hesitation. It is amazing when God calls His sheep. The sheep know and should always respond to His voice with great enthusiasm and assurance. One of the greatest defense mechanisms sheep have is to discern and obey the voice of their shepherd. Being unable to hear or obey the shepherd's voice puts the sheep in great danger of becoming prey for predators. It is imperative the sheep know without hesitation the voice of the Great Shepherd. The sheep cannot afford to become stagnate or confused when they hear the voice of their shepherd calling them.

Like sheep, the urgency of fulfilling the mission when God calls us into service is such an important task that there is no time to waste. The preaching of the gospel of Jesus comes with great responsibility, accountability, and consequences. Women who have been called into the gospel ministry must not allow anyone to make them miss or deny their calling from God. Stay strong in the power of His might, and be courageous as you fulfill your purpose in life. The best appreciation you can give to the God that gave you life is to fully obey His words without compromise. Whatever God has commissioned you to do, do it to the best of your might under the power of the Holy Spirit and God will do the rest for you. If you remain faithful to the words of Jesus by going into the world and make disciples, God will protect you, provide for you and promote His agenda through you as you fulfill His mission of teaching all nations about Jesus (Matthew 28:19-20).

Furthermore, when God calls people into His gospel ministry, failing to answer or respond in the affirmative is not an option. When the Master calls a person, it is greater than when a federal judge summons a person to court to testify. When a person has been called to preach the gospel, literally the person has been summoned to appear before God Almighty! No one or nothing has a better track record for turning a loser into a winner than God. God's grace and mercy are the proof we are champions in Jesus! When you stand up for Jesus under the anointing of the Holy Spirit, what other proof do you need?

Furthermore, God is the only force I know who can take people who have been classified as losers by society or given up as hopeless by others, and give them new beginnings with new identities. God, like no other entity or power on earth, turns the defeated into victors and champions. Here is the final verdict. The only thing sheep needs to do in order to reap the blessings and benefit from God is to have a willing spirit and obedient heart to follow the voice and guidance (instructions and examples) of the Good Shepherd. When God calls a person into His ministry, answering the call at one's convenience is not an option either. Answering the call of God is always the most important thing in life.

Keep in mind some miracles in our lives will pass our way only once. We need to be ready and assertive to claim our blessings when they come our way. When the angel came down from heaven at a certain time of the year and stirred the water at the pool of Bethesda, the man kept missing his blessing because he could not get into the pool when the angel of God troubled the water (John 5:1-9). To maximize your potential and blessings, you need to take advantage of the moment because it may never come your way again.

As a young man, I missed opportunities and miracles that God had brought to me. I did not have vision to see what God was trying to do in my life. I reiterate, when God calls a person into His gospel ministry, He demands an immediate, and affirmative answer (Yes, Lord!). Remember, the calling of God is like being called to His emergency room to minister His love to hurting and dying people throughout the world. You cannot afford to miss out on the greatest opportunity in life, being a voice for God.

Since you know God has called you into His ministry, why debate your answer or calling in sanctuaries and classrooms across America? When you are convinced God has made the call on your life, what is there to debate? Since God is the only one who does the calling, this should settle the issue—whether others believe it or not! The overwhelming anointing of God's Holy Spirit will prove to be the most powerful evidence of His calling for your life and ministry.

On the other hand, keep in mind that more than likely you will never be able to convince anyone or prove anything to people who see things in a carnal manner. The Apostle Paul lets us know there is enmity between the Spirit of God and the flesh (carnality), and the flesh is constantly at war with the Holy Spirit (Galatians 5:17). People who live in the natural realm are unable to see the mantle of God resting upon your life.

When people attempt to make you question or abort your calling from God, they are not spiritual minded. Only the devil will tell a person that he or she has not been called to do the will of God. Only demons will put the thought into a person's mind or heart to disobey the calling of God. Only those who are without relationship with Jesus will tell a person to take a back seat when the Holy Ghost has given you a frontrow seat.

So, debating your calling with people holding onto the law and the world will never materialize into anything productive for the kingdom of God. We who are willing to listen to the voice of the Great Shepherd must never lose track of the fact that God's will for our lives is to move us from the natural world to His spiritual kingdom. When a person has been called by God, all he or she needs to do is obey Him and then watch the fruit of your labor speak in your life as the power of God validates your calling with miracles, signs, and wonders. Just believe and these signs shall follow you (Mark 16:17).

The best way to present to the world that you have truly been called into ministry is by preaching, teaching, and living the gospel daily with humility. Remember, some people will never believe in you no matter what you do or accomplish in life. Some people never believed Jesus was the Messiah or the Christ, regardless of what He did or how many miracles He performed. This does not change the fact God called you, just as Jesus is still the Messiah and Christ regardless of what people believe or think. You must continue moving forward in life with your marching orders from God.

My advice is to do whatever God has called and commissioned you to do. I beg you to please leave the debating and antagonistic rhetoric about whether God did or did not call women to the gospel ministry to the so-called self-righteous, modern-day Pharisees, Scribes, and Sadducees. Please know this about these groups; as you waste your time trying to prove to them God endowed you to preach His divine gospel, they will never accept you or believe God has called you into ministry. Think about this dilemma. If Jesus could not enlighten the Pharisees, Sadducees, Scribes and some of the others who rejected Him concerning God's words and actions, surely neither you nor I will be able to tell these people anything about His decisions and actions.

In the same way, there is a sector of people who will believe anything but the truth about God's Word. Even within the borders of America, there are those who will remain serial killers no matter what you do to try and transform them. There are rapists and child molesters who will not heed the laws of humanity, society, or God. Therefore, institutional incarceration is the best thing for some in our culture who threaten the safety and welfare of others within our society. No matter what we do to rehabilitate these people, the end results are always the same criminal and deviant behavior of destruction.

Likewise, the people who rejected Jesus' notion that He was indeed the Savior of the world are the ones who got angry when Jesus decided to extend compassion to sinners by allowing them to eat dinner with Him. Keep in mind the same "flamethrowers" who resisted Jesus wait anxiously to set us on fire if we do not follow their instructions and play by their rules (Matthew 9:10–13). To them, you either abide by their rules or lose your seat at their table. If you have truly been called by God, then regardless of the push and pressure to deny you of your calling, you will fight to find your place in His kingdom. You have to make up your mind to follow Jesus and accept your calling or play by the rules of those who will make up bias and unfair rules for you as they go along.

All I can say to you, my sister, is to make up your mind as to whose team you are on. Remember, you cannot play on both teams. Either you stand with Jesus or fall with the Enemy. As Jesus says in Matthew 6:24, "You cannot serve two masters; either you will hate one and love the other, or you will be devoted to one and despise the other one."

Matter of fact, modern-day religious taskmasters would have you believe they are so smart and brilliant that they have all the answers straight from the mouth of God. Yet they offer no solution for the fire burning in your bones and the fear you have about disobeying God if you do not preach His most holy Word. They offer no wise counsel for telling you how to scratch the itch that will not let you rest day in and day out.

Believe it or not, the people who try to talk you out of accepting your calling from God cannot explain the conversation you had with God, because they were not present during the conversation. They offer you no clear reasons why you cannot preach except for the explanation God does not call women to preach but only to teach in certain situations. Yes, they have lots of philosophical reasons, educational training, and theological education but no practical, biblically sound evidence why God does not allow women to be called to the preaching ministry.

The day God summons you to stand before His mighty throne, who will be able to stand in front of God and defend you? What man will plead your case for disobeying God? What person is willing to take your punishment for disobeying almighty God? What person can tell the almighty Father why he or she created or made you instead of God? I challenge you to name the person. If it does not spell God, ignore the sabotage. I charge you to plant your hands and feet to the gospel plow, and do not ever look back or let anyone or anything distract you (Luke 9:62).

Finally, religious elitists have the audacity to turn to one or two Scriptures to try and prove their point why women should not enter the preaching ministry while neglecting the whole truth of the matter concerning God's call for women ministers in the preaching ministry. They neither point out nor explain the Scriptures showing women being used in the preaching ministry. It is my desire to help enlighten you with a greater understanding where the Holy Bible lays Scriptures demonstrating the female role as ministers preaching the gospel of Jesus Christ. Once you have seen and read the evidence, you can witness for yourself the world of beauty that theological heretics do not want you to know. God takes the full liberty to use anything or anybody in His creation. With God, purpose is greater than the person or the personality of the individual being used for the glory of God!

Above all, we must remember the Word of God is the greatest ophthalmologist in the entire world and human history. The Holy Spirit allows the Word of God to open your eyes in such a way that it will give you better than 20/20 vision and clear understanding. The authentic Word of God is the most liberating, fascinating, rejuvenating, and soul-stirring experience you will encounter on this side of heaven. The thought of being able to preach and live your purpose on the earth as a preaching vessel for the kingdom of God is an exciting fulfillment beyond the comprehension of this world. Many people will not be able to understand the call of women to the preaching ministry because they are yet to move from the carnal to the spiritual world, where the Lord can allow them to witness the beauty of the vision.

Howbeit religious gurus (Pharisees, Sadducees, and Scribes) never accepted Jesus. Yet they ended up being the strongest advocates for nailing Jesus to the cross with trumped-up lies and plans of deceit laced with the vicious sting of jealousy and hate. Yes, the Devil used religious leaders to convince the Roman government that Jesus was an insurrectionist and needed to be crucified. Jesus' enemies convinced Roman leaders He was a threat to the Roman rule in the region and the peaceful stability in then Palestine, under the Roman occupation.

During the days of Jesus' earthly ministry, Israel was conquered and renamed Palestine by the Roman government. Yet in the eyes of God, the territory remained the Promised Land of Israel that God Himself deeded to the Hebrews (Matthew 23:13–39; 26:47–68). When God gives you a promise, no matter how many times the title or deed changes hands, it will eventually end up back with the promised person or people. In order for the promise to end up back in the hands of the blessed, the blessed must stay obedient to the promised giver and the promised keeper (God). What God has for you, it is for you. All you have to do is keep the faith, stay obedient, and trust the Lord and His Word!

Whenever God makes you a promise, He does not take it back. According to the Holy Scriptures, God is not slack concerning His Promises (2 Peter 3:9). And if God says your sons and daughters will prophesy in the last days after He pours out His spirit upon all flesh, and then they shall prophesy in the last days (Joel 2:28). Why would God pour out His Holy Spirit on all flesh if He did not intend for men, women, boys, and girls to be utilized in the fullness of His Holy Spirit and preach His Holy Word? Before we can read our mail or even get the mail into our possession, someone has to first deliver the mail to us by electronics (e-mail) or by some human intervention (mail carrier).

The mail's delivery process plays a vital role between the sender and the receiver. When the sender takes the time to write and mail a letter, he or she does it with the hopes of the receiver receiving the letter. Once the letter carrier delivers the mail to the intended person, then the sender of the mail expects the receiver to read the letter and respond to the letter in some way. The person sending the letter mails the letter with expectation of the letter reaching its final destination even in the midst of rain, sleet, snow or storm. Some letters and packages are sent certified or with delivery confirmation as a way of letting the sender know the message, letter or package was received on the other end.

Therefore, when God sends His Word out, he does not expect it to return to him void (Isaiah 55:11). When God calls a person, He expects a harvest of humility, obedience and righteousness. God understands this process better than anyone or anything. He is more concerned about the message getting to the receiver than the method He chooses to deliver His message. God used a dove to communicate His message to Noah. He used a cloud to lead the children of Israel across the desert, and he used a raven to feed the prophet Elijah while in the wilderness. Finally, God used a donkey to communicate his Word to Balaam (Genesis 8:11; 1 Kings 17:6; Numbers 22:28–30).

I would rather live with nothing, than to die with everything.
—Alvin E. Miller, Sr.

Women Preaching the Kingdom of God

The preaching ministry for the kingdom of God helps build God's kingdom on earth in such an unprecedented manner that it is beyond the grasp and control of humanity. The preaching of the gospel of Jesus Christ has riddled the minds, hearts, and souls of humanity across the ages. The recipe for the preaching ministry is unexplainable. Whenever it is conducted under the grace and anointing of the Holy Spirit, it is a wonder to behold. Though at times we try, humanity really cannot explain the miraculous power associated with the preaching ministry of God.

Moreover, if it were up to humanity to control the selection of who is chosen to preach, many of the great preachers across the pages of history would have been disqualified by justice and the law. Just think about this scenario I am about to share in the following sentence. Under grace and mercy, it is people like you and me who, under any other terms, would not have been considered for the job. Yet through the blood of Jesus, God puts out the call into His glorious kingdom to revamped sinners by the Holy Spirit.

Preaching is something any called-out person has the ability to do, regardless of the sound or pitch of his or her voice. Not everyone with a voice can carry a pleasant tune when it comes to singing, but every voice can be used to preach and teach the gospel of Jesus. From soprano to alto to tenor to baritone to bass, all voices can be used to preach and teach His gospel. Preaching is how God tells His creation that freedom and salvation are ours for the taking. All we have to do is grab them and hold onto them for dear life.

Also, the awesome beauty of the preaching ministry for the woman or man who has been called by God is so colorful, like the paint an artist uses to make scenes come to life on canvas. Never let anyone stop you from expressing the beauty of the preaching gifts and talents God has put in you for His glory. Even if you have to preach to nature, preach Jesus to the birds, bees, and flowers. Hopefully somebody is standing by and listening to you as you preach the Word of God. You just never know how God will use an obedient and willing heart.

The preaching ministry is a validation license only God can give. Although a person may go online to get various degrees or certifications or may even go to seminary to get credentials, only God can qualify a person through the Holy Spirit to preach the gospel of Jesus Christ. Even an ordination ceremony can only be validated by God as a result of the fruit a person produces for His kingdom. Regardless of the decisions of humanity, denominational affiliations, councils, boards, and/or institutions, the authentic call to ministry comes from God.

Institutions, councils, boards, denominations, and associations may be able to give papers, licenses, degrees, certificates, and ordination rights, but only God can give His anointing to fulfill a calling into the preaching ministry. A person's ability to wear the shoes of greatness does not mean he or she has the gift or ability to walk in the footsteps of greatness in the kingdom of God. Only Jesus and the Holy Spirit can lead a person to the only well where living water is plentiful.

The beautiful sound of the good news can come in good sounding voices to the ear or bad sounding voices to the ear. Yet the sound is still good news because God has willed it. The quality of the voice does not affect the message that conveys an important communication from God. When people are in need of miracles and blessings from God, they do not care which postal carrier delivers the message, blessing, or miracle. As long as the message gets to the right person in a timely fashion, both the sender's and receiver's needs are met as things line up for the good of the whole. It is up to God to decide which postal worker (male or female) will deliver His awesome messages to His people.

I challenge everyone who has a problem with women ministers to take the issue up with God, and let's see if your prayers get answered. Keep in mind God is not in the business of caring about whether the Devil is happy or angry. So if preaching God's Holy Word angers some, just remember your aim is to please Jesus and not to cater to the wishes or desires of men or women and other things that are apart from God. Whenever we in the church get into the business of pleasing people, then we have lost our focus on Jesus, and kingdom building becomes a chore instead of a joy.

When we reflect on gentleness, righteousness, holiness, awesomeness, and compassion of Jesus during His earthly ministry, we see established religious entities in the region never accepted Him for what He offered to the world and the kingdom of God. As a minister of the gospel of Jesus Christ, the first thing you must come to grips with is the understanding that not everyone is going to accept or appreciate you as a minister. Some people will even be angry because you did not get their approval before accepting your call into the ministry. Others will reject you because they can no longer control your destiny. A few will embrace you and encourage you with unselfish support and excitement for the braveness and the determination you have shown as you sacrificed all to follow Jesus, just like the early disciples wholeheartedly followed Him after the resurrection and ascension.

According to the Holy Bible, it was the chief priests and elders who took counsel against Jesus to put Him to death. (See Matthew 27:1, 17–35, 40; Mark 14:53–65; 15:1, 10, 11–24; Luke 22:52–67; 23:1–7, 13–26; John 18:3–14, 22–24, 28, 35–40; 19:6–18.) The same wicked spirit that conspired to kill Jesus during His earthly ministry is the same diabolical spirit conspiring to kill the zeal, dreams, and ministries of women who have been sanctioned by God to preach His divine words. This attitude is an evil spirit designed to create a stumbling block in lives of women and the life of the church in order to keep women from excelling in the ministry.

My sisters, there are many pastors and preachers out there who believe the Lord has called you to serve as one of His leaders. So please do not lose heart and allow some contrary spirit that is totally against God's plan stop you from fulfilling this divine mandate God has entrusted you to handle for Him. Hope and obedience are always greater than doubt and disobedience.

Moreover, failing to exercise the authority and rights God has given you is a sign of walking in darkness and not in the marvelous light of Jesus. Since Jesus came to liberate us from the law, why should you allow its enforcers to continue to make you live under the law. If we continue to live under the law, we shall die under the law, which offers us no salvation (Galatians 3:10–25). What sense does it make for God to send us His Son to die on the Cross so we could go free, yet we make the choice to continue living in the deplorable conditions of the filth of sin? If this is the case for some, then why did Jesus die on the Cross? Each individual that has been called to preach the gospel of Jesus must answer the question whether to live under the law of spiritual and personal bondage or in the Spirit of God through grace and truth.

Men and women who insist you are not to preach because you are a female possess the same spirit that the apostle Paul had to combat when the religious zealots told Gentiles they needed to become circumcised before they could become saved by Jesus (Galatians 5:1–15). Keep in mind the Evil One will use any person or thing that will submit to him in order to confuse you or put fear in your heart and keep you from carrying out the will of God. If you give evil an audience and listen to the Devil's agents, he will make you think you are walking against God's will for your life. The Devil will not only have you questioning your call into the ministry, but if you listen to him rant and rave, he will even have you second-guessing your salvation.

As a strong woman of God, you must be willing to stand boldly for Jesus, look the bully in his eyes, and tell the Devil, "I will face and conquer my fears because Jesus Christ is always here with me" (Matthew 28:19–20; Luke 8:50). The Devil's intimidation tactic is why it is important for a person to know without a doubt who has called him or her into service. Also, it is imperative to the minister's stability that he or she has truly processed the discipleship journey in heart, mind, body, and soul.

Likewise, it is even more essential for you as a minister of the gospel of Jesus to be prepared for the battle that awaits you. It is a war you neither picked nor volunteered to fight; you just want to be a disciple for Jesus and serve His earthly kingdom as best you can. Yet you fail to realize that the very second you become a born-again believer, it is like raising your hand to take an oath of office to serve in the military forever. Your calling to serve as a minister for Jesus is an everlasting calling, and God has moved you to the front lines so you can help build His kingdom on earth.

Whatever the case may be, you cannot stand down and succumb to the Devil's ego and power struggle to silence the preaching of the gospel through you, as you serve as the vessel. The preaching of gospel ministry is going to be like a raging battle. At times you will have some success, winning souls for the kingdom of God, and at times you will have some losses. Through it all, however, the benefits and victories far outweigh the risks and losses. As the old song says, "You just cannot beat God's giving no matter how you try."

As for me, I would rather be wrong for doing right than to be right while doing wrong. In other words, obey God rather than the cultural mores, denominational standards, religious traditions, and theological interpretations and practices. Sometimes society norms will try to make you think you are wrong when you are right. Other times, you may even be persecuted for doing the right things in the eyes of God. Whichever way the tides turn, you just have to be prepared to stand on holy ground for God.

Sometimes it seems as though some people the Devil uses to distract or discourage us from seeing, listening, or obeying God are those we love the most. Some of our greatest discouragers are people we are closest to (relatives and friends). For some unique reason, our guard tends to go up when we enter the presence of our enemies because it is a fact our enemies do not desire the best for our lives.

Yet we tend to let our guard down around family members and friends, either by natural instinct or through learned behavior. If the truth be told, many of us have been hurt and terrified the most by family members or those we consider friends. We often let down our defenses for those we like or love, simply because somewhere in the back of our minds, we tend to think they love us and will not hurt us.

Sadly, we sometimes find out later that our false sense of love was our imagination playing tricks on our reality. Many times those we love with great intensity are the ones who cause us the greatest hurt, pain and shame. It seems like we tend to love them more than they love us. By human nature people are selfish and self-centered without Jesus ruling in their lives. Although they may not mean to hurt you, they will indeed hurt you when there is no solid relationship with Jesus.

Sometimes it is in our family and friendship settings where our feelings and emotions are abused the greatest. Yes, people you think would be excited about you being called into the ministry will shun and scorn you the most. People you look to embrace your calling will sometimes end up being the ones to reject you and your calling. They may reprimand you for even thinking in such a deranged manner. This is why the preaching ministry sometimes ends up a lonely place to reside. Do not allow the opinions of others to sway you from the calling of God.

If you ever start feeling lonely about your calling or while serving on the preaching trail, this is the time the Devil will take the opportunity to try and convince you that you are out there by yourself. No one cares about your happiness and well-being like you. As a woman minister of the gospel of Jesus, you cannot afford to let anyone evade the comfort zone where you meet with Jesus for solace. You need to follow the example of Moses. When Moses, in the book of Exodus, went up the mountain of God to speak with Him, he left Aaron behind. You, too, need to leave Aaron behind so you can hear from God without any distractions.

Our loved ones or closest friends sometimes cross the line by attempting to give us words of advice or encouragement about how we should go about accepting our call to the ministry. I shared with my Sunday school class how it amazes me when people try and tell pastors how to pastor within the various churches though they have never served as a pastor. Nor have they been trained in the theological arena. Yet they have all the answers for pastoring or leading a church or congregation. All I can do is advise you to be careful and watch out for agitators and great debaters. Some will approach you with their own rendition of what "thus says the Lord" means based on their personal thoughts and opinions.

One thing that puzzles me the greatest historically and biblically speaking, God does not call people into the gospel ministry through other people or based on other people's recommendations or sanctions. God is driven neither by the crowd nor the individual but only by His divine will. There is much greater value when someone takes and passes the test, rather than when he or she has someone else take the test and accepts the passing score of the other person's efforts. There is a greater legitimacy and opportunity to convince others in the process when you speak for yourself, rather than when someone else speaks for you about your salvation. Your experiences and relationship with Jesus are the passport you need to board the salvation train and make the trip to the Promised Land.

I am blown away by the pompous attitude of some people who feel they have the right to select or give God input about who He should select into the preaching ministry. I want to know what gives a sound-minded person the audacity to think God has commissioned him or her to put people in order (a sort of chastisement) or in line as to their willingness to follow and obey the leading of the Holy Spirit. This act of disrespect by some people is proof that people are selfish and seem to care about accomplishing their own agenda even if it means ruling and ruining the lives of others.

When God calls someone to His ministry, the initial negotiation and meeting is between God and the person. The person being called is probably already going through a range of emotions and does not need any additional stress, pressure, or roadblocks put in his or her way. Answering the call into the gospel ministry is such a powerful, serious, and sacred moment. The person being called probably needs as much peace of mind and tranquility as possible in order to have the necessary capability to chime in and hear the voice of God.

It is imperative that the listening ears of those being called by God and their ability to hear not be compromised in the least bit. Hearing God's voice with urgency, clarity, and precision is crucial to the life of the minister being called by God. The ability to hear God's voice clearly will have a significant impact on the minister's relationship with God. When God speaks in the lives of others, there is always another voice that comes to bring confusion, chaos, disobedience, and division in the lives of those God is speaking to.

As human beings, we are given individual lives and born into the world by ourselves (one by one). Although you may be an identical twin or more, you were born at a different time than your sibling. When we are called by God into the gospel ministry, it is not as a package deal, like two for the price of one. Each person God calls comes as an individual agreement and commitment. Every person must decide for himself or herself whether to follow His beckoning or try to run and hide, like Jonah. Even though there are some husbands and wives who may serve as copastors in various ministries, when all is said and done, neither can vouch for the other about his or her calling from God. No person can validate another person's calling into the gospel ministry.

The call to Christian ministry is proven by the godly evidence of the fruit someone renders while serving in the Master's vineyard. The called-out person's testimony is proven by his or her actions in the kingdom of God. The self-worth of the minister is not by the person's past sins, which took place in the world of darkness he or she left behind and where sin reigned as the master chef. The value of the preacher becomes connected to the Cross where Jesus died for the sins of the world. The commitment of the minister must prove to be invaluable like the treasures the wise men brought to Jesus.

The best way to determine if a person can cook is to put him or her in the kitchen and then let the results speak for themselves. A sign of an experienced and good cook is the ability to make something good happen every time he or she enters the kitchen with a cooking task at hand. Even if the professional cook does not have all the necessary tools to prepare a meal, he or she will improvise and come up with a method or means to turn a shortfall into plentiful and a deficit into opportunity. This is the success story of a good cook. When God calls you, your excuses will not exempt you from answering the call to duty.

Regardless of the kitchen or the circumstances, he or she has the innate ability to prepare a good meal, no matter what ingredients you give. The cook makes great things happen in the kitchen without complaining or making excuses about what he or she did not have to accomplish the expected task at hand. Ministers who have been called to the ministry should not complain about what they do not have in order to feel equipped for the gospel ministry of Jesus Christ. When God calls a person into His ministry, He provides the person with the things that are needed to succeed. God is greater than what you know and believe. He is the All Powerful!

When a person is called into the ministry, he or she becomes like a professional cook/chef. The called-out one cannot sit aroud and procrastinate about fulfilling his or her calling from God. Once he or she has gotten the revelation concerning God's demand to produce quality service regardless of supplies and equipment, then he or she will have a better understanding that is not by his or her might to prepare a sufficient meal, but it is by the grace of God that renders the power to succeed. With the cook, he or she must have a keen understanding that the people are hungry, and they must be fed the Word of God.

Therefore, if the cook does not feed the people of God a well-balanced meal that is able to feed the souls of men and women, then the people will eventually suffer from malnutrition and possibly die of starvation. Anytime people anywhere die of starvation, it is an indictment on the entire human race, especially considering the plentiful resources the world has to offer. When people die because God's chef refuses to answer the call from God and feed His sheep, now the cook has to answer to the Master Chef of the kitchen.

God is more concerned with the minister's obedience to teaching the sheep about His righteous living than the supplies that are lacking in the cook's kitchen. God can do more with an obedient chef with a little food than He can with a disobedient chef with a kitchen running over with food, experience, training, instruments, and equipment. The Lord is looking for servant workers who will stand in the gap to lead His sheep to the Promised Land. Are you willing to serve as one of God's chefs, even though the kitchen will sometimes get very, very hot from the heat of persecution and hatred?

The person who has been called into the gospel ministry must understand the clock for his or her examination period starts the moment God makes you aware of His call on your life. The clock of divine responsibility for accepting your personal invitation from God does not start from the moment the person accepts God's calling, but from the time God makes the initial notification to your heart. Example: God's calling on one's life is like making a long distant call back in the olden days. The cost of a long distance telephone call started when the telephone on the other end started to ring and not when the person picked up the telephone.

When God calls, your clock starts ticking, whether you answer the line or not or become obedient to the call or not. The most important thing to remember is it is a *call from God*. It is a good thing to never forget it is God, through the Holy Spirit, that equips us with the necessary tools to promote His divine gospel, even though we are nothing but frail and sinful beings. This alone is a reflection of the awesomeness and beauty of God the Father; we are still sinners, but He continues to use us for His divine glory. Amen.

Moreover, I am blown away by how the grace of God allows us to transform and gives us the power so we can become in God what we could never become separated from Him. The Holy Bible teaches us that even when our hearts condemn us, God is greater than our hearts and knows everything (1 John 3:20). Sometimes in life you may not feel like you are worthy to serve as a disciple for Jesus. But, through the grace and mercy of God the Father, you end up being counted as one of the saints.

Furthermore, we must never forget to keep the faith and trust that our God is much bigger and more powerful than our hearts, feelings, minds, and emotions. It is imperative we know the force that is constantly trying to make us turn away from the love of the Father. The hate and jealousy of the Devil is no match for the Holy Spirit. All we have to do is believe and trust God, and in the process of the journey, enjoy the blessings of Jesus as He fights the battle for us. As I have said over and over, the victory has already been won on Calvary. All we have to learn to do is celebrate in the joy of the Lord!

Imagine if God allowed men to have input or determine if women could preach the gospel. What would stop men from deciding a certain ethnic group could also not preach, similar to the way ministers of African descent were held captive and denied the right to fulfill their preaching calling by some of their Caucasian slave owners (masters). Yes, they were so-called masters during American slave era, which lasted over three hundred years. What would stop another ethnic group from ruling supreme over another ethnic or racial group by refusing to recognize its citizens as authentic ministers of the gospel?

The Lord seems to make the call personally as to who will minister the gospel through some kind of divine intervention. When God personally makes this call, it tends to reduce the confusion about who is doing the calling. It gives receivers ammunition and willpower to stand strongly against critics who question and challenge their bids for acceptance of their calling in the Christian ministry.

Thank God humanity has not an ounce of control when it comes to the distribution of grace, mercy, and salvation. I am so thankful to God that no one but Jesus holds the key to accepting or denying the calling of a person into the gospel ministry. If this were not the case, the Hebrew brothers probably would have rejected Saul/Paul when he initially accepted his call from Jesus in chapter 9 of the book of Acts.

God is responsible for determining who will serve as ministers. As a result, He makes the call to the person being summoned for a lifetime of service on God's team. The recruiting role God plays is very significant, especially if the person later wants to develop amnesia or ignores the voice of God somewhere during his or her journey on the gospel mission to preach. Once the person has agreed to the terms and conditions of the everlasting contract from God, there is no turning back without some type of devastating consequence. There is no such thing as opting out of your contract without stiff penalties. Once God has drafted you there is no free-agency rule after the term of your initial contract; because your contract with God is for eternity. Jesus has already negotiated the salary for you on the Cross.

Another reason it is important for God to personally make the call is because in some cases, things intensify while the person is on the ministry trail. When God makes the call, the individual's personal accountability and responsibility commitment cannot be shifted to someone else. Some people tend to want to hide behind the success or work of others. However, with God serving as the rater and grader, it is impossible for anyone to hide or attempt to shift the blame or responsibility to someone else.

By God allowing things to be controlled by His hands, no one can blame anyone else for failures, shortcomings, or disobedience to follow Jesus. Once you accept your calling from God, be prepared to walk through the valley of the shadow of death without fear. When the group you thought loved you begins to turn on you, you will see and feel the pain the writer of Psalms 13 and 22 endured when he felt rejected by the almighty Creator. Although you may have to walk through the shadow of death, it does not mean you have to die. Keep living in Jesus is the best advice I can offer you.

When you become part of the greatest team in history, you become a threat to the most evil Enemy throughout time. He is a hater of humanity and has levied the greatest attack on God's creation. Once you accept your personal calling from Jesus, you become the bull's-eye on the world's largest target. Claiming to be a Christian or disciple of Jesus puts you on the market for attacks from the Devil as well as greater blessings from the Lord Jesus. Remember, greater is He that is in you than he that is in the world (1 John 4:4).

A reminder to those doubting God's call of women ministers, it was not too long ago that people argued against women's right to lead as entrepreneurs, politicians, business owners and managers, supervisors, head athletic coaches, presidents of universities, and so on. Some opponents said women could not be pilots on major airlines, and even went as far as restricting them to serve only as stewardesses (not flight attendants, as they are referred to today). Women were not allowed to fly fighter jets in combat. Nor were they allowed to serve as mission commanders aboard NASA space vehicles headed to the moon or on other space missions.

Furthermore, many women were forbidden from serving in the medical field as doctors. Women were confined to serve as nurses and in other technical areas in the medical field. Women were also forbidden to serve as police officers. Women were shortchanged, not by their lack of abilities and talents, but by a sexist and bigoted society that refused to give them opportunities to excel as a respected member on the team of creation and humanity.

I will explain later that it has not been too long ago that the U.S. Military started allowing women to serve in combat units and go on the battlefield as combatants. It was during President Obama's Administration that an Executive Order was issued allowing women to serve in combat branches in the U.S. Military. The Commander-in-Chief's Exective Order lifted all combat restrictions prohibiting females from serving in combat related fields and roles that in the past only males could serve. This change from the Oval Office is a positive change for the overdue progress of women and America.

Also, many states during the middle and late 1800's, had laws on their books against women being at the helm of government agencies and serving as positive representations in public life as governors, senators, court judges and Supreme Court Justices. It is this kind of practice that led to the Women's Suffrage Movement with Susan B. Anthony, Elisabeth Cady Stanton and Sojouner Truth. Just as those old Jim Crow laws would not allow African American/Blacks to excel in key positions in society, the same diabolical force attacks women ministers in America simply who only want to preach as God has ordained them. These women of the cloth only want to fulfill the task God has given them without discrimination, bigotry, or some sexist stalemating or human stumbling blocks standing in their ways.

Oh, by the way, did you know Sojourner Truth was one of the first recognized women ministers in America to preach the gospel of Jesus Christ? According to an article written in 2003 "This Far by Faith, Sojourner Truth" by the Faith Project, Inc. somewhere between 1826 and 1828, Sojourner Truth claims to have received the baptism of the Holy Spirit and walked to Freedom by leaving the Dumont's farm (former Plantation) in rural New York. Around 1828, Truth moved to New York City and soon thereafter she became a preacher in the Pentecostal tradition. It was her faith and preaching that brought her into contact with abolitionists and women's rights crusaders.

Let us not play games and act like women were not degraded and denied the opportunities their male counterparts had. We now live in a time when women are allowed to excel in ways like never before in America. Women still have bias and sexist hurdles to face, especially in the religious arena. Under the leadership of President Barack H.

Obama, women probably have been granted more opportunities to excel on levels comparable to their male counterparts, especially in the workplace, and have access to a wider range of health-care benefits and in the U.S. Military. As of 2013, President Obama signed an executive order lifting the ban on women serving in combat roles and positions once off-limits by military regulations.

Women must allow God to navigate their destinies in the kingdom of God. Women standing boldly in the gospel ministry cannot let men or anything other than the will of God control their destinies in God's kingdom. Yes, the Holy Bible teaches all of us to submit to our leaders, but *never* at the cost of disobeying God the Father. Spiritual leadership that is in tune with the Holy Spirit will never encourage anyone to go against the "move of God."

Also, the "move of God" seems to always do something totally different from what we think the natural order of things should be, according to our experiences and understanding of God. God has a tendency to defy the natural order of things for His glory. The natural order says when you die and are dead for three days, you are not coming back to life. But for the glory of God, Jesus rose from the dead on the third day. He defied the natural order of creation when the grave could no longer hold Him in the shackles of mortality. When the Holy Spirit calls you to preach whether male or female, God releases the person from the shackles of the natural order and takes the person to the spiritual realm of His glory.

Likewise, throughout biblical history, God has always had a way of confounding the wisdom of this world with His own way of doing things. God does not have to follow the same recipe, road map, directions, or instructions as humans in order to get holy results. Everything God does is holy, and He does not have to worry about passing anyone's inspection or test. Men in ministry should keep in mind when the veil of the temple was rented in twain, it abolished the fiduciary relationship or direct human representation between God and humanity. The splitting of the veil of the temple took the legal representation from the priest under the Law to plead your case to God, and put you at the throne of God to plead your own case by the grace of Jesus. The separation of the veil meant all humanity has the same relationship with God as the high priest or any other male representing the priesthood (Matthew 27:50–51).

When President Abraham Lincoln signed the Emancipation Proclamation, it should have freed all the African slaves across America on January 1, 1863. The truth of the matter is not all of the slaves got the message, at least not mentally. Like many former slaves, their minds were so conditioned to the diabolical acts of slavery that they were never able to recover from slavery. When a nation enslaves a group of people for hundreds of years and releases them, keep in mind the abolishment of slavery is not washed away by the stroke of a pen. One must never forget the mental, spiritual and environmental conditions of slavery have an everlasting effect on people's lives for generations like the deadly radiation of an atomic bomb.

Yes, to some degree *physical* slavery ended with the Emancipation Proclamation, but in all actuality, slavery in the mind and heart won out in the lives of many former slaves. Nearly everywhere in the South where the former slave went, there were constant reminders of the cruelty and dehumanizing conditions of slavery. Even today, in the year of Lord and Savior 2014, there are still reminders within our culture and society that slavery is just around the corner, lurking to rule as king again.

According to the teachings of the gospel message of the Holy Spirit, God gave grace to the disciples of Jesus. No longer are we bound by the practices under the law. We are now free to live under the blessings of grace and mercy. The splitting of the temple's veil from top to bottom signified to the world God was doing a new and fresh thing in the lives of His people (all those surrendering their lives to Jesus). The separation of the veil of the temple is God's way of allowing all humanity (participants) to see what is behind curtain #1, rather than just the high priest who was there to make atonement for our sins.

Under the new covenant Jesus has allowed all of us to become priests. Through the Holy Spirit we now can bring our own sins and issues to God. Everyone not only has a right to the Tree of Life but can also venture into the ranks of the Holy of Holies with a relationship with Jesus, something only the high priest could have under the law. God's grace has given us safe passage to His throne and presence, without a middle man acting on our behalf (Hebrews 9:3–12). Praise God for the liberation and joy grace brings to our lives through the Holy One of Israel. Amen. What a wonderful friend we have in Jesus!

Furthermore, under grace, mercy, and salvation in Jesus Christ, God has given all of us the opportunities to become high priests in a sense of servanthood for the kingdom of God. As priests in the kingdom of God, we now have the right to bring our sins, issues, problems, and concerns to God's altar, regardless of whether we are male or female. The powerful and enlightened teaching ministry of Jesus has given us a more practical image of how God respects and loves all His creation and especially the endorsement of women in ministry. Jesus' teaching has taught us God is more concerned about the heart of the person rather than the sex or ethnicity of the vessel. His love is greater than our limited abilities and understanding about who He decides to use to fulfill His plan by making disciples of men and women, as the Holy Bible instructs us in Matthew 28.

According to the teachings of Jesus and the Holy Bible, please tell me where has gender status become more important than recruiting people into the kingdom of God, where lives and souls can receive salvation? If our roles in life are to help bring lost souls to Jesus, why should we ever get bent out of shape about the vehicles used to tow damaged automobiles and wrecked vehicles to the automotive and collision shop for repairs? It seems a very selfish and prideful act on the part of those opponents that seems to be laced with the lethal poison of self-righteousness to reject a messenger of God because God has chosen her to be a woman. Hopefully this is not the signal Christians wish to posture as a position in the family of God and throughout the world.

According to the Pharisees and the traditions of men, the woman who met Jesus at the well in chapter 4 of the gospel of John had no business being at the well at the same time as Jesus. By the traditions of men, the woman was too unclean to be in the presence of a Jewish rabbi. Local congregational rules forbade the woman from having a conversation once she found out about the priestly role of Jesus. However, since Jesus is in charge of the entire universe, He has the right to make the rules and change them at will, and no one has the power to usurp His authority. People seem to forget God is in charge, and if He did not want woman in His presence, conversing with Him, or for her to play a major role in the history of the gospel message, Jesus would have done something more permanent after the fall of man to prevent women from preaching His divine words.

What confuses me the greatest about the entire matter concerning women ministers is when I see male ministers reject the notion women are called to preach based on their sexuality. Yet, they turn around and preach sermons of encouragement to women about the woman at the well with Jesus and tell inspiring biblical stories about how women were the first disciples to tell other disciples Jesus had risen from the dead. They fight the very thing they preach about. How can you slam and tear down women's self-esteem on one end, and then turn around and attempt to build them up on the other end?

The only time the Holy Bible recalls that God reprimanded women as a whole for being out of order was in the Garden of Eden. Eve and Adam disobeyed His commandment not to eat from the Tree of the Knowledge of Good and Evil (Genesis 3). Even during the punishment of man and woman in the Garden of Eden, God still extended a great deal of grace and mercy to both the man and the woman. I believe if God never intended for the woman to preach the good news about Jesus, He would have implemented the curse sentence during this very crucial time in the life of humanity. Other than this episode, God has never cursed women across the board.

For men to coerce women to accept an unjust law that God did not call women to the preaching ministry of Jesus Christ is a blatant abuse of pastoral leadership and powers by male pastors and ministers. To deny God's calling is to accept the devil's curse of disobedience. For women not to accept their calling to preach the gospel of Jesus Christ due to humanity's fear is a greater curse. So, with this being said, all I can tell you godly women is, "Preach, my sister, preach." And do not stop preaching for anyone! Do not even look back once you have put your hands on the gospel plow, because there is much work to be done, and God has called you to prepare the field for a great harvest. Amen.

When God uses someone to help build His earthly kingdom, it is not due to the physical or mental attributes the person brings to the table. If the individual's physical ability or mental might were the criteria, none of us would be good enough prospects for the Holy Spirit to use because we all have been contaminated by sin. As the writer of Romans 3:23 says, "All have sinned and fall short of the Glory of God!" Therefore, God is more focused on the "plate of humility" one can bring to the banquet table to share in a feast with God. Men and women who are truly called by God will not bring their own "ego-dish" to God's table. They will surrender under the helm of obedience to the Holy Spirit and recognize they are only at the table because grace and mercy, through salvation, advocated for them to have a seat at His table.

Over the years, I have observed people who appreciate life with the understanding it is a very special gift from God. These people are some of the most warmhearted and appreciative people on the earth. I am convinced appreciative people do not allow themselves to get caught in fights without any kingdom value or spiritual blessing. Neither do appreciative people involve themselves in struggles or battles that diminish the gospel of Jesus Christ. Appreciative people will be so grateful they are invited to the dinner feast of the Lord that they will not have time to look over their shoulder to see who else is at the banquet. They will not want to look over the guest list to see who was or was not invited to the feast of the Lord. They are just happy God did not leave them out.

By not trying to dictate to God who He can or cannot call into His ministry is another way we demonstrate to the Lord our attitude of gratefulness. People who have a humble spirit of gratitude always tend to demonstrate their most sincere thankfulness by having a willingness to stay in their respective lanes. People who have good driving records tend to stay in their lanes and follow traffic signs and signals with integrity. When men and women become intoxicated on something other than the Holy Spirit, they become reckless and deadly to the plan and will of God.

We must keep in mind that God gives gifts and talents to all of us as He deems necessary according to His choosing. None of us has the privilege, right, or authority to sit down with God and handpick our gifts and talents. God does not run a Burger King operation, whereby you can order from a menu and "Have it your way." Whatever gifts and talents God gives us can only produce the desired results if we have faith in Jesus. Believe it or not, the mistake many people make with their gifts and talents is failing to recognize all gifts come from God, so we can glorify Jesus. Whenever a holy gift is used for unholy purpose or things, it becomes contaminated and loses its sense of direction. On many occasions, the gift or talent never finds its way back to its original purpose or home station.

Over the years, we have witnessed so many talented and gifted people's lives destroyed simply because somewhere along the road, they got off track and could not find their way home to God. Many of the great voices of soul music during the civil rights era—produced by Motown Records, Stax Records, and Atlantic Records—came out of the church and into nightclubs and other venues unrelated to church music. Many of these precious and anointed vessels God gifted with awesome talents never made it back to the church, where they received their starts.

No matter what your gifts or talents are, they will not produce their best results apart from the anointing of the Holy Spirit. At times, many gifts and talents might produce great results only *because* they come from God, who is the giver of all good and perfect gifts (James 1:17). But a person will never give his or her best effort or produce the best product apart from the Lord. God has set it up so that He will never allow us to give our greatest praise and glory to the Devil.

However, if you want the greatest results over the long haul, only Jesus has the omnipotent power to bless the fruit of your labor. With the anointing of the Holy Spirit, your gifts and talents will not only produce great results. God will allow them to produce awesome dividends for His glory as well. The residual dividends from heaven's blessing fall downward with an awesome overflow, which blesses others around, above, and beneath you. God gives believers overflowing blessings that just keep on coming. This is one of the greatest blessings that come with serving God. One thing I can almost guarantee you is you will overflow with blessings of great joy when you totally sell out for Jesus Christ.

If a person's calling was validated by his or her physical characteristics or mental status, the law would take precedent over grace. God forbids such a thing from happening. Under the law, there seems to be greater emphasis put on humanity's inability. Yet under the era of grace, in which we now live, emphasis is put on Holy Spirit empowerment, which allows us to overcome our human inabilities and shortcomings through the already shared blood of Jesus. Under the power of grace, we can become something we could not accomplish apart from the presence of God in our lives. Under the grace of God, we become more than just human beings. Under the grace of God, we become anointed human beings because the mantle of the Son of God has been passed on to us. This is why the Holy Scriptures say we are more than conquerors through Christ Jesus, who has loved us from the very beginning (Romans 8:37).

Therefore, our calling to the gospel ministry is about God's grace and should never be viewed as the contributions of our own works. When we put the focus on grace by our works, remember the works of the flesh will always point to works without grace or faith. The Holy Bible teaches us this philosophy is a deadly combination because the minute we think we have arrived because of our own doing, pride and failure become the evidence we cannot accomplish anything without the hand of God in our lives (Galatians 2:19–21). The calling of humanity to the building of God's kingdom is not about what we bring to the table. It is about the wisdom and lifesaving tools provided through the grace of God that we take away from the table and others will benefit from as we humble ourselves under God's mighty hand.

God has an awesome way of blessing us with supernatural and divine gifts once we enter His presence and sit down at His table of compassion and humility. Once a person has been blessed with the opportunity to sit and eat with the Holy Spirit, he or she will continue to hunger and thirst for this divine meal that only God can give to humanity. At God's table of compassion, the laws of bondage no longer reign king over our mortal bodies according to the words of God (Romans 6:12–14).

When we walk in the will of God, it is the most wonderful feeling and safest place in the world. When a person is in the presence of God, it is a time when the person is relieved of fear, guilt, or shame. The woman at the well, the woman they said was caught in adultery, and the woman with the issue of blood were all relieved of their guilt, pain, shame, and sins. These emotions have such strong holds on people's lives that they often choke the joy and life out of people before help can reach them. Jesus came to liberate us from the shackles of oppression and to give to us the spirit of freedom so we might serve in the kingdom of God with honor. When we submit to God's will by rendering all glory to Him, this is pleasing to the Father, Son and Holy Spirit. The local church can only move forward with godly leadership that is willing to follow Jesus to the Promise Land where bondage ceased to live.

Whenever we look at a divine calling, mission, or task and attempt to measure our success ratio based on physical or natural attributes of the person, it means we have lost touch with God somewhere along the way. When someone walks with God, he or she recognizes that self has been denied, and the Holy Spirit rules supreme. When a person turns to human knowledge and personal strength for spiritual security, there is a grave disconnection between God and that individual. Sizing up a situation based on a person's physical status or material gifts is not rational or sound judgment, to say the least.

When we make decisions based on what we know or do not know, or respond as a result of our physical or emotional buttons, unless God intervenes, more than likely the results usually end up contrary to His will. Whenever God calls or employs a person, He does not want the individual to bring a résumé or references to the interview. The truth of the matter is God will never check your references or look at your résumé because all of us are underqualified for what God is calling us to. God knows He cannot hire any qualified candidates or applicants unless He makes them worthy.

More important, it is God through His grace who gives us the job, even though we are not qualified. It is not until He gives us His stamp of approval for greatness as servants that we become equipped to carry out His mission. All God needs from us is to show up on the job and be ready to go to work for His kingdom with willing hearts. God prepares all employees with on-the-job training, using various trials, tests, and tribulations we encounter while on the job. I do not know of any company in the world where you can come to work with your mess and still get a blessing.

In spite of all our human frailties, did you know when you work for God you can make blunders and mistakes by the millions and not get fired—as long as you have a willing attitude and obedient heart? As God's employee, you are given a mentor/helper who never leaves your side. It is the motivator that makes you a successful disciple for Jesus. Always remember that a willing heart is a reflection of a motivated attitude accompanied by commitment, integrity, loyalty, compassion, and humility. This is the way God wants us to come to work every day. When kingdom employees with this attitude toward life come to labor in God's vineyard, it makes a world of difference to people looking to come out of darkness to the marvelous light of Jesus.

Theological debate in many churches is connected to the issue that God has not called women into the preaching ministry. So, are you also willing to say that every woman who is preaching the gospel of Jesus is out of the will of God? Or, are you saying that because women are preaching the gospel of Jesus Christ that they all are headed to hell because they are walking in disobedience to the Voice of God, the Holy Bible? It is amazing to me that such an idea is based on the called-out vessels being females in the natural (the flesh), but more than males or females in the spiritual eyes of God. I am convinced your decision to uphold such a thesis is driven either by pride, arrogance, ignorance, fear, sexism, bigotry, disobedience, or chauvinistic posturing. Your objection to women preachers is a position that seemed to be charged by energy or power laced with a deep disrespect for women. If the truth be told, there is a type of superiority complex driving the train producing such a disfigured interpretation or position for understanding Holy Scriptures.

Furthermore, condescending ideology and inferior actions or practices that are designed to dehumanize women from accepting their calling into the ministry are what some people use to rationalize their strategic methodology to keep women out of their pulpit. These religious pitfalls against women ministers are only attempts to control their movement within the local church or denominational environments rather than a hand to help lead them to submitting to the will of God with humility. Humility and tolerance have a way of teaching all of us to respect each other for the sake of peace, even if you think a person is wrong or has an opinion different from yours—as long as the person's actions do not violate the ability to save a soul. Even then, it is only your responsibility to warn the person about the assumed infraction or issue.

However, once you have warned the person about the perceived infraction, I encourage you to let God render the verdict, not you. When we put ourselves in place as accuser, jury, and judge, we have, more than likely, already lost the case because we begin to play the role of a demigod. God only wants us to obey Him and He will do the rest. If you have been called into the gospel ministry by Jesus, all you need to do is stand up and go, and God will meet you there at the place He has prepared for you.

According to Romans 8:1–10, if we allow the work of the flesh to rule anytime during our journey with Jesus, it will have us thinking we are right when we are wrong because we can no longer see through the eyes of the Holy Spirit. When we think we are the only ones entitled to the upper-management section, for some reason, this thought process ends up causing a rebellion within the ranks of the people or society. The philosophy that women are not called by God to preach His gospel insinuates that men are superior to women. This tends to minimize or isolate women's self-worth in the kingdom of God based solely on their gender. Thinking like this forces women and some others to believe women are inferior to their male counterparts. Although our roles may differ, our goal of sharing the gospel of Jesus with every creature should remain the same.

When men endorse such a negative belief or opinion about women, they endorse a philosophy that claims one group has a superior nature. This anti-female philosophy is not a good example of the New Testament movement Jesus led while on earth. The sexist idea that women are not called to preach is one the Devil developed in his laboratory of division and separation. Within the Devil's laboratory of destruction, hate and evil rule as the supreme arsenal in distracting God's people. If the church is to ever become like Jesus, especially to the population of women who minister in the gospel, we must become fair, genuine, and always open to God's unconventional moves when handling or dealing with kingdom assignments.

Moreover, we have to stay humble by remembering we do not know everything there is to know about God. I would like to see the first person who stands and says he or she knows everything there is to know about God. I would get down on my knees and say, "Welcome back to the earth, King Jesus." With all truthfulness, we know only the Devil would make such a foolish claim.

As a result, when we use discriminatory tactics and practices to assign positions in local churches, it ends up a travesty. God must be summoned to act on behalf of justice for those who are treated with injustice, inequality, and unfairness. When God's dinner table is not open to every disciple of Jesus, there will always be unrest in the atmosphere. If Jesus was gracious and compassionate enough to allow guests to come from everywhere and eat at the dinner table of God, what makes men think they can produce any less than this example of equality and fairness for women?

When people try to suppress other people based on Holy Scriptures, this becomes the foundation for establishing the idea of superiority and cults. In God's kingdom, whenever we attempt to classify positions by gender or ethnicity, we move away from the principles of God's grace and move back to the old neighborhood of sin under the law. Believe it or not, the thesis to segregate men and women in God's kingdom based on gender is an attempt to force a person back under the bondage of the law.

On the contrary, why should we have to go back under the law, which God has already delivered us from by the sacrifice of Jesus? The idea that a person is limited in God's kingdom because of his or her physical makeup or condition puts a person right back under the law of bondage, where many of Jesus' opponents continuously tried to keep the people during His earthly ministry. According to Romans 8:1–3, if there is no condemnation in Jesus, why do some pastors and ministers use gender to bar women from the preaching ministry of the gospel of Jesus?

As you read Romans 8, you find the law was designed to exploit a person from the outside and then move inward based on what the person could or could not accomplish in the flesh. It served as that old, brutal taskmaster, treating the person with disrespect and evoking the feeling of condescension, no matter how hard you tried or worked to become good. Even when you gave your very best under the law, it was never good enough. And you received little or no reward for your worthy labor.

Or should I say our unworthy labor under the law is not worth a penny to God. It is no secret the law was aimed at restricting or handcuffing people, so they would not allow their fleshly desires to kill them or others. It was put in place to prevent evil people from getting worse and hopefully prevent them from self-destructing as a human race. Under the Law, only the good God intended could come out of a person's life. If God did not deem anything as good and pleasing in His sight, then it did not happen.

The Holy Scriptures teaches that no one could become righteous through the law. Only through the Son of God could a man or woman consider himself or herself righteous. According to the Holy Bible, if righteousness could have been obtained through the law or by any other means, the death of Jesus Christ on the cross was a waste and a useless act of God's eternal love for humanity (Romans 8:3–8; Galatians 2:21).

A segregated gender pool for employment in God's kingdom is a barrier devised by the minds and hands of the Enemy. The Enemy uses human beings from all walks of life to attack God's plan by discouraging the saints. When someone or something tries to strip women of their inheritance at the King's table, we know this takeover attempt is not a divine appointment plan from the Almighty King of the universe. The Enemy of God is responsible for bringing disruption into the kingdom of God.

In God's kingdom, when God calls and uses a person under the anointing of the Holy Ghost, the person's gender, or ethnic background, or age, or size and weight or physical characteristic is probably the least important to God. To God, it seems like a person's humility to obey the Holy Spirit is the key for doing the things that are pleasing to Jesus. The motive, intent, and purpose by which a person submits to the will and call of God stand out the brightest.

More importantly, if God has the power to take vessels from the animal kingdom (especially like the ass and a whale) and use them to deliver His Holy Word (Numbers 22:27–32), surely He does not have to think twice about using women to deliver His words to His people. As people of God, we must learn to take our eyes off the creature and focus on the Creator. It is the Creator who gives us all things beyond what we can ask or imagine according to His power, glory, and honor at work in our lives (Ephesians 3:20). We need to move our attention away from the vessel and focus on the vessel creator and maker; here lies the truth of the whole matter.

Until we can focus our attention on God and not on the opinions of men and women, we will not be able to fully see God's move in the lives of women ministers, as we do with their male counterparts. Let the butterfly loose, observe the beauty of its graceful motions while in flight, and you will be mesmerized with wonder and excitement on the behalf of the butterfly's Creator. Even if you think you are right about the women in ministry issue, name some other things on your job, in relationships or in life you felt right about, but for the sake of peace you either work it out or refuse to fight and buck the system. Whenever love, humility, peace, respect and survival are foundational in the lives of people, we work out our differences by agreeing to disagree with compassion and understanding.

God made all of us, and His Holy Spirit is able to compensate for whatever physical, mental, spiritual limitations, or other shortcomings we may have. So why do some people try to use a physical trait to disqualify a certain group of people from the preaching ministry? I believe God is setting the record straight about His awesome power and His intention to use whatever and whomever He chooses to use when the Holy Bible says, "when the fullness of time had come, God sent his Son, *born of a woman*, and *born under the law*" (Galatians 4:4; emphasis added). This small portion of God's Word says a lot about God's intention and plan to use women to help liberate His creation from sin during a crucial phase of His creation.

Also, I find it intriguing how men would fight women on the idea of becoming preachers, but on the other hand, some of these same men, including men of the cloth, have no problem working with or even uniting with women in order to make a life on this earth. Men need women and women need men in every area of their lives, including the ministry. I would like to challenge pastors who are against women ministers to stand up in their pulpits and tell women they have no place in the preaching ministry or preach a sermon why God does not call a woman to preach the Gospel of Jesus, and stop cowardly hiding behind local ministerial alliances and denominational rules, etc.

For some reason it seems like God is saying to all of us that though he could have chosen any method or vehicle to bring forth His Son into the world, He selected a woman. Yes, God chose a woman when He did not have to. God could have allowed Jesus to come as an angel or just ride down on a cloud, similar to the way He ascended into the heavens. Yet God chose to give the honor to a woman. When allowing Jesus to come to earth through a woman's womb, was God making a powerful statement about forgiveness that goes back to the days of the Garden of Eden? Oh, do not forget we are talking about *the* God and not just *a* god. Keep in mind we serve a God who is not limited in anything. He has the whole world in His hands.

In the meantime, all I am saying is God did not have to use the expected method to usher His Son into the world. Just like He did not use an ordinary method to impregnate the woman (Mary) who gave birth to Jesus, He could have done a similar process in selecting how Jesus would enter the world. The mere fact a woman was chosen for the mission is certainly a divine act of selection that establishes great creditability for all women on the earth. It demonstrates that in God's eyes, women have significant value in His kingdom.

Also, for God to choose a woman as the mean to bring His greatest blessing to the world and humanity speaks volumes concerning the love and respect He has for women. If a woman is worthy enough to carry God's words in the flesh, she is worthy to carry the Word of God from the pulpit to His people. If a woman is worthy enough to nurture the most awesome life ever to be born, surely she is worthy to minister to and nurture God's sheep. There seems to be a powerful, underlying piece of irony in the philosophy that promotes and supports the idea women are not supposed to preach the Word of God to the people of God.

If men and women continue to focus on and fight about which gender is the appropriate one for God to use in the preaching ministry, then the belief that salvation is acquired by an act of faith rather than works—will send a mixed signal to the church and the world. While we are fighting so women ministers can have the same acceptance and respect as their male counterparts, there is a waiting world standing by for their opportunity to render their lives to Jesus. Also, while we waste time waging the war for women to have equal rights in the ministry, just imagine the people who are probably losing their souls to sin while church members bicker over whether women should be allowed to preach or not preach in pulpits throughout the land. If this is the case, what a tragedy this would be for the kingdom of God.

Accordingly, if we truly believe the Christian movement or disciples for Jesus is based on an act of faith in Jesus and not by the actions of work in the flesh, then a person's gender should not matter when it comes to serving or eating at the dinner table of the Lord. Men and women are called into the gospel ministry not based on their works but because each person has expressed the faith and a commitment to follow God. Such divisive theology supported by those who believe otherwise is designed to bring separation in the body of Christ and create a caste system within God's family. If grace does not rise as the central theme of salvation within the local church, Christendom is in for a terrible in-house power struggle. The belief that a woman is not allowed to preach tends to promote salvation from the school of thought that is geared towards a faith that is work centered rather than God given.

The Holy Bible teaches salvation is not an act of works but an act of faith in Jesus. Faith says if God granted a miracle for someone else, surely He can do the same thing for me. All the disciple needs to do is wholeheartedly believe in the words of Jesus. Faith says if my ways are pleasing to God, He will give me the desires of my heart, even if it means preaching God's most holy words (Psalm 37:4).

Let's look at Ephesians 2:8–10, where it states, "for by grace are we saved through faith, and not of ourselves: it is a gift of God; not of works, lest any man should boast. For we are his workmanship, created in Christ Jesus unto good works, which God has ordained that we should walk in them." Here lies the truth to the whole matter. It is not our call to decide who should or should not preach the gospel of Jesus Christ; it is God's decision! Only God should and will continue to exercise the right to call whomever He wants into the preaching ministry. If God is the one who created the test, He should be respected as the one who will grade the test. Allowing God to handle His business without human interference is having godly respect for the divine.

2

Women Called to the Gospel Ministry, Should Be Viewed as a Unified Front by All Women

Women's roles in the gospel of Jesus Christ have always been of great significance. Women will continue to play pivotal roles as long as salvation is needed on the earth by the human race. As we study the Holy words of God from the Holy Bible, we can easily see how women fulfilled a much greater role in the God movement than the stereotypical ones where male directors have cast many women in society today. With so many sweeping changes in the world, especially women's rights groups demanding changes in society, it is the right time for women to take advantage of the opportunity for equal rights and take a proactive stand to express their gifts as preachers, ministers, leaders, and teachers in the most powerful movement in the history of the world, the Christian church.

Furthermore, women who have been called to minister the gospel of Jesus Christ must believe without a shadow of doubt their calling is a faith journey with God rather than by the approval of a person, people, or denomination. Your calling into the gospel ministry should never be looked at as some work of the law, as some men would try to convince you. The fulfillment of the law is based on what you as an individual are attempting to do to please God by your own actions. If you decide to become a victim of the law then so be it.

However, if you have decided to live under grace, then you need to know that liberation and salvation belong to you at no cost except obedience to Jesus. Please do not allow yourself to go back into bondage of slavery once Jesus has freed you. Do not let anyone or thing strip you of the joy of salvation and its many benefits to include the preaching of the gospel for some. Believe it or not, many people get sucked into the deception of fame, wealth, power, control and the mountaintop experience life has to offer. The Devil tried to deceive Jesus with all the so-called things of the world that people often go crazy over. He took Jesus on the pinnacle of the temple and made Jesus an offer he may have thought Jesus could not refuse (Luke 4:1-14).

Sometimes people would rather enjoy the pleasures of this world rather than suffer the joys of a better world that awaits them in Heaven. The Enemy will attempt to keep you in bondage with the fine and glamorous things of the world when Grace has removed your shackles, guilt, and shame. Hold your head up and drive on. God awaits your arrival at the finish line with a crown of joy for you.

Some people actually sell their souls to the Devil just to enjoy the riches of this world, which is a reason why they decide to stay in bondage. They live for the right now and not tomorrow. Some people do not believe there will be a day of judgement where God is going to judge all of humanity. Finally, some people would rather stay in bondage rather than taking up the commitment and responsibility of living a saved and holy lifestyle. When the Emancipation Proclamation was signed by President Lincoln, not all slaves were happy to leave their plantations. When the Iraelites got angry with Mose during the Exodus, some wished Moses would have left them in bondage in Egypt (Exodus 16:3 and Exodus chapters 15-17).

Under the law, only a chosen few could begin to feel the thrill of victory, but under the gift of grace, all are given the opportunity to experience the thrill of victory. Under grace, we do not have to live out our lives with the "agony of defeat." Whenever we try to live up to the standards of human beings, we travel in the wrong direction and without God's blessings. We are not only fighting a losing battle, but we are also depriving ourselves of many blessings and opportunities God has already extended to us by the invitation of Jesus. God has placed on the table of salvation things like compassion, peace, love, joy, prosperity, happiness, goodness, kindness, patience, modesty, self-control and a host of other things for us to enjoy as His servants (Galatians 5:22-23). When we spend our lives trying to please others or prove to them our worthiness in life, we miss out on the awesome blessings of God because we waste too much time trying to please other people before we can please God. This is a terrible waste of God's time and a lost opportunity for you.

There is so much we can learn about grace if we are willing to stand boldly on the promises of God and Jesus. There is so much we need to learn about grace and the way God unselfishly gives it to us, even when we do not deserve it. Just think about all the precious moments people have wasted running behind lies, foolishness, or even trying to prove things to people who do not have their best interests at heart. Chasing other people's opinions about one's life, especially when it applies to being called into the ministry, is futile to say the least. How dare a person seek confirmation concerning the final 'rite of passage' from someone after God has called the person into a higher calling as a minister of the gospel of Jesus Christ.

Instead of checking popular opinion polls, spend this precious time communing with God about the direction He deems necessary for your life. I am not saying you are not to inquire or discuss the matter with your spiritual leader. I am saying no human being has the authority to deny someone from preaching the gospel of Jesus after God has given His stamp of approval. People do not have enough power in their bones to make this type of judgment call for the Holy Spirit, Jesus, and God. It is impossible for sinful individuals to call a person into a holy kingdom with a divine mission. Only God has the power to call a person into the ministry and sustain him or her during the journey. Even if a person is called by his or her denomination or pastor, but not by God, the person will not be able to stand the test and last to the finish line regardless of the earthly training.

Believe it or not, some people spend their entire lives going backward and forth like a ping-pong ball, bouncing from one end of the table to the other, looking for love, approval, and acceptance from anybody. Some of these people are knowledgeable about the words of God, yet they end up becoming prey for the Enemy by believing the ideology that God did not call a woman to preach His gospel. Such people become confused or dogmatic about theology and lead others down the wrong path. They are of the impression since it comes from a pastor or minister and they should know the Holy Bible, then surely these persons would not mislead people in the wrong direction.

Yet they fail to realize God's grace is always extending its hands of compassion to rescue them with education and understanding. The Holy Ghost would not have us to go wrong on such an important issue about women preachers. God is a Redeemer of acceptance and not a father of rejection. I am amazed how God's grace will accept you when no one else is willing to offer a listening ear or an open heart. Each day I live on this beautiful earth, I realize that we, as humans, can never elevate to God's standards without Him lifting us up. His grace and mercy are the means, or mechanisms, by which He reaches down and pulls us up to Him.

We do not have the strength or power to become what God wants us to become without the Holy Spirit ruling our lives. For us to get in tune with the will of God, we need the Holy Ghost to rule supreme in our lives. Here is the most comforting thing I love about this great phenomenon we call grace. Grace has the powerful ability to wipe away our sores, scars, embarrassments, shames, sins, weaknesses, and shortcomings, so God can use us in a greater capacity apart from ourselves. God continues to look beyond our sins and faults and sees our needs.

In contrast, under the law of bondage, a person has to constantly look out for the deadly and ruthless lion called sin, which constantly keeps lurking nearby, waiting for us to make the wrong move. Once the wrong move is made, then the demons of sin will come pouncing on us with a swift bite of destruction. Immediately after we make the wrong move, this savage monster, sin, takes the opportunity to crush us in it jaws and then grabs and holds us into submission in its claws. The brutal beast of sin has no sympathy or compassion for God's creation. Sin has the dubious duty of separating us from God, who is our greatest helper. Once sin has removed us from God's holy presence, it viciously destroys whatever is left of us by ripping us to pieces.

As discussed earlier, the law is not a friend to people desiring to live under grace. Grace is the friendliest and most compassionate neighbor in the neighborhood. Grace never travels alone. Each time I see grace, he is always escorted by mercy, peace, joy, and happiness. The thing I love about grace is He does not render himself to be unfriendly to the person because of the lifestyle he or she has chosen to live.

Moreover, even if we are in the wrong, grace is always in the right but will never persecute you. Grace will always try to reason with you, take Jesus' hands, and walk with Him to the freedom land of life and prosperity. Grace does not tell everyone in the neighborhood you should be treated as a second-class citizen, because grace loves you and because God first loved you and will always love you. Grace respects you because God demands grace respects and honors you. Grace gives you the opportunity to exercise your gifts and talents because God has given grace the opportunity to exercise its gifts and talent across the broader spectrum of time and creation. You can see grace extending himself to Adam and Eve in the garden, after the fall of humanity. When you look at the beauty of a rainbow, it is a reminder of God's grace for humanity. Whenever you look into the sky and see the sun, moon, and stars—all this is a reflection of God's marvelous grace to the world, and especially to the human race.

It is evident the act of *grace* is what Jesus uses to purify things in your life when you honestly begin to reflect on all your faults, limitations, and shortcomings as human beings. Yet through the working of the Holy Spirit, you are able to please God the way He desires to be pleased by His creation. Human beings are sinful by nature. Without the blood of Jesus washing away our sins, there can be no good works produced by sinful human beings. The precious blood that forgives humanity of its sins is the same blood that allows women to preach the divine gospel of Jesus. With grace, the Holy Spirit empowers a person to accomplish things and excel in areas he or she ordinarily would not be able to, simply because of the impossibilities and restrictions we have as human beings. No matter how far we come in Christ, sin is always a step behind us and waiting for its opportunity to cause our swift demise.

You see, we must understand the ill working of the law. God gave us the law to prevent the desecration of the human race by sin and disobedience. Under the law, the attainability of righteousness was impossible because it was centered mainly on the work of human flesh rather than the righteousness of God through grace. Putting trust and faith in works and accomplishments made by the sinful hands we present to God is an act of pride and a disaster in the making. Boasting of our so-called accomplishments without making Jesus the center of attention is a recipe for failure.

When a person boasts or brags about personal success apart from God, it is only a matter of time before the bottom has fallen out of his or her plan. The bottom will only fall out of your plan when Jesus is not its foundation. A plan based on Jesus stands on the most solid foundation in the world. It will never sink or crumble. Though the winds may blow and the ground might tremble, the foundation will never break, because Jesus is the Rock that cannot be shaken, broken, or moved (Psalm 62:6–9; Isaiah 28:16; Matthew 7:24–27).

For this reason, as servants of the Lord, we must never forget there is no righteousness in humanity apart from God. Beware of those who think they have the power and authority to tell others God has not called them into the ministry. Such people are like people playing with matches around a petroleum tank. God has already won the battle of the sexes as it relates to preaching His divine words.

The force behind the preaching phenomenon is so powerful that even the Devil cannot stop it. So what in the world makes men—and women—think they can stop women's ministries from excelling within the churches of Jesus Christ? The people in the anti-women preacher movement would rather beat you down with arguments about why women cannot preach the gospel rather than take the initiative to welcome sisters into the ministering fold of God.

Hence, all I can say to you is let the Holy Spirit speak for you, and please do not get caught up in the idea of being rejected by others. Here is the bottom line—only God has the stamp of approval and final report card waiting for you at the end of the journey. All you need to do is stay obedient to the Word of God and graduate with honors. Walk across the stage of life with humility, loyalty, commitment, and dignity, and receive your honorable recognition from God and not the audience. Through the grace of the Holy Spirit, you are the one being called to do the work, so please do not let anyone else steal your joy or cause you to forfeit the blessings and prosperity God has for you as a servant of His ministry. Amen.

It is Jesus, through faith and grace, who gives hope to humanity that was once lost in the darkness of a world filled with sin. God extends His love through Jesus and turns us into a righteous people for His glory. It is Jesus who gives us the gift of eternal life by the sacrifice He made on Calvary, when He died on a cross for the sins of the world, including yours and mine (Galatians 2:15–21). No one else was worthy enough to make such a universal redemption for humanity, even across all the ages of time. Only Jesus fit the description and had the DNA to liberate humanity from an eternal death sentence (Romans 3:23; Galatians 3:7–29). Prior to the ministry of Jesus, there is no record of a person coming forward and announcing he was the son of God and sent from heaven to die on a tree for the sins of the world.

Prior to Jesus' birth, no one walked on water, healed blinded eyes, made the lame walk, gave voice to the dumb, gave hearing to the deaf, and healed people of leprosy. No one prior to Jesus' arrival was able to feed thousands with two fish and five barley loaves of bread. Never in the history of humanity was there a person who could make the dead rise after being in the grave for four days. There was never a human being who said he was from heaven, and he and God were one in the same in the spirit, mission, mind, and heart. Even the foes of Jesus had to respect His audacious powers and wonders, which He so gracefully performed as the crowds gazed in great amazement. What an awesome Man, with so much humility and compassion for the human race.

The Pharisees, Sadducees, and Scribes tried to deny the divinity of Jesus, even after observing many of His mighty acts and miracles. Jesus performed miracle after miracle, yet His enemies refused to accept the fact He was the chosen Messiah, sent from God. Even after Jesus told audiences no miracles could be possible unless His Father granted Him the power, many religious leaders still denied the divinity of the Christ. It is Jesus who made claims to all the signs and wonders, as well as to many more astonishing acts, only because of His relationship with God, His Father. The message Jesus was sending to the world is without God, we, too, are useless and powerless in all our efforts and thinking. It is through our faith in Jesus that we receive the motivation to believe in signs and wonders beyond this world.

Moreover, it is by our faith that God gives us the grace to achieve the impossible things in life. Yes, with faith in God, all things become possible. With your faith in Jesus and obedience to the Holy Spirit, God will see you through your trials and tribulations with the signs of victorious praises. All a disciple of Jesus has to do is hold his or her peace, and allow God to fight your battles (Jeremiah 32:27, 17; Matthew 19:26; Ephesians 3:20).

It is imperative for us to understand the struggle women face daily while trying to fulfill the mission (calling) God has called them to perform. We must not be afraid of those who try to stand in our way when it comes to carrying out God's commandments. We also must learn to show patience, tolerence and discretion while exercising divine wisdom when addressing the saga about the calling God has for women in the gospel ministry. Never allow anyone to push or pressure you to get you off course with the teachings of Jesus. Stay a Christian at all times by following the teachings of Jesus and His apostles.

Just remember, if the Devil can continue to draw us into fights and/or debates that bring discord among the people of God, he has outwitted us and scored a major victory for hell. When our attention is drawn away from Jesus to the carnality of things, including our self-centered way of thinking, our kingdom-building efforts suffer a negative blow rather than a stroke in the affirmation that shines with the joyful lights of victory. The Evil One has an agenda to keep us arguing, which causes us to lose focus.

Believe it or not, once we start spending valuable time on nonessential issues concerning salvation, then we limit the power of the Holy Spirit in our lives. The Holy Spirit wants to save souls and not waste time arguing about things that have nothing to do with a person's salvation in Jesus. For example, a person's height and weight, or skin color, or cultural background has nothing to do with his or her salvation in Jesus.

Since these things do not matter to Jesus as it relates to a person's commitment to Him, why waste time debating or arguing about such issues? Imagine who would waste time trying to figure out if someone is too short or too tall to enter the gates of heaven? There is no merit or sense with debating this issue, so why limit yourself and become drawn into a fruitless conversation as such. Physical stature has no relevance to qualifying or disqualifying for eternal life in paradise. If any of us depend on our physical or natural gifts, talents, or deeds to open a special door for us with God, we have truly deceived ourselves.

Furthermore, the kingdom-building process for Jesus is so important that we cannot afford to become split over who is preaching or teaching from the pulpit on Sunday morning. The debate that surrounds the issue of who is called to preach the gospel is a small point when you think about the real meat of the matter, which is who gets the glory when a vessel brings a soul to Jesus. It is not the gender of the instrument conducting the preaching and teaching. If I did not know any better, I would think the fight is not about who is doing the preaching but more on the subject of who is the undercover vainglory person seeking praise and glory for his preaching. The fight seems to be more about recognition than winning and nurturing souls for Jesus.

The preaching of the gospel of Jesus was never designed to separate the kingdom of God. God gave the gift of preaching as a vehicle to bring together His kingdom and not as something that would be used to divide His people. As you reflect over biblical history from the days of Noah all the way through Revelation, preaching was used as a lightning rod to bring together the saved and unsaved in the spirit of unity. The preaching of the gospel of Jesus is also used to call people to repentance and to accept righteousness with God.

For this reason, I have come to the conclusion that as long God uses the vessel, why should I fuss or reject the message or the messenger? When I lay on an operating table in the operating room, it does not matter to me which medical school the doctor or surgeon attended. All I want to know is if the doctor is qualified and can fix my problem.

Furthermore, we must never allow anyone or anything to draw our attention away from the gift of God's grace. When we allow things in life to distract us from the principal things of grace and cause us to focus on our works (personal attributes and physical characteristics) under the law, we become no better than the Pharisees who lifted themselves above the grace of Jesus. When people lift themselves above God's compassion and seek to become rulers and not servants, they have lost touch with the reality of the wonderful grace God provided us through Jesus Christ. If God's people are forever entangled, fighting issues that bring no glory or honor to God, the Devil has not only thrown us off course but made a mockery of something that is holy and just in the eyes of God.

Why should the body of Christ allow the Enemy to drag the community of faith into battles Jesus fought and won for us over two thousand years ago? There are many kinds of winds at sea that push sea vessels off course, but the captain of the ship is there to make sure the ship follows its plotted course. When on course with the Holy Spirit—regardless of the winds, storms, or currents you may encounter during your travels—you must never lose track that your mission in life is to promote the gospel of Jesus Christ. You can always stay true to the directions God has mapped out for you if you are focused and committed to the calling. Let the Holy Spirit teach you how to pick your battles, and always follow the lead of Jesus. Some battles you should turn over and allow your big brother to fight the fight of faith for you. You should just enjoy the victory.

Remember, God is the captain of your faith and the Master of your soul, and the Holy Spirit is like the guardian angel that watches over you to make sure you safely sail to your destination. If you keep your faith in Christ, He will make sure you arrive safely ashore. If we follow the path Jesus plotted for our lives, He has guaranteed we will reach our destination safely with Him by our side. Jesus' promise should give all hope for safety. God told us that He "will never leave us or forsake us if we only put our trust in Him" (Deuteronomy 31:8; Matthew 28:20). Just like when you know God has a calling on your life, it is important you do not let anyone interfere with this very important duty, the preaching of the gospel. Making disciples for Jesus is probably the most important job you will ever have on earth and the preaching of the gospel is at the center of making disciples for Jesus.

God's calling on your life is what drives your purpose for living, even though you may not always know exactly what is going on in your life. Your purpose for living is the thing that connects us to God and His plan for our lives. Without a plan from God, we have no purpose for living, and without purpose from God, there is no purpose for us to unite with God to receive our mission in life.

Furthermore, I recommend you study and become very familiar with the following Scriptures during your daily devotional. They serve as a great platform for understanding the argument Satan is using to discourage women from accepting their call into the gospel ministry. Who, other than the Devil, would not want to be a part of a labor force that tells the legacy and glory of God with such great excitement? Not only is this labor force able to share God's glory with great enthusiasm and excitement, it is also able to share the wonderful news about His Son, Jesus, in such a magnificent way that both heaven and earth rejoice at the celebration of such awesome news (Romans 4:1–25; 8:1–17; 9:1–13).

The Scriptures listed in the above paragraph open the door for women to rise up with freedom as they release the shackles of bondage and accept their calling into the ministry without the guilt and shame that was once the case under the law. If God can bring life to the decrepit body of a man of faith like Abraham while under the bondage of sin, surely He can use women as vessels to promote His plan of faith during the era when His grace and mercy are the only lifelines for humanity on a daily basis. Under the law, we could only do the things the law allowed us to do. Under the law, we could only become the things the law allowed us to become. Under the law, we had limited range of movement towards Heaven. But under grace, we are given unlimited potential. Under the marvelous act of grace, everyone can freely have what only a few could possibly have under the law. Thank God for King Jesus!

If God did not sanction women into the preaching ministry, the entire idea of women preachers would dissipate like a fading fashion trend. However, if God deemed it mandatory for women to preach His gospel, no power on earth or in hell could stop this powerful move of the Holy Spirit. No pushback or rejection from humanity can ever stop a move of God on the earth or elsewhere. I echo the words of a great Jewish theologian named Gamaliel, who was a doctor of the law. He had a good reputation among the people of Israel for reasoning on the side of God. Gamaliel admonished the religious council at Jerusalem not to take counsel to kill the apostles of Jesus for preaching, teaching, and carrying out the ministry of Jesus.

Gamaliel also cautioned his brothers, elders, priests and leaders of Israel that sat on the council with him not to interfere in what could be the work of God. Gamaliel pleaded with his colleagues to allow more time to see if the new Christian had been sanctioned by God. He was convinced that time will tell if God was behind the new Jesus movement, because if it was not of God, then it would crumble like kingdoms and fads of the past. Gamaliel concludes his point by saying,

> Ye men of Israel, take heed to yourselves what you intend to do as touching these men. For before these days rose up Theudas, boasting himself to be somebody; to whom a number of men, about four hundred, joined themselves: who was slain; and all, as many as obeyed him, were scattered, and brought to nought.
>
> After this man rose up Judas of Galilee in the day of taxing, and drew away much people after him: he also perished; and all, even as many as obeyed him dispersed. And now I say to you, Refrain from these men, and let them alone for this counsel or this is of men, it will come to nought: But if it be of God, ye cannot overthrow it; lest haply ye be found even against God (Acts 5:33–42).

In the same way Gamaliel stood up for the disciples of Jesus, I, too, stand up and challenge the Christian community to stand up and give our sisters respect and the opportunity to serve as fellow members of the clergy. Only God has the right to serve as supreme judge as to whether women are called by Him. I believe if we adhere to Gamaliel's humble request, then in the end, when our journey on this earth is over, we shall receive a smile from God and an embrace from Jesus for being a team player. When we all work together without fighting over the issue of whether God calls women to the gospel ministry to preach His Word, all of us will receive a greater blessing by the Holy Spirit for our cooperation. Given the opportunity, we will recognize women ministers as important agents of God, who bring a host of nurturing talents and gifts and a diverse flavor to the ministry. The following idea, proposed by one of my male minister friends, is quite interesting: "Women ministers are just another 'monkey wrench' that the Devil has thrown into the ring to see how long the church will fight over the issue." It is a cop-out for not wanting to deal with the issue on the side of what is biblically right and just.

The women in ministry issue is an awesome opportunity for the people of God to view the kingdom of God from an out-of-the box perspective and begin to experience things from the other side of God's wonderful creation story. One of the unique things about a window is you can usually look in or out and view things from both sides. Many people in the local church probably viewed women in ministry from outside the window rather than from the inside. When trying to look in a window from the outside, you tend to not be able to see things as clearly as when you look out of the window from the inside.

Accordingly, the gifts and talents women bring to the gospel ministry should be appreciated and embraced by Christianity as a whole. It is not fair to other people within the Christian faith that women are ridiculed and rejected from the gospel ministry simply because of their gender. Women bring perspectives from their experiences and backgrounds men cannot bring to women. Women bring a caring and motherly perspective to the body of Christ unlike their male counterparts.

Furthermore, women bring insight on how to minister to women that their male counterpart cannot gain in theological school or from life's experiences. Women know how to meet the needs of other women better than men. Women know how other women feel about issues better than men do. Women have a way of connecting with other women in a way that many men cannot understand or grasp. Women embrace other women with affection and a platonic relationship that is sometimes difficult for some men to handle.

Also, it is no secret women analyze and resolve issues with a different approach than many of their male counterparts. By design, God created the woman to be more of a nurturer than the man. Even women's soft physical features are more conducive to their role as the apex caregiver within the family. God has given women the gift and ability to invoke emotions in situations where many men would invoke reason and logic to analyze and address issues. I am not saying there is something wrong with this. It is just the nature of the beast, as men and women are different and view the world from different perspectives. The difference between men and women is like the artistic creativity of the right brain versus the logic reasoning of the left brain. It is not saying one side is better than the other side. Each side has a different function for the way we function, see, and do things in life.

The bottom line is women are women, and men are men! We are different and were created/made to be different. It is our unique differences that attract us to each other. God knew what He was doing in the Garden of Eden, when He created humankind and made us to be different yet so similar. There are still some people who will not accept the fact God made us different. Our differences are the things that cause us not to become boring to each other. Our differences challenge us to become more like Jesus and less like each other. Being different is not a bad thing, because even with our differences, we can have compassion, respect, and appreciation for each other.

Furthermore, women ministers as preachers of the gospel of Jesus have the innate gift of providing us with a balanced image of God's family. They also serve as mentors for equipping other women for the battlefield by providing a woman's perspective on things and issues in life. When local churches and ministers refuse to allow women to articulate their calling as full-fledged ministers, with the same rights as their male counterparts, it is possible that the dark shadow of bigotry and sexism have infiltrated the ranks of the local church or denomination. The people of God must ensure the shackles of bondage (bigotry and sexism) do not take root in the church especially among the ranks of the leadership of the ministry.

There is great danger when denominations and local churches make decisions about the call and salvation of people based upon their sex, ethnicity, and nationality or culture; because only God should render such an important verdict. Hopefully, the following examples will help you understand the danger when people step up and try to rule God's affairs from their personal experiences. As humans living in a world where wickedness has run rampant for thousands of years, it is imperative we understand the hands and thoughts of sinful men and women have contaminated our culture. This in itself is a recipe primed for disaster, even before the chef goes into the kitchen to prepare the meal.

For example, though the American slave trade was something God never approved, many churches, denominations, pastors, and ministers advocated for the institution of slavery. To be honest, America did not seek God's advice when it came to slavery in America. No, whenever a people want to do wrong, the one entity they always leave out is God because they already know His answer. People seeking to do wrong and thinking they benefit from doing wrong or evil never seek God's advice—until they get in trouble or into a predicament they cannot pull themselves out.

The American slavery system was wrong. Yet many churchgoers said it was the will of God for Africans and their descendants to be enslaved in America. The American slave turmoil was a time when humility was traded and sold for greed. It was a time when selfish pride reigned in the lives of the people of a country that preached freedom but lived as hypocrites. It was a time when idol worship was practiced in the North as well as in the Deep South.

The American slavery dynasty was a period when love and respect for God's creation was traded for hate and the false sense of feeling superior to another group of people. It was a time when many Americans lost their integrity for greed, bondage, power, control and much sin. American Slavery was an era when men and women across America traded Jesus and salvation for religion and hate. As we discuss the issue about women being denied the opportunity to preach in male dominated pulpits across America and the world simply because they are females, maybe there is a lesson we can learn from the American Slavery Holocaust that can help us solve the discriminatory practices women ministers are facing in some Christian churches.

During the American slave trade era, true worshippers of God were persecuted with physical and cultural bondage. The religious Pharisees gloated in their lustful pride. The wicked were in control, and people groaned and mourned for God's Liberation (Proverbs 29:2). When people operate with the mentality of being superior to others, the atmosphere is filled with mistrust, pride, greed, hate, deception, and anger. Eventually, there is a total collapse of the unjust system that many tried to justify as being just and righteous even in the eyes of God.

You see, American slavery is an example of people rebelling against unjust rules and laws. It represented the epitome of unfairness, whereby a certain group was allowed to fill its minds with vain imaginings by allowing itself to set up a make believe superior culture. At the same time, the group put down the descendants of Africans as their slaves and servants. Teaching people to worship and call men and women masters based on skin color of the person is idol worship in the truest sense. Only God should be referred to as a Master.

God has taught us in His word that no one should serve or have two masters, because a person will love one and hate the other one (Matthew 6:2; Luke 16:13). Idol worship is when a 90 year old black man has to call a 5 year old Caucasian boy sir and mister simply because he is white. The elderly man has to do this not because it is the right thing to do; it is forced upon him against his will because he lives in a racist society that teaches its citizens racism and pass and enforce laws that perpetuate the ideology that white skin is superior to black skin. A racist and unfair society led to total rebellion, which caused great chaos throughout the nation, leading to great division and destruction like this country had never experienced within its shores. This slavery epidemic is one of the root causes of the Civil War. The irony of the Civil War is that it brought America to its knees and nearly destroyed the nation that boasted it was "One nation under God."

Furthermore, proponents of slavery later found out they were wrong about the slave issue because slavery was a travesty that nearly ripped this nation from the fibers and cords that held it together. Some of the ministers and denominations endorsed the institution of slavery as a good thing and felt they were in the will of God. There was a great deal of disunity in a nation that said it stood for unity by respecting the rights of all people. The issue concerning the fight to try and keep women ministers from preaching the gospel of Jesus is one that can rip the heart out of America like the Civil War of 1861.

American slavery was the Judas that betrayed an entire nation and a people for thirty pieces of silver. Overzealous men and women sold their souls down the drain of human corruption for the pride of superiority and the greed of currency. During the American Slavery Era, the nation split over the issue of slavery. The physical identity of a certain group of people stirred a great controversy in southern states starting first with South Carolina, the first of the southern states to secede from the union on April 12, 1861. Yes, it was skin color that set this so-called Christian nation apart and divided families and friends to the point of war.

Today, it is the women ministers' gender argument within the churches like the slavery issue in the 1800s that is wedging a wall of separation between Christians. Within the next few years, if something does not give, it could ignite a war within the trenches of our churches and denominations. There has to be a way we can embrace, respect, appreciate, and accept women called to the gospel ministry, rather than reject them simply because they are women.

The bigoted spirit that controls many male pastors who are refusing to embrace women as legitimate preachers of the gospel of Jesus Christ is as deadly as the lethal poison of slavery. It is deadly because it is designed to dehumanize women and to kill all their hopes for the preaching ministry. The excruciating pain and terror from this type of rejection by an organism/institution that is supposed to love and embrace you is hard to overcome. Without doubt, this type of rejection from church leaders is designed to leave its victims psychologically and spiritually damaged for life. Or, at least dead when it comes to fulfilling dreams and the calling God placed in the heart of the worshipper, the person praising and serving as a servant of the Most High God.

Women ministers of today may have to mobilize a force within their local churches and outside the church to help them protest for their rights, as Sojourner Truth, Susan B. Anthony, and Elizabeth Cody Stanton did during the Women's Suffrage Movement in the late-nineteenth and early twentieth centuries. This women's freedom movement for equal rights culminated in the 1920s, with the passage of the Nineteenth Amendment to the U.S. Constitution, which provided, "The rights of citizens of the United States to vote shall not be denied or abridged by the United States or any state <u>on account of sex</u>."

Jesus mobilized a force within the boundaries of Israel to protest the unjust laws and rules of the Pharisees, Sadducees, and Scribes that were poisoning the minds and hearts of the people in the regions where Jesus was ministering. Let us remember the burdens placed on the people by the Pharisees, Sadducees, and Scribes were mainly of the traditions of men and not God. They offered neither a cure for sins nor the gift of salvation. God's calling always trumps the protocol and procedures of humanity.

In other words, the grace of God always supersedes the rituals of individuals. You see, the rituals and traditions of society often change over the course of time, but God's grace never changes. The awesome grace of God is still saving lives, as it did back in the days of Noah. The grace of God has a proven track record throughout the course of history on the earth that illustrates God's love is much greater than our physical limitations and the mistakes we may make in life. God's grace and mercy prove the Holy Spirit is more concerned about us fulfilling the commandment and mission of God than the gender of the vessel He uses to bring life and knowledge to His people.

Moreover, male preachers are fighting a losing battle by trying to intimidate or forbid women from ministering as they obey their callings from God. Some men try their best to use their male dominance to prohibit women from preaching in the pulpits across America. I equate such futile actions of ministers and people against women preachers/ministers with a group of men trying to stop the birth of a child after the woman has gone into labor and her water has broken. It is time for delivery and not time to hold back. Even if someone tries to prevent the baby from coming, God has already ordained the birth of the child.

More important, this is a time for the Christian community to experience great jubilation and not for some people to experience theological constipation as a means of rejecting women ministers. For men to really understand why it is necessary for women to obey the Holy Spirit and preach the gospel at any cost, they must begin to understand a basic principle about the anatomy of a woman's body, especially the powerful gravitational force in operation as she gives birth. Once the water has broken, it is inevitable that new life must come forward. Men need to understand when God has truly called someone to preach His divine gospel, it is impossible to stop what He has put in motion. When God puts His preaching anointing on a person's life, male or female, the Word of God must come forth from the vessel that has been chosen by the almighty Creator of the universe and all life forms.

In the same way, imagine what it would be like for a woman in full labor to try to hold back the birthing process. This would create a catastrophic problem for the mother and the child, when the 'fullness of time has arrived' as the words of God spoke abut Jesus coming to the earth (Galatians 4:4-7). Sooner or later, it becomes impossible for a woman to keep in what God intended to be released. Your chances of trying to catch or stop a bullet in full motion are better than stopping a mother in the final seconds of her delivery.

First of all, the labor pains are too great, and second, the force demanding the baby come forward is too powerful for the laws of men and women to hinder life God has called to come in to being. When God calls a person to step forward, he or she will step forward or suffer the consequence of disobeying the almighty Creator and Savior of the world. The same godly force that brings forth a baby in nature also applies to women ministers or anyone else being called by God. As I have said earlier, the force of God is too powerful to prohibit female ministers from taking their rightful place at the table of God with their male courterparts.

The fact of the matter is no human has the ability or power to prevent the dawning of a new day. Nor does humanity have the power to stagnate the move of God in the lives of women ministers as they take up their preaching crosses to follow Jesus. Have you ever known a man to stop the dawning or the setting of the sun? Do you know of anyone in human history to stop the moon from shining in the dark night? Please tell me his name. Other than God, no one possesses this type of power, and the same goes for the calling of a person into the gospel ministry.

Just like when floodwaters are in a position to breech the levies and dams, you have to open the floodgates and release the water pressure from the structures and prevent a catastrophe. So I say to all women ministers and men who are obedient to the move of God, let's open the floodgates and release the water that has come from God Almighty. Amen! Believe it or not, when a person humbly submits to the move of God, it keeps everyone safe upstream as well downstream. When we submit to the Holy Spirit in this way, people tend not to get out their respective lanes. When the people of God stay in their lanes, more kingdom work for Jesus is accomplished and God gets glorified.

I am more than convinced that by the leading of the Holy Spirit women will persevere and find ways to defeat the obstacles and rejections aimed at denying them access to many church pulpits across America. Over time, they have found ways to master situations and circumstances with a grace and poise only God and life's experiences can bring to the table of faithful servanthood. One would prove to be ignorant if he or she thinks women have not figured out ways to survive in a world (the preaching ministry) dominated by men who believe women are out of order for even attempting to enter pulpits with the idea they have been called by God to preach His gospel. It is my most sincere prayer that male ministers realize the great gift they have in women ministers, reach out to them, and commit to helping train them, so we all can serve in the kingdom of God as co-laborers.

Women have the right to preach the gospel and tell men and women about the beautiful message God has to share with them concerning His most holy words. The atmosphere or environment in churches for women ministers should be as friendly and conducive as that for male ministers. People should not get up and walk out of a service because a woman is ministering or preaching. This is an act of total disrespect for a sister in the family of God that you say you love and respect.

Well, please answer the following questions. Is love cold and disrespectful? Is love degrading? Is love kind? Is love patient? Is love uplifting? Is love racist? Is love sexist? How does God allow you to see the world you live in? Do you see male or female only? Do you see the world from the perspective of black or white only? Or do you truly see the world and life from the mind of God and through the eyes of Jesus? Do you actually believe Jesus would tell a woman to go and sit down because she cannot proclaim His words to the masses because she is female? I am curious why the Holy Bible calls Miriam, Moses' sister, a prophetess if she was not to serve as a minister, delivering God's words to the congregation of Israel (Exodus 15:20).

Many of us have friends or know people we may not agree with on every issue. Yet we extend to them the respect to be heard and the right to express their own opinions. We, too, allow them the space to follow their own dreams, no matter where they may take them. I would love to one day see women ministers have the same freedom, respect, and comfort to share the gospel with men the way they have the freedom to share their feelings in an environment with other women. When women are given the opportunity and freedom to let down their guard with chauvinistic male pastors and ministers, it will be a great day in the kingdom of God on earth. Then I will know we have arrived at a place that is pleasing to God.

Some women ministers will probably never reach their full potential in God as long as their male colleagues continue to cast the dark veil of rejection upon them as they go about fulfilling their appointed assignment as a preaching minister of the gospel. I have learned this one thing about love; it is not so much concerned with where you came from but is more interested in where you are going in life. When we learn to love our sisters like we do our brothers, the gender issue between male and female ministers will cease to exist in the congregation of God.

Yes, I know there will always be ministers and people who will never accept women as ministers, like there are those people who will never accept biracial marriages. Regardless of what one may say to persons in any of these groups, their minds are already made up, and there is no changing them or their mindsets. I believe people who reject people because they are doing their best to fulfill God's plan for their lives will probably never understand the meaning of true love until they learn not to equate race, gender, or ethnicity with love! If love is the greatest principle, please tell me what is the fuss over ethnicity or gender?

Ignorance and hate will continue to be stumbling blocks for many people, even beyond the return of Jesus Christ. Some people would rather lose out on spending eternity with Jesus than to accept women ministers or marriages between different ethnic groups. You probably would come out better trying to pull a piece of meat from the mouth of a ferocious beast than trying to convince some antiwomen legalists that God has approved women to preach the gospel, or a racist that God approves of interracial marriages and biracial children. Better yet, that all nationalities, ethnicities, and genders will be in heaven.

Many people will not accept the fact God has called women into the ministry. Some cannot fathom that God has given women gifts such as preaching, teaching, exhortation, and other talents to use within the church like He gave male ministers. The same should hold true for the human vessel God uses in a like manner. If God can give the gift of speech to things in nature other than humans and convince people that a supernatural act of God has taken place, then the female vessel the Holy Spirit uses to minister the Word of God to His church should be celebrated with amazement, like all miracles performed by God. Amen.

When God calls someone into His ministry, it is a great honor and a mind-boggling phenomenon. Think about it. When God saves and calls a person into ministry, He is not only purging the person from the filth of sin but also taking the person from his or her natural habitat and using the person in such an awesome and powerful manner that the person's actions are beyond human comprehension. The humanness of the person is lost in the divine transformation process of the Holy Spirit. It is the Holy Spirit that becomes supreme in the person's life, and no longer can the individual take any credit for the miraculous things occurring in his or her life. Unless God gives revelation to a situation, we will never grasp the message at hand.

Many students attend school, but not all students are in tune with what the teacher is teaching. Some students come to class, but they never participate during class discussions or exercises. Salvation is a classroom, where all learners must participate to receive a passing score for promotion to the next level. The students which refuse what the teacher is teaching or disrupts class, will more than likely end up being suspended from school or receive some other type of disciplinary action.

Some people go to college and get a degree but leave school without understanding their journey, profession, or the degree or certification they acquired. They went through the motions and received the gift of education with some basic knowledge, but they never learned the skills of the trade or profession. This is like how the Holy Bible says, "Some people will be forever learning, but never able to come to the knowledge of the truth" (2 Timothy 3:7). Such people will forever deny the truth about God using women in the gospel ministry as preachers, so they will never have to explain the great mystery and awesome phenomenon of how the Holy Spirit uses women ministers to touch and change lives of people who were once lost in sin but are now saved by the grace of God through the ministry of a Christian woman.

There is still so much about God we do not understand. Humankind cannot even begin to scratch the surface about God's awesome nature. When we think we have figured out a small portion of God, He rolls out one of His awesome acts and puts us back at square one again. The move of the Holy Spirit is so majestic in nature that it often catches us off guard because we expect God to move in a way we have preprogrammed in our minds. Just because a person may not be able to explain or understand something does not mean it did not happen. The female or male vessel is only able to speak as an anointed oracle by the power of God.

Traditionally, male ministers are afforded the opportunity to share their thoughts and opinions about the gospel with the entire congregation. Yet many women ministers are rejected in many mainstream denominations and churches simply because they are female. Many times when women ministers are given a platform to speak, it is usually to a group of other women. The sting of rejection felt by women ministers is forcing many to leave mainstream denominations and churches to start their own ministries, which will allow them to fulfill God's calling without the bondage and red tape of traditional denominational beliefs.

Women ministers should be given the same window of opportunity as male ministers. They should be given the chance to preach on all special days or occasions. Women ministers should be given the opportunity to preach before an audience during annual men's and women's day celebrations. Women ministers should not be restricted to only preaching women's annual days, but given the respect to preach men's annual days as well. In the family of God, Jesus is all about inclusion and not exclusion, like so many churches and denominations practice today. Learn to do things out of the box when ministering to the people of God, and observe the nurturing and feeding of God's sheep help them to grow into spiritual giants.

Many women are at a standstill in churches, knowing they have been called by God to preach His Word. Yet because of the human fear factor, being afraid of the things people might say about you or what they will probably do to you sometimes strikes fear into the hearts of people. The fear becomes so overwhelming for some that it literally makes people buckle to their knees with the spirit of surrender rather than exercising the will power to stand up and fight for God's calling to preach His Holy word. The peer pressure especially coming from loved ones, societal expectations, and social isolation, forces some women to sit down and either avoid their calling or submit to the selfish and deceptive power of humanity, which causes some women to eventually doubt they have been called out by God.

Just think about this, if a bird God has given wings to fly only sits in a tree and watches other birds fly, sooner or later, that bird will become prey for some predator. The same goes for women ministers who sit around and refuse to fulfill their calling from God. Sooner or later, they will become prey for the Enemy. When men and women fail to do what God has called them to do, there is a great void in their lives that only obedience to God can solve. Whenever people walk in disobedience to the will of God for their lives, they will never experience the peace and joy God has in store for them. Do you want to submit your loyalty to humanity or experience the peace and joy of God? One day of obedience to God is better than a thousand years trying to live without Jesus.

We must never forget that Satan is an abuser and has ruled in the arena of religion with an iron fist for centuries. Nothing has changed about his style. The Evil One made his mark by promoting and embracing fear and intimidation. The Devil uses fear and intimidation so forcefully that many of the sisters called into the gospel ministry will not move toward the pulpit because they do not want to rock the boat. They fear putting a strain on some of their relationships and people who will not understand their move to step up and preach God's divine words of wisdom.

Also, their concerns are not about how to step up and comfort the people of God. It is how to keep their relationships intact if they decide to obey God's mandate. This is why obeying, trusting, and believing in God is a bold move, and to preach in the midst of great opposition is an even bolder move for the kingdom of God. Many of us are called to do it, but only a few are chosen to preach God's Holy Word, even amid great opposition. A word of caution to the wise is when we allow fear to rule or control our lives, then there is really no room left for Jesus to take control of your being. We have to turn over our fears to the Lord and let the Holy Spirit remove the cyst from our spirits.

Keep in mind that once God puts His calling on someone's life, He never lifts the responsibility of the calling. Attempting to live the rest of one's life avoiding the calling does not relieve him or her of the responsibility of the calling. God's calling is more permanent than someone's birth certificate, birthmark, or Social Security number. It is a person's greatest identity. A person's calling is tied to his or her purpose. One can never understand or be true to God's calling without first understanding God's purpose for his or her life. It is true when certain persons in the Bible—like Cain, Jonah, and Saul—refused to obey their calling from God, a death warrant was issued for their lives. Just the thought of having God issue a death warrant for their lives should let people like us know the seriousness of trying to avoid God's calling.

Furthermore, purpose is everything, especially when you do not know what your purpose is in life. Knowing your purpose provides security, confidence, direction, identity, and a destiny as you journey through life. Your purpose acts as your global positioning system and if followed correctly, it will get you safely to your destination. Purpose is what sustains our lives even when we do not know our purpose. Sometimes while driving your vehicle you may not know where you will end up but you still go. Even while driving we sometimes get lost and have to redirect ourselves to find our way back on the correct path. Purpose points us in the right direction to Jesus.

Nearly everyone wants to know about the ending of his or her life. Purpose answers the question about your ending before you can hardly get out of your beginning. Once a person begins to operate in his or her purpose, the reservation for destiny is being finalized by its originator. The beauty of obeying a calling from God is you will always be able to know where you stand with God. Knowing you are in the best hands ever is another reason it is important a person learn his or her purpose in life.

Only the Creator has the key to your purpose in life. Everyone desiring to fulfill his or her purpose must come through Jesus to get confirmation and instructions about his or her purpose in life. It is impossible for anyone to fulfill his or her divine purpose without the anointing of Jesus. Only the Holy Spirit can take you to the King.

Although someone may claim to know and fulfill his or her purpose without coming to Jesus, no one can ever fully complete his or her purpose without Jesus. Jesus said in John 15:1–5, "I am the Vine and you are the branches, and God the Father is the gardener ... and you cannot do anything without Me." Jesus is letting us know that even though someone may think his or her achievements in life came as the result of personal talents, it is all by the grace of God!

Women who have been called into the gospel ministry of Jesus Christ must decide if they are going to be a frog on the log or swim as a fish in the water for Jesus. We have this familiar saying within the church that says, "Only what you do for Jesus will last." This idea supports the fact we have all been put on the earth with the mission of building the kingdom of God. It is humanity's duty to labor for the kingdom of God because the bottom line is Jesus is the only One with the power and authority to give us our final grade in life. Your calling is not between you and humanity; it is between you and God. Your calling is not between you and your local church; it is between you and Jesus. Your calling is not between you and your denomination; it is between you and the Holy Spirit.

I charge each woman of virtue who has been called by God to preach the words of God, and then stand and take your rightful place in the kingdom of God. He is looking to receive glory from you as you minister to His sheep. There is no better calling or duty given to men or women than to preach God's Holy Word. So consider yourself blessed and not among those who are cursed, as some would have you to think. The Devil will have you think you are out of order for accepting your calling into ministry, but you must understand the dynamics that surrounds calling into the ministry of Jesus. Stand strong, and do not spare the lightning rod of God's Holy Word, because it is the right time for you to preach, my sister, preach the gospel of Jesus Christ.

Your calling into the ministry by Jesus is a direct threat and attack on the Devil's wicked kingdom. The Devil knows Jesus has invested His power in you so that you will be used as a vessel to expose and defeat Satan's wicked schemes. Accepting your calling into the ministry of Jesus is a constant reminder to the Devil that his time is running out. God is using the same humanity Satan deceived back in the Garden of Eden to fight against him and to tear down his kingdom. It is amazing that the woman played a significant role by helping to usher sin into the world.

Yet men do not give her the credit as ministers of the Gospel to also help usher sin out of the world through the preaching of the gospel. If man is going to blame woman for the caterpillar that introduced sin to the human race, why has he become a stumbling block for helping her to eradicate sin from the people's lives? There is something gravely wrong with this picture. Until men of the gospel respect women of the gospel like Jesus and the Holy Spirit do, the Devil will continue to divide the family of God with an unprecedented gender gap in ministry. Like it or not, change is inevitable and waits for no one except God.

Always remember, it is Jesus who calls you into the gospel ministry with great assurance. Jesus is the Master of the universe that will always get the glory and honor for your labor in His kingdom. It is always up to God to decide if He wants to share some of His glory with humanity. Some people may come into the ministry for the wrong reasons, but in time, He has a way of weaning or pruning leach branches from the fruit-bearing branches on trees the Holy Spirit nurtures. Even as a minister of the gospel of Jesus Christ, you were first born into sin to spread and emulate the ways of sin. Sin is a contagious disease that spreads across the land like the curse of death spread across Egypt during the plague of the death of the firstborn in Egypt when God told Pharoah to let His people go in the book of Exodus (Exodus chapter 11). Sin is worse than the most lethal and out of control wildfire or the deadliest bomb in the universe.

To my sisters in the gospel ministry of Jesus Christ, I charge you to accept your calling from Jesus and begin the process of becoming a branch on the tree of life that brings forth good fruit for the kingdom of God. This is what Jesus would have you do. Never become consumed with those who will reject you, because you have been accepted by the King of Kings and given an invitation by the Lord of Lords. Who can stop you? God's calling is greater than any agenda in the world. God's calling is more important than life itself. God's calling into the gospel ministry is the key to life that opens the door to eternal life in heaven.

I cherish the idea that when you became a born-again Christian, you were reborn and transformed by the Holy Spirit to be like Jesus.

When we stand up for Jesus, God can use us in ways beyond human imagination and far above our own and others' expectations. Women ministers must be willing to stand for whatever is right in the eyes of God. In order for women ministers to survive the anti-women attitude against them, they must demonstrate a commitment and loyalty to Jesus beyond all else. Women ministers, like their male counterparts, must stay focused on the fact it is God, not humanity, who has called them into the preaching ministry. The only thing God asks of women ministers is to cast fear aside and obey Jesus, regardless of who tries to stop them from accepting their calling into the gospel ministry.

Women ministers need to decide they are going to give birth to the preaching baby God has given them. It is sad how some women allow others to encourage them to abort the most precious thing life has to offer, doing God's will. Sisters, please do not allow these modern-day Pharisees to discourage you, because at the end of the day, God is going to ask you, "Who or what hindered you from doing My will?" When men, women, or any other creature try to prevent women from fulfilling their ministry, it is an attempt to abort a life that God has placed within them. Any person who comes to steal, kill, and destroy your baby, your dreams of serving the people of God, or your life is not your friend; neither is he or she a friend of God. According to the Holy Bible, the Devil is nothing but a thief who comes with the mandate of stealing, killing, and destroying the things God has given you as blessings (John 10:10).

If women ministers would just obey God, then the Holy Spirit will work on their behalf and destroy the yokes of bondage. Not only will the Spirit of God destroy the yokes of bondage, but it will also protect and defend against those who attempt to stand in God's way as these women render service to the Holy Spirit. Women ministers have to make sure they believe and trust God at His word regardless of how things may look. God asked you and me that if He is for us, then who can be against us?

Keep this thought in mind, when God is for a person, He is more than the whole world against the person. When God is for a person, the person cannot lose (Romans 8:28–31). For this very reason, you have nothing to fear because God is standing with you and holding you up. Remember, God is your great protector and defender against the opposition you face in life as you do His will.

Women ministers must exercise the courage to stand against opposition and stop caving in to fear or rejection by those who try to discourage and rule them by intimidation. If women ministers allow fear to cause them to sit down or give up, it will more than likely rule supreme in their lives. If women do not stand up for themselves, the Devil will feel as though he has been granted permission to abuse them at his leisure. When we avoid what God has commissioned us to do, we become like a fugitive, running from justice. If the Devil can make you run from a fight in which God has given you the victory in advance, then he feels he has the authority to control your destiny by creating fear in your life or situation.

Some people do not like conflict, and instead of facing conflict, they would rather run from it than face it head on. When a person becomes a child of God, no longer does he or she have the right to run from conflict, especially when God has put you in the middle of the battle. Becoming a light of life for Jesus automatically puts you in the middle of conflicts for the sake of the kingdom of God. So running from a fight where God has placed you is not an option. The women ministers issue, fight, conflict, saga is a battle that we cannot run from because God demands us to carry out His divine will regardless of the person, people, churches, and denominations fighting against it.

No matter how hard or fast you run, sooner or later the moment of truth will arrive at your doorstep, looking for you to give an account of your actions, talents, and gifts (Galatians 2:15–21; 3:26–29). When the truth of God arrives at your doorstep, asking for your personal testimony, what will you say about your journey in the ministry of Jesus? Or will you be one of those who make excuses as to why you went off and hid the talent or coin the Lord gave you to invest and bring back a return from your wise investment (Matthew 25:24–30)? Will you try to blame others for preventing you from obeying the voice of God concerning your calling into the gospel ministry?

With thirty years in Christian ministry as a pastor or army chaplain, I am convinced women, like men, bring unique gifts and talents to the ministry that are beneficial to the entire congregation. These gifts and talents can nurture and empower the sheep in ways that are sometimes beyond the grasp of their male counterparts. One of the unique ways women approach the ministry is from a heart-to-heart approach rather than a mind-to-mind approach. Many male ministers seem to use a more logical approach to their ministries as they deal with issues and solve problems. I am amazed at the insightful perspective women bring to the table, which sometimes eludes many men. It is a great blessing to have that second set of eyes to help nurture and protect God's people from the Devil and his army.

Furthermore, the way a mother's intuitiveness helps protect and nurture the natural family should not be taken lightly, because it is an awesome asset for ministry. God's wisdom and might are so amazing that He uses the same gifts to bless Jesus' disciples in ways that are mind-boggling to many people. As recorded in Revelation 4:11, Jesus created everything for His purpose, and nothing was created without God's approval. God gives us gifts and talents, and it is God who should be the one deciding how we use those gifts and talents. No humans should overstep their boundaries and try to possess such authority or power like they are the Deity. When mere men and women try to assume God's throne, they deflate the faith and create confusion. It is this type of confusion and division that unlocks the door for the Devil to enter into the family of God with the intention of conquering and devouring the flock of Jesus.

The problem with the king of Tyre, the citizens of Tyre and Lucifer in Ezekiel chapter twenty eight is they all got carried away in their own lustful pride. When men and women continue to cross over out their lanes and attempt to do God's job without His approval, I would argue that pride is the principle thing that is causing the rift. In Ezekiel chapter twenty eight, God shares with the Prophet Ezekiel the trust, respect, love, perfection, beauty, wisdom, authority and anointing He had given to Lucifer caused him to get lifted up in pride. Lucifer became so prideful that he tried to overthrow God by attempting to take over God's throne in Heaven. Men ministers that reject women ministers on the notion they claim the Holy Bible does not support the idea, need to be very careful they do not end up with the same pride that overthrew king Tyre, the city of Tyre and Lucifer as also recorded in Revelation Chapter 12 and Isaiah Chapter 14.

Women ministers bring unique gifts and qualities to the preaching ministry that only come from being a woman. For example, over the years, I have noticed young people have a way of ministering to other youth that comes out of the creative minds of youthful thinking. No one understands a youth like another youth. For this reason, God has taken it upon Himself to call men, women, girls, and boys into the preaching ministry. It takes all parties working together to make the kingdom of God on earth an enjoyable experience, which brings about an exciting ride for everyone. There is nothing hard about riding the joy train for Jesus if we all render due respect to God, Jesus, the Holy Spirit, and our brothers and sisters in the gospel ministry. Once we respect the fact it is God who calls all for His purpose and by His might, there will cease to be the issue or debate about whether it is right for women to enter the preaching ministry.

When we talk about the table of brotherhood, does this only mean those of the masculine gender? Does the conversation within the Christian faith and local church settings about brotherhood only apply to male ministers or does it also apply to the sisterhood within the Christian faith? When God says He created man in His image, is He only talking about men or women as well (Genesis 1:26-27)? When the writer of the book of Hebrew says, 'Follow peace with all men, holiness without no man shall see the Lord,' was he only talking to males or does this message applies to females as well? (Hebrews 12:14). Or, when Job said if a man dies, shall he live again, was Job only referring to men? (Job 14:14) Finally, when the Apostle Paul says to Timothy, "I will therefore that men pray every where, lifting up holy hands, without wrath and doubting" (1 Timothy 2:8). These few examples encourage me to ask the question are women ministers welcome to sit at the same table as the men of God? Or does this mean women can sit down at the table but are not allowed to speak? Can there truly be a table of true brotherhood, as God intended from the beginning of creation, if Eve is not represented in the garden?

Even after the great disobedience in the Garden of Eden, Adam and Eve were allowed to tell God their sides of the story prior to God expelling them from the Garden of God. If God has enough respect and love to listen to a man and woman even after they messed up His great creation plan for humanity, surely we can exemplify this same kind of compassion, since humanity is made in the image of God. Where do men and women draw the line for their authority in the local church, denominational settings, and religious circles throughout the world, but especially here in America?

I am amazed how in God's houses of worship, everybody's gifts should be appreciated and respected mainly because the gifts and talents are devotions to God and not humanity (James 1:17). The sanctuaries of God should be sacred places, where all people should be granted the opportunity to bring their respective sacrifices and gifts to the altar of God. How is it that when a certain group, like women ministers, brings their God-given gifts and talents to the altar, it is the place where chauvinism attacks them with great disapproval and rejection? God's altar has always been where the individual came to present his or her offerings, gifts, or sacrifices to God. Under the law, in certain circumstances, no one else could be present at God's altar for the individual except the high priest. Is this the case today in many churches across America? Like the priest under the law, are we telling women only males are called to address the sinful issues plaguing God's people today?

Whenever a person stands in the presence of the Almighty God, he or she is responsible for his or her own actions and decisions. Regardless of the situation, the person is required and expected to present his or her own contributions to God. No one else can stand before God and plead your case except Jesus. When people try to stand in the way of women fulfilling their calling into the gospel ministry, they are forbidding others from presenting their gifts, sacrifices, and offerings to God.

Furthermore, throughout the history of the Holy Bible, we witness corporate and individual worship in the lives of the Hebrews and the people of God. God requires that we give gifts and sacrifices as individuals and as a community of believers. For example, in Genesis chapter twenty two, Abraham was tested to offer Isaac, his son, as a personal sacrifice to God. Then in Genesis chapter fourteen, Abraham turns around and offers Melchizedek, the king of Salem and priest of the Most High, a tenth of all he had gained from battle after defeating Kedorlaomer and the other Mesopotamian kings of the east (Genesis 14:2). When female as well as male ministers accept their call from God, it is a personal sacrifice being offered up to God.

Here is a basic fact you need to know before you decide to step into the waters of the preaching ministry, or if you are already swimming in the waters of the preaching ministry. Please understand the way by which males and females are sometimes viewed and classified within our society. Too often people are treated differently because of the color of their skin, gender, or physical looks rather than by the person's performance (skills and abilities), etc. or the person's persistent testimony including the genuine and repeated attempts to prove he or she has been called by God to preach the gospel of Jesus Christ. Whenever you weigh on the scales of fairness, the difference between the ways male ministers are treated versus female ministers are treated within the local churches; there is significant unbalance in the scales. Such a dysfunctional and unbalanced trend in these scales of justice will more than likely give a false reading about women pastors, women preachers, and women ministers.

The unbalanced scales of the gender clash are always in favor of the person or persons calibrating and reading the scales. In this case, men think they are balancing and calibrating the scales, when in reality, God is the One in charge of balancing, calibrating, and controlling the scales. God invited women ministers to eat with Him at the table of His New Testament church, where grace is extended to all, regardless of sex, ethnicity, or age. Whenever God's grace is the chef and server of the meal, you never have to worry about meeting people's expectations. Just be willing to please God.

In the book of Proverbs we are taught that when you use an unbalanced scale or weight to hold people back from exercising their God-given gifts and talents, we are treading on dangerous grounds with God. Proverbs 11:1 reads, "A false balance is [an] abomination to the Lord: but a just weight is his delight." In Proverbs, 20:23, God's Word says, "Divers weights are an abomination unto the Lord, and a false balance is not good." These two Scriptures, along with all the others cited in this book, ought to serve notice on people who are forbidding women to preach based on their gender.

Furthermore, men and women are given gifts and talents to make the world a better place to live. They should be given the opportunity to share them with all God's creation and not just an isolated group of people. Unjust scales are detrimental to all creation because they take away the very thing (the freewill to choose heaven or hell) that God has given to humanity, which separates us from the rest of creation. We are given gifts and talents to use for the kingdom of God, and everyone, regardless of male or female, should be allowed the opportunity to help advance the kingdom of God here on this earth.

A scale that measures social or religious acceptance based on human identity is no match for grace and mercy. God uses a corrective measure that is not made by human hands or intelligence. Neither does He use any other natural means to determine if a person is worthy to serve as a preacher in His kingdom. By God doing it this way, only God has the right to grant grace and mercy to whomever He decides to favor.

I challenge each of you to step out in faith and exercise the lifeline of grace God has given you. Only until a person moves by the faith of God and under the obedience of the Holy Spirit can she go and preach His Word to all who will listen. Some will not listen, but do not allow rejection to become a stumbling block in your ministry. After all, many refused to listen to Jesus, and He was the Christ Savior, who came to liberate them from sin, death, and destruction.

If humanity closes one door for you to preach God's Word, then you best believe God will open many more opportunities for you to proclaim His Holy Word. Through the ages, Satan has done everything within his power to stop God's Word from going forth but has failed repeatedly to stop the promotion of the gospel of Jesus and the Word of God. The Devil's attack against women ministers is another failed attempt to prohibit God's words from going forward to free people from their sins. It is essential that you do not allow fear to stop you from fulfilling the dream God has birthed in you and the child He must birth through you. Remember, if you do not preach His Word, He will raise another to take your place at the great banquet.

Also, when God calls you, no man can hinder you from accomplishing what He has called you to do. When God equips you, no one can take your tools or gifts from you. Your calling, gifts, and tools are unique; they were given only to you for a divine purpose. When God anoints a person, whether female or male, the anointing will validate your legitimacy through signs and wonders surrounding your life and ministry. When God calls a person into the gospel ministry, the Devil is the only force in the world that will fight it and deny it. Accepting your calling to the gospel ministry is no easy task. This is one of the main reasons God called you; He calls great people for awesome tasks in life.

God already knows you are capable of succeeding with the mission. Otherwise, He probably would not have called you. You just have to know you will succeed in the mission and prepare yourself for battle. To preach or minister God's Word is unlike any other battle known to humanity and creation. When you submit to preach God's most holy words, the Enemy will come after you, like a perfect storm that makes land with vicious winds and an assault full of destruction. Yet the city residents live to tell the story of how God spared their lives and instilled hope in them to rebuild their city.

However, regardless of the ferociousness of the battle at hand, you must charge on with the faith and belief God will see you through the journey. Always know your reward is not given to you by men or women but by the hands of God. The peace of knowing God is in charge of your calling to minister should be encouraging enough to motivate everyone *called* to run the race all the way through the finish line, like a track runner or swimmer trains to continue all the way to the end. These athletes know they must cross the finish line without looking back for their competitors because many have lost the race by the split-second they took to look back. There is no joy or victory until you have crossed the finish line. The feeling of knowing God is the captain of your ship should be the emancipation proclamation that will encourage you to step out of your old bondage and shackles. Preach, my sister, preach!

I pray you never buy into the false notion that another person has control over your destiny when it comes to God's plan for your life. God does not give human beings the glory to decide who can become a part of His priestly court. No one has the right to tell you whether you can or cannot preach God's divine words of faith, hope, liberty, and salvation. God is the only judge who sits on the bench when selecting ministers for His kingdom.

Sadly, some people have refused to accept their calling because they have allowed other people to control their destiny in the ministry. Only later do they find out their calling into ministry is a covenant between them and God. Your calling to ministry is your soul, and I beg you to never turn your soul over to anyone except God. No one knows what is best for you like God does, and no one else has your best interests at heart like God. Preaching the gospel of Jesus Christ should be your number one passion in life because life is all about pleasing Jesus!

When you are a child of God, Jesus has negotiated a covenant with the Father on your behalf. The covenant allows only the Holy Spirit to control your destiny. The Holy Spirit will always do what is in the best interests of God and Jesus. Heaven's agenda is always more essential than the desires of humanity or your personal agenda. As disciples of the cross, we must never forget we are here to serve God and submit ourselves as servants of the Most High God. We were not given life for God to serve us, even though He does serve us in many ways. The choice of what He does for us is left to God. He allows Jesus and the Holy Spirit to serve us only because He loves us so much that He does not want to see any of us die and go to hell.

Moreover, whenever God puts a triumphant message in your heart, the Holy Spirit fuels it with an explosive power that cannot be contained by humans or any other force. When this happens, the mouth can only serve to release the overwhelming, bubbling power that carries the keys of liberation and the joyous reality of hope for so many people who are willing to listen and submit to the gospel message. The preaching of the gospel message ignites an explosion in the hearts of humanity that directly connects God with humanity like no other experience in life. Not even the birth of a life or the wonderful sounds of wedding bells can compare with the celebration of salvation. It is the greatest feeling, the greatest response, the greatest decision, and the greatest destiny in life.

When we allow God to set up business in our lives, the Holy Spirit becomes the managing supervisor for the actions of your heart. It immediately begins producing a joy and peace like none other in this life. When we obey the Word of God, the Holy Spirit gives us a joy that is unexplainable to this world. It is a peace that passes all understanding. It is an assurance that is always punctuated with hope and faith and without any doubt. God has never had to reduce his workforce because of lack of business. You do not need a specific length of service on the job or with the company to qualify for retirement. You are eligible for full retirement benefits the day you accept Jesus' salvation plan. Even if you are on the job for one minute and have to retire, you still get full retirement pay with benefits from Jesus.

Also, when you live for Jesus He will never leave you or forsake you. If you should die, you will live again in heaven. You do not have to worry about tomorrow or the future or where your next meal is coming from because God is going to provide it for you. Jesus and God will give you peace even in the midst of trouble. You do not need to worry about the wars and rumors of wars, because Jesus is your protector, buckler and shield (Psalm 18:2, Psalm 91:4; Matthew 20:9–16; John 14:1-31). This is the awesomeness of the power of the God we serve.

You have to blow your gospel horn, even if it is going to make some people angry with you. Never allow another person to forbid you to do something God has already told you to do. Do not allow anyone or anything to cause you to break covenant with God, especially after you know what God has done for you. Remember, you are not just blowing your horn because you are a part of the band.

Furthermore, you have a much greater reason to refuse to remain silent. You are blowing your horn for the drum major of salvation, Jesus Christ. You are blowing your horn because it is an instrument that proclaims God's righteousness. If you do not blow it for Jesus, wickedness will continue to spread its lethal flames of corruption across the universe. Sin ruins lives, and God has given you an instrument to help save lives, as a doctor is trained to help save the lives of his or her patients. If you refuse to blow your horn, how can they hear holy words of God without a preacher like you, who has been sent by God?

More important, never ever forget that Jesus is the person you must aim to please and not humanity. You will more than likely always have a listening audience whenever you blow your horn, but never forget the reason you are part of the band. You only made the band because Jesus selected you as one of His faithful ones, not necessarily because you are a talented musician. Keep in mind that humility is a much greater asset in the kingdom of God than a person's talent or gifts. Jesus is why you have the strength, gift, and power to blow your horn. So I charge you, my sisters in the gospel ministry, blow your horns for Jesus regardless of the audience.

Whenever you please Jesus, He makes your enemies your haters, as well as those jealous of you your footstool (Psalm 110:1; Isaiah 66:1; Luke 20:43). When you please Jesus, He makes you and your enemies have peace with whatever He has called you to do, and if you truly trust in the Holy Spirit, nothing can ever stop you (Proverbs 16:7). Things may strike at you, but they will never bite you. Some people and things may attack you, but they will never defeat you as long as you trust and obey Jesus.

When Jesus calls a man or woman to preach His Holy Word, the calling has priority above anything else in life. This is not to say Jesus desires you to drop everything else, like your family responsibilities, job, and commitments, to attend to His business. It does mean the Holy Spirit demands to become the most essential person or thing in your life. On accepting your call to ministry, not only will you make time for Jesus, but He now becomes your primetime! Of course, this is the way things should become when we totally commit our lives to Jesus.

Even though some may continue to fight against you as you fulfill the mission God has birthed within you, their attacks will have no relevance to the success God has in store for you. If you can only believe in Jesus and not the critics, you can achieve greater things through faith. If you can allow yourself to push without doubt, hope will guide you into the arms of Jesus. When your ways are pleasing to God, the Holy Ghost will serve as a force field, protecting your surroundings as though your enemies never stood against you. This is how God will make things for you when you stand up and obey His divine calling.

When a person makes the wise decision to surrender to God's will by accepting his or her calling into the gospel ministry, it signals God that you are totally giving in to heaven's highest calling. Ministering as a humble servant in the ministry of God is probably the greatest calling of servanthood on the earth. The ministry of Jesus offers a challenge to bring all your strengths and weaknesses under the submission of a hope and belief you are doing a greater good for humanity as well as yourself.

Please keep in mind women ministers and pastors will probably always be judged by a more ungracious audience than their male counterparts. Also, women ministers will more than likely always be challenged to work in an environment with stricter standards by people in the world and those within the church community. In comparison to their male counterparts, women ministers have had to do more to prove their calling as an authentic one from God. Women ministers have also had to endure more ridicule within local churches in order to prove and validate their calling into the preaching ministry.

Furthermore, it is like being in a particular ethnic group and regardless of the great accolades and accomplishments you achieve in life, you will never be accepted as equal to the group that thinks it is superior to you. No matter how brilliant you are, how well you can perform a craft or art, or how well you can preach and teach, you still do not make the cut as one of the elite. This is why women ministers have to learn to accept their calling and move on into the mission field where God sends them. When you know you are right by God, there is no need to fight.

Unfortunately, some things in life, especially in the religious world, are very unfair to women and especially to women ministers. The women who have made great strides in their ministries are those who trusted God regardless of the obstacles facing them. Like many of the oppressed ethnic groups in America's history and history across the world, women allowed their faith, determination, and hope to propel them to press on through various hardships in life. They were determined never to give up, regardless of the pain or shame that accompanied their experiences. When people become oppressed, they discover innovative measures and ways to denounce their oppressors. When denominations, religious associations, and individuals conclude it is within their authority to decide, based on gender, if a person has been called to preach the gospel of Jesus Christ, what would prevent them from taking it farther and say they will also determine who will be allowed to preach based on ethnicity, class, education, financial hierarchy, or family name?

Oppressed people also have no problems risking their lives for freedom and to make the lives of future generations better than what they have experienced. The drive or will to die for an idea or purpose is nothing new in American history. It is the determination to be liberated from unfair taxation and second-class treatment by Great Britain that drove Americans to protest and fight for its independence. While America was under England occupation, Great Britain was the world's greatest empire as far as economics, power, resources, territorial control, and geographic boundaries. History teaches us to never underestimate the fortitude people will exemplify when their rights as free agents of God's creation are at stake. The good in people will always find ways to defeat evil and get around man-made barriers that will try and hinder what God has put in place to liberate people from oppression.

Many successful women ministers understand that in man's sinful and unjust kingdom, they will probably never get a fair assessment of their calling into the ministry. Yet women ministers should not put on the brakes, because they are faced with bigotry and sexism. Women ministers must know they can survive in a religious kingdom where the leadership in times past has been dominated mainly by male ministers. What I admire and love about Jesus is He is a God of change. His presence on earth represents and demanded change starting from the inside and moving outwardly. Just the thought of Jesus means change to me. Accepting Jesus in our lives is the beginning of the ultimate change that will occur in our lives here on earth.

God gives grace to the humble and rejects the proud. As you read this particular text, keep in mind God did not isolate this statement to a particular sex (James 4:6). It says He gives grace to the humble and not just to the males. Males and females who prove themselves as humble beings to God are the ones who will reap the benefits and blessings from God in supernatural ways here on this earth. Women ministers, humility is not you sitting down on God when you know He has called you to preach His divine gospel. Women ministers, humility is not you hiding in the shadow, filled with fear and intimidation, because your pastor has stepped out of his lane by telling you God does not call a woman to preach His gospel. Faith and humility show your willingness to obey the voice of God regardless of the cost! Humility and faith are two ingredients that move the Holy Spirit to quick action for you whenever you are in need. According to God's holy words, faith is one of the most powerful influences in the life for the believer, because God is able to do wonderful and great things through a person's faith and without faith it is impossible to please God (Proverbs 3:34; Hebrews 11:1-19; Philippians 3:3-9; 1 Peter 5:5).

I challenge my sisters to never forget in God's kingdom, the playing field is fair for all who accept the mission to preach the gospel of Jesus Christ. Yes, it is true that under the law, mainly the Hebrew people were given special privileges to excel beyond human expectations and limits by the power of God. Thank you to the almighty God that times have changed, and we are no longer under the law, which seemed to favor men over women and Jews over Gentiles. Under grace, this is where we now live, and our greatest reward is connected to our obedience and commitment to live wholeheartedly for Jesus.

Here is the bottom line. None of us is worthy to stand in God's presence apart from Jesus. None of us can become pleasing to God, even at our very best, without the guiding of the Holy Spirit. Although it is an Old Testament Scripture, Jeremiah made a statement several thousand years ago that without the justification of the Holy Spirit, it is impossible for anyone to make the cut with God. As proclaimed by the prophet Jeremiah, the Holy Bible teaches us that "the heart of humanity is wicked and deceitful above all things" (Jeremiah 17:9).

Our only hope is to obey the voice of God against all the odds. The reason you should step out in faith and deny the odds is because God is the odds breaker. Reality and common sense tell you it is impossible for you, but faith, hope, and trust in God say if you only believe, you can accomplish impossible things through Jesus. There are only two ways a person can walk in life: the natural (foolish), or by faith in the Spirit of God (wise). Which way do you want to travel in life?

3

God Has the Power to Break Down Walls

God has the power to break down the pieces of anything that exists. God, the Maker and Creator of everything, can break anything all the way down to the point where it no longer exists as it was. He can make it into a whole and even give it an entirely new identity. Only God has the supreme power to turn a small human seed into liquid form, and as it passes through the process of forming life, God allows the seed to turn into a full-grown, solid woman or man. God's way of working with fractions is to turn all equations into whole numbers, which are signs of everyone being completed in Jesus.

Our fullness in life and the world to come can only be achieved by the grace of God. To experience this wonderful grace, one must accept Jesus as his or her Lord and Savior. It seem like the people I have met during my life have a drive to become complete in some fashion or another. They look for others to help make them complete by the giving and receiving of love in marital relationship. Some people have children and families to fill a void of loneliness in order to help them feel complete. Yet the truth of the matter is only a submissive and genuine relationship with God can bring total completeness to a person's life.

Furthermore, as Christians, we must learn to be careful and not just follow our hearts' desires and the voices of others. We must commit to obeying the words of God above all else. For those of us accustomed to following our hearts' desires before we accepted Jesus as our Lord and Savior, and when we walked in the darkness of the world, we ended up getting ourselves into trouble time after time. We thought we knew what was right and best for us, only to find out in the end that we landed in the wrong drop zone. The embarrassment, scars, pain, and suffering from some of the trouble we encountered lingers to this day for some of us. When we line up with the will of God, we are no longer the underdog; we now become the "superdog" because our hero, Jesus Christ, is the greatest superhero in the world. Jesus has a way of giving a powerful voice to those without a voice. All you have to do is trust in the Lord, your God, and Jesus will move mountains out of your way so you can accomplish the mission He has called you to perform.

Women in the gospel ministry must be able to quickly spot and avoid people who will make every attempt to oppose their ministries. They have to recognize their callings from the eyes of God's grace instead of the letter of the law. If women ministers allow themselves to buy into the philosophy that God does not call them into the preaching arena of His ministry, then they have to be very careful not to become brainwashed into disobeying God like Eve and Adam did at the request of the serpent. Once a person has an appointment with God to preach His Holy Words and he or she refuses to do so, then the person starts living in the land of disobedience. Whenever a person ends up living in the land of disobedience, he or she can also become infected with the same condescending spirits as some of their detractors have convinced themselves with the delusional belief that God forbids women from preaching His gospel.

If women ministers cannot exercise an overwhelming amount of grace toward people who reject them and refuse to recognize them as called-out ministers of the gospel, then it could become very easy for bitterness to set in their hearts. If women allow bitterness to take center stage in their struggle for fairness in pulpits across America, then their bitterness and anger will eventually detract from the awesome glory of God. You now become fighters of the flesh instead of allowing God to fight for you by His Holy Spirit.

God desires to receive the glory and honor as a result of a test of faith and perseverance by calling you to preach the words of liberation and life to people who will die in the emergency rooms of life. By approaching the situation from the ranks of humility and wisdom, women ministers can extend much-needed mercy and hope in a pious world that only God has the power to change. The word pious in this conversation is the adjective that refers to devoutly religious but no relationship with Jesus the Son of God. We must never forget just because a person looks a certain way or acts a certain way does not mean the person has a relationship with Jesus. In the following paragraph you will see a group of people that had all garments, practices, words and tools for pietism, but no relationship with Jesus Christ the Son of God and Savior of the world.

When I talk about being pious, I am talking about making a hypocritical display of virtue, insincere, self-righteous, holier-than-thou and sanctimonious like the biblical day Pharisees, Sadducees, and Scribes were according to the teachings of Jesus (Matthew 23:13-36; Mark 12:38-40; Luke 20:47). The exclusion and disrespect women ministers have endured over the ages taught women ministers how to live and coexist in a world where they will get very little support from their male counterparts. Yet they find ways to survive and excel in a jungle-like profession, where fathers have mastered the trade of sabotaging and slaughtering the lives of their own daughters in the gospel without question or hesitation.

The women preachers' struggle in America is similar to the African American and Women Suffrage Movement struggles. The key success to the women ministers' plight will be their ability to handle each relevant situation with wisdom and compassion. Women ministers must never allow emotions to dictate their actions or responses, no matter what happens in the struggle for their freedom in pulpits across America. Neither should they become discouraged to the point of giving up. Sisters in the clergy who are willing to make the sacrifice by carrying the flaming cross for Jesus must do so with grace and dignity. As frontline warriors for the Lord, women ministers must always analyze the entire battlefield with the wisdom, grace, boldness, patience, and compassion of God, while demanding their God-given rights for equality in a male-dominated environment that, at times, has proven to be hostile toward women ministers.

Some things and situations in life can only be changed by the power of God. This is why it is so important for all of us to understand that moving on God's time is essential in any struggle for liberation or to gain human or civil rights. Whenever conducting God's business, it always a matter of moving by the leading and guiding of the Holy Spirit and not on our own accord. We have to be willing to plant seeds where God tells us, even if it means planting them in the scorching heat, freezing cold, or the bitterness of a lukewarm religious atmosphere.

Sometimes in the fight for justice, physical or spiritual conditions may not feel favorable toward your mission. This is when your faith should kick in like a turbocharger and allow you to accelerate and fly as the Holy Spirit guides you through unfamiliar and uncharted territories in your life. You have to dig down within your soul and connect with the Spirit of God to be ensured all is well because your destiny has been ordained by God and not by the hands of men or women.

As God's change agents, women ministers have to make sure they do not get caught up in being controlled by emotions. They must stay focused on biblical reasoning and not respond only with human logic and reasoning. Women ministers fighting for the right to exercise their gifts in many of the local churches across the land must learn to wait for the Holy Spirit to guide them in every situation. Even if the situation looks right, sounds right, feels right, or seems right, still wait on the Holy Spirit to verify it is the right thing to do, and more important, the best thing for the kingdom of God.

When women ministers begin to inspect the way some male pastors and clergy have treated them, it becomes a hard pill to swallow when you know someone is violating you. It probably is a very difficult thing to process when you are being discriminated against simply because the way God has chose to make you. I can imagine it is hard to embrace people when the people endorse rules that say you are less than what they are simply because you are a woman. Yet you have to still handle rejection with the love of Jesus and wait on the Holy Spirit to perform the operation for you or give you the go ahead for the right direction to travel or things to do.

Hopefully, women ministers can begin to see things more clearly from the lens of grace and mercy rather than from the dark shadows of anger and revenge. Many of the women clergy I have befriended over the years continue to suffer from the unjust sting of sexism they have suffered over the years from some of the people they love and respect most. I pray there is a balm of peace and reconciliation in Gilead for the healing of the land because it hurts to be rejected by those you love simply because you have been called by Jesus to do the will of God. The great tragedy to the whole matter is women ministers are being rejected by many male pastors who were once in the same boat. They were rejected because of their physical appearance as being from African American descent.

It is the Spirit of God that liberates us from the shackles of traditions of others. Without His guidance and assistance in our lives, we are constant failures, without any hope of ever winning anything. This is why it is so important for women ministers to move by the grace and Spirit of God when dealing with the issue of fair and equal access to pulpits across America. Wise women and men conquer adversity through humble and constructive actions and usually end up getting what they want in life. The measure of a man or woman is not in how loud he or she is in life; it is the quietness by which he or she successfully allows others to gain access to a greater success by exposing persons to opportunities for the commitment of diligence and unselfish sacrifices.

Troubling as it may sound, women ministers need to understand there is strong resentment against them in many churches across America because of their persistent determination to stand boldly and press on to occupy their rightful places in pulpits throughout America. They must not become consumed by the hostility of others but, rather, focus on the love and grace of God! It is God's love that brings healing to tense or volatile situations, especially those dealing with issues we might not fully understand, like women in the pulpit. By understanding some of the twisted ideology and theology concerning women ministers, women ministers are better prepared to handle and combat some of the strong anti-female factions in many local churches and denominations.

Some of these opponents will continue to refuse to accept any inclination that God has called women to preach His gospel. The good thing about the whole matter is the answer does not rest with women or men. Such an important decision is always in the hands of God, Jesus, the Son of God, and the precious Holy Spirit of the Almighty God.

Women ministers must be very careful not to allow people to draw their focus away from the mission of Jesus with discussions and issues that have no relevance to the kingdom of God. I encourage women ministers to stay focused on the gifts, talents and abilities the Holy Spirit has given you and be loyal to your calling in ministry. Also, women ministers need to be prepared to maneuver around and navigate through distractions in their particular ministries. Since the Holy Spirit has broken the shackles of bondage for women to preach the gospel of Jesus, women ministers need to move forward and enjoy brighter and bigger things God has prepared for them in His kingdom now on the earth.

I share this information with women ministers who receive their calling with great jubilation and overwhelming excitement, but also as words of caution. Some women ministers will discover not everyone shares the same enthusiasm about their calling into the ministry as they do. Remember, Jesus never called us to sit around in the boat; He called us to get out of the boat and come to Him. In obeying His commands, we do not allow fear to overtake us.

Likewise, it is better to know upfront the animosity in the room before you enter than to walk into the room and be oblivious to the discord among the people there. When you understand the disagreement that exists in the room, you can better maneuver on the side of peace, justice, and compassion for the kingdom of God. It is always a good and wise thing to warn people about the hostility and danger they will probably encounter as a result of deciding to stand up for Jesus and obeying their calling from God. Even Jesus told His disciples about the danger on the evangelistic field where He was about to send them to promote His divine gospel.

Jesus told His disciples He was sending them out as sheep among wolves into a world of hostility toward Him. Jesus cautioned they would be confronted with the similar hatred He had to endure for the gospel message (Matthew 10:16; Luke 10:3). I charge and caution you to prepare yourself for demonic attacks against you unlike you have ever seen in your life. The hate and ill-treatment will be real and mind-boggling. The pain and hurt will be unbelievable to the point your faith will be tested like never before. Yet, you cannot stop or retreat from the battle. That is what Jesus was talking about when He said, "A man or woman that puts his or her hand to the Gospel Plough and looks back, is not worthy of the kingdom of God" (Luke 9:62).

Why do people think the storms in their lives will subside when they give their lives to Jesus? The truth is when you give your life to Jesus, the storms, wars, fights, and hatred toward you escalates simply because you have become a disciple of Jesus. Once a person becomes a disciple of Jesus, the Devil puts out this message on you: "Armed and dangerous; shoot to kill!" When someone gives his or her life to Jesus, he or she has just become armed with the greatest weapon in the world: the Holy Spirit of God. God gives His saints a love that is more powerful than any bomb, world military, military equipment, mood or feeling, or any group or gang. Having this kind of ammunition against the Enemy of God is what puts you at the top of the Enemy's most wanted list. To leave the protection and safety of Jesus is a dangerous and disastrous road for any person, especially someone who is running from God's callings.

The Enemy of Jesus is very angry that you gave your life to Jesus. His intelligence has already told him that on accepting Jesus' mandate to preach His divine gospel, you have become a warrior, a skillful fighter, to help expose and destroy the Devil's evil kingdom on the earth. The Evil One knows Jesus has just equipped you with an indestructible weapon that he cannot defeat. Satan knows once you learn how to use the power of God, he can no longer push you around and bully you as he once did.

The Enemy knows once the power of God embraces your life, you become the most powerful agent in all creation and the most destructive force to his kingdom. The Wicked Serpent knows the anointing of God ruling in your life is a perfect match for the love of God to guide you to help destroy his kingdom. The Great Dragon knows once you are in a relationship with Jesus, you are the happiest you will ever be in life.

When people do things pleasing to God, they are the happiest in life. God gives fulfillment to humanity that is unchallenged by anything in the world or universe. The joy and self-worth God brings to people's lives is uniquely His. I am fascinated about the joy people testify about after giving their lives to Jesus versus the hell they lived in prior to Jesus becoming their Savior. Regardless of the person's predicament, Jesus is the best choice for whatever you need.

Think of it way. For every wedding or marriage that is filled with great excitement, there is probably someone somewhere around the world who is angry it is taking place. The person might feel left out or jealous about the joy the newlyweds are sharing with each other. Or the individual may even feel someone has gotten something that belongs to him or her. Whatever the case might be, the feeling of joy is not mutual. Even some of the wedding guests might experience some jealousy or envy about the excitement or blessings of the wedding couple.

Also, every newborn baby does not bring joy to others. We can verify this truth by the births of Moses and Jesus, when the reigning powers were busy trying to destroy their lives. Even today, some people are successful at destroying the lives of babies before they are given the opportunity to live. There is an evil system among us to prevent women from preaching the gospel of Jesus. As children of God we must stand united to prevent this wicked system from taking over the churches of God.

Remember, some people will accept you as a woman minster while others will not. Do not view the opinion of others as the traffic light or signal that tells you when to go or when not to go, especially when the Holy Spirit is the traffic cop in your life, giving you instructions as how to proceed. When you receive the green signal from God, accept His calling, move forward, and do not look back. If you refuse to move forward once God has giving you the green light, you hold up traffic, especially traffic waiting to reap the benefits of your harvest.

When God puts a calling on someone's life, He also gives the person an audience somewhere that is ready to listen. Only through your obedience and willingness will God lead you to the congregation or audience awaiting your arrival, or your rejection. Rejection does not always mean God did not send you. Sometimes God will send you somewhere, knowing you will be rejected.

Finally, you may not be aware of the traffic you are holding up, but this one thing is for sure; God has so many vessels waiting to hear an authentic and powerful word from the Lord. You just might be the vessel God wants to use to make a thunderous sound for Him at a particular moment. This reason alone is enough motivation for you to accept the calling into the gospel ministry. God has chosen to put His mantle upon your life because the Holy Spirit looks for men and women who will stand for Jesus without a flinch or wince.

For over three hundred years in the new land, the descendants of Africans have fought for equality and justice but continue to struggle with injustice caused by wickedness of pride and sin. Like the entangled tension that continuously surrounds race relations in America, there will probably always be an attitude of rejection toward women ministers from the conservative religious sect.

During Jesus' earthly ministry, He was constantly greeted by even greater rejection by the same condescending and prideful spirits that are trying to stop you from fulfilling a commandment God has called you to complete. It is just the nature of the beast when it comes to women ministers in the local churches and within the Christian movement throughout America and the rest of the globe. An oppressed people or group that sincerely wants freedom and equality can never give in to wrongness or give up on the fight or struggle for righteousness, justice, and equality. If women do not stand up for God and bring a gender balance to the preaching ministry, who will?

Regardless of our struggles in life, remember God is always greater than the obstacles people try to put in your path or battles you may face in your ministry. Never forget when you have preached your last sermon, taught your last Bible study lesson, preached your last funeral, dedicated your last baby into the world, or perform your last wedding ceremony or made your last visit to the hospital or nursing home to care for the sick and shut-in, it is time at last for you to stand before the great throne and answer to God. When you stand before the throne of God, will God be convinced that you gave your very best in His kingdom? Will God compliment or reward you for being a loyal and bold soldier for His kingdom while on the earth? Will God say to you well done my good and faithful servant; come and sit down on my right side?

Standing before God is a very serious matter that I believe more people seriously need to consider. If more people knew they are really going to stand before the judgement seat of God, maybe there would not be as many murders, killings, drug abuse, lowliness, or hate for other people because of their gender, ethnicity, religious beliefs, nationality, etc. Have you thought about what your mode of operation or temperament when it is time for you to answer the roll call from heaven? When you have to give an account to God for your actions and deeds, what will be your attitude? Will you be the one who starts your oration to God with a bunch of excuses about why you failed to complete what the Holy Spirit told you to do? Or will you stand empty-handed because you did not obey God? Will God say to you, "Well done, my good and faithful servant," because you refused to bow down to fear, pressure, or the opinions of others about the life Jesus has granted you?

When you stand before Jesus on that great day, none of the parties protesting or promoting your call to ministry will be able to testify for or against you. It does not matter what someone else says or thinks about you when it is your time to stand before the throne of God. Thank God for Jesus!

You will stand before the God who called you. You will give an account how you allowed the Holy Spirit to use you to stand against all the odds and proclaim the wonderful gospel of Jesus to the dying and lost souls. My sisters, here lies one of the great beauties of grace and mercy. God calls us knowing we are not perfect or mature beings. God loves to works miracles and wonders with broken hearts and spirits that have been abused and crushed by sin. Even in the midst of a world with great wickedness God's power is so awesome that it can give you comfort and protection in the world that has caused so much shame and pain at the expense of sin. Jesus is the only one who can release us from sin's ruthless and heartless death grip.

In Jeremiah 35:12–16, the prophet Jeremiah, through the Holy Spirit, lets us know it is natural for the nature of humanity not to be in tune with the will of God. If the Holy Spirit does not tune a person's dial to the right station or channel, the individual will not be able to connect with Jesus. A person must have the right equipment in his or her life to pick up the Holy Spirit's frequency or call signal. If the person is off the dial by even a fraction of a hair, more than likely the individual is still a little too off the station to pick up and hear the voice of God. Sometimes, depending on where you stand in your home determines whether you can pick up a signal on your cell phone. A slight move to the right or left could cause you to lose connection, even though you are in the same general location. The same goes for the kingdom of God.

People can be in the same family, church, choir, Sunday school classroom, service and have a totally different signal or no signal. When the cell phone cannot get a signal of any sort, we call this a dead signal or a dropped call. A dead signal frustrates us because we wish to connect and communicate with our loved ones, friends, business acquaintances, and so on. The most disturbing thing about modern technology is we have all the gadgets, bells, lights, and whistles but no signal to communicate. You have the service but no signal that will allow you to retrieve your call with clarity of heart, mind, body, and soul. When we do not obey the calling of God, we walk around with things and gadgets but have no communication with God. Until one has a personal line to the voice of God, he or she will continue to experience dropped calls in life.

Furthermore, connecting with God is a very serious and delicate relationship, and it could become disrupted by even the slightest outside interference. Never allow anyone to break or disrupt your line of communication with God. You have to be very deliberate in ensuring this never happens because some will interfere unintentionally while others will purposely interfere with your relationship with God by obeying commands from the Devil. As ministers of the gospel, it is our responsibility to stay alert, stay in tune, stay focused, and stay in communication with the Holy Spirit, regardless of how hectic things might become in our lives.

Remember, wars do not stop because soldiers get headaches, become angry, or become hungry. Wars continue even though we have personal crises. We must never allow our lives, missions, or journeys to ever lose communication with the central control tower. Regardless of the storms that may arise on the sea, let's stay focused on communicating with the main tower because the lighthouse leads us to safety, regardless of how boisterous the storms in our lives may become. Jesus is our beacon for salvation and strong tower in the midst of good or bad weather.

Please keep in mind that some people have their own selfish agendas and often rebel against the plans and desires of God, especially if He does not meet their demands at the specified time they requested (Romans 5:12). The apostle Paul tells us there is an ongoing struggle, battle, or war between our carnal minds (the flesh) and the Spirit of God that dwells inside us. It is the spiritual person who lives inside that connects with God when the decision is made to carry out God's instructions with obedience while under the complete influence of the Holy Spirit.

The Holy Bible teaches us that the flesh has been conditioned to rebel against the will of God as a result of the curse of sin way back in the garden of Eden (Galatians 5:17). The Holy Spirit has to chastise and train the flesh before submitting it to the working of the Spirit of God. Since the fall of humanity, the flesh has been conditioned to submit and obey the Devil and do things that are displeasing to God. Since the Devil has been so successful by controlling the thoughts and actions of people, he relies heavily on the flesh to control his slaves who continuously submit to the laws and rules of sin. The Devil looks to get his glory from the sinful nature of the flesh that is continuously in motion to disobey God. Satan will do everything within his power to prevent people from producing anything that will bring honor and glory to God. The Devil is determined to ensure you and I do not glorify God in our flesh or spirits.

God gets the glory when we bring forth good fruit by living under the guidance and direction of the Holy Spirit. When the Holy Spirit of God converts someone, the Holy Ghost immediately starts remodeling the old shack, transforming it into a home of peace and love, where the presence of God abides (1 Corinthians 2:11–16; Romans 7:17–24). Since Jesus has invested so much in the resurrection of our lives from the deadly sting of sin, it is the right thing to show Him that we are indeed appreciative of His sacrifice by following and obeying His commandments. Like the fig tree in Luke 13:6–9, when death was our expected course, Jesus stepped in and begged His Father for a stay of execution for our lives. It was granted to the fig tree as a result of Jesus' pleading its case to the Great Creator of the universe.

It was Jesus who stood and pleaded with His Father that the fig tree be given another year to prove itself under His care and nurturing. It was Jesus who recognized the fig tree had the potential through faith and hope to produce good fruit for the kingdom of God if given the right nutrients (words of God) and fertilizer (Holy Spirit) to feed it. Jesus always looks for opportunities to sustain our lives, even when we do not bear the kind of fruit that is pleasing to God. He is constantly on the witness stand in heaven, pleading our case for a brighter today and a greater tomorrow (1 John 2:1-2).

Whether we believe the playing field is fair or unfair has nothing to do with the power of God. We know God is self-sufficient and does not necessarily move by what we think or what we do in terms of our personal lives. However, when God gives us a mission in life, He wants us to operate against the odds in order to test our faith. Many times when God sends us on a mission, He has already prepared the playing field or removed obstacles that will try to hinder you from achieving the great mission of obeying His calling. When someone is truly determined to please God, he or she will not let anyone isolate his or her faith and hope by forcing the person to withdraw into a corner of disappointment.

More importantly, how can we prove our trust in God if we are never put in situations where our faith can be tested and proven by success? To prove our faith, we need to put it in positions where adversity tests and challenges faith. Anyone can claim to be your friend when peace and prosperity are escorting you to the banquet; but will they remain your friend when war and poverty uncontrollably ravage the land? Regardless of the situation or the crisis, Jesus is always your friend.

We must never lose touch of the fact God has the power to take situations we consider deficits and turn them into profits. God can take our shortcomings and make them success stories. God can take an unjust situation or environment and cause you to become the catalyst for change and then allow you to be the person to help usher in justice where injustice once roamed and ruled. God can take something that was meant for evil against you and make it turn out for your good. God has the authority, power, and ability to take your enemy and make him or her bless you, even when he or she does not intend to bless you. This is the kind of God we serve. Then He turns around and serves us with His awesome grace, mercy, and love, which are filled with great blessings and kindness beyond human comprehension.

You could end up being like powerful preachers such as Sojourner Truth, Harriet Tubman, Joyce Meyers or Bishop Vasti Murphy-McKenzie, Dr. Samella Junior-Spence, Brenda Harris-Haywood, Juanita Bynum, Paula White, Elizabeth Miller, Liz Mentor, or Monica

Mitchell as God graciously gives you His anointing. Believe it or not, God is just waiting to use faithful and dedicated warriors in the gospel ministry to stand boldly without fear to preach the Truth (Jesus) about the kingdom of heaven. You must be willing to move to the next realm, where God wants to do greater things with and through you. You just have to make up your mind that if fate would have it, you are willing to give your life and soul to become the next sacrificial lamb for the kingdom of God.

Remember, there is always a sacrifice prior to celebrating and enjoying victory. It seems that with nearly every joy, someone somewhere had to share a tear and suffer pain so you and I could enjoy the blessings. Even with sports, the arts, religion or any other genres of life, somewhere behind the scenes someone shared some tears either as a result of failures, mishaps, injuries, pains, disappointments, losses, or joys. When we watch national and world championship competitions, somewhere along the way the competitors shed tears so we could enjoy the blessings and joys of the victory along with the competitors. Just think about all of the emotions surrounding the Super Bowl, Major League Baseball World Series and NBA Championships. Even the joy that goes along with the celebration of a new life comes with the price of a mother having to endure great pain and tears before the jubilation of a newborn baby.

Since Jesus has already made His sacrifice, now is the time for you to make yours. Are you willing to endure the hardship of carrying the bull's-eye of the gospel message around on your chest and head? Are you willing to endure the hard road of persecution for the gospel of Jesus Christ? Are you willing to die for Jesus if it comes down to it? What is your decision? Are you willing to sacrifice your gift at the altar and celebrate the victory by the preaching of God's most holy words?

Women serving in the kingdom of God as ministers must make their presence known by continuing to demonstrate they are assets to the ministry rather than liabilities. There are men who possess the view that women invading the ranks of the ministry are more of a crisis than a solution to the many ills in the world and the local church. When people in society tag you as an "underdog," you have to come out of the blocks full throttle to your labor in ministry. You have to hit the road running full speed simply because of the fact there are people around that believe you do not belong in the big league. If the hearts and mind of people are going to ever change about women ministers, women ministers are going to have to lead the way by the guiding of the Holy Spirit with authentic, powerful, anointed and humble service to the world and people of God.

Even if you have to work overtime for less or no pay, do it for Jesus. If you have to take the backseat just to get into the meeting, do it for Jesus. If they strip you of your official title for the moment, do not fuss or fight. Allow it to happen for Jesus because He will allow you to go through a test of your humility before He can trust you with much. You must know many male ministers view women coming into the ministry as competitors or foes rather than partners or teammates serving the same franchise and owner.

Furthermore, there are some male ministers who use the opinion that even the apostle Paul had issues and problems with women serving in the ministry, and that is why he did not advocate for women to go into the ministry. I beg to differ that the apostle Paul had problems with women in the gospel ministry simply because they were women. If he had a problem with women in ministry, why would he write to the Christians community at Philippi and instruct the congregation of believers to "help those women which labored with me (him) in the gospel, with Clement also, and with other my fellow-labourers, whose names are in the book of life" (Philippians 4:2–3)?

Also, it is very important for women ministers to give God their very best effort in everything they do in ministry and their personal lives. The women ministers of the twenty-first century are trailblazers, charting new territory that women ministers of the past were prevented from exploring. Today's women ministers are breaking new ground for generations of women ministers to come. Women ministers of today have to be committed to the success of living in a special calling so those who follow will have a solid, authentic legacy from which to draw strength and hope.

God has called you to prove a point to the Devil, and to cause an uproar in the minds and hearts of people who refuse to believe that God can use any vessel including women ministers to preach His divine gospel. It is your duty to give God and humanity results navigated by the Holy Spirit. Unless those who doubt your calling from God can witness the overwhelming preponderance of power and evidence by the Holy Spirit in your life, they will never believe you are the vessel being called out by God.

Therefore, you must allow God to use you in such an extraordinary manner that it leaves no doubt in the minds of people that you have been called and empowered by the almighty Father. On the day of Pentecost, some will believe and some will not. The moment of truth is not about what the skeptics believe; it is about how you will submit and allow the Lord to work through you. Trust me, there is no problem too hard for our great God. If you allow God the opportunity, He will do exceedingly awesome things way beyond the imagination of human beings.

The prophet Jeremiah tells us to list something that is too hard for God because according to his recollection, nothing is too hard for God. Even though Jeremiah sounded the alarm thousands of years ago, his message served notice on people who will try and stand in your way today as you obey your preaching calling from Jesus (Jeremiah 32:27; John 10:10). If you truly stand as a disciple of Jesus, I guarantee the Holy Spirit will do the rest for you, regardless of the situation. Do it for Jesus!

Let us keep in mind Jesus specializes in doing awesome things that are impossible for humans to fathom. This is one of the reasons we call it faith and allow it to lead us to places we do not have the ability to go. With faith, we have to trust in things we do not understand and cannot explain. Faith allows us to walk with blinders on our eyes, yet arriving safely wherever God directs us.

When women ministers deny or suppress their calling to preach the Word of God, they become liabilities to the kingdom of God. They often do not know they have become liabilities. Anytime we refuse to obey God or procrastinate in carrying out a command or mandate from God, we become risks and possibly liabilities rather than assets to the kingdom God and humanity. Any person walking contrary to the Word of God cannot ever say he or she was a blessing to the kingdom of God. Sin does not produce productive fruit from its wasteful labor. Whatever the outcome, sin cannot ever be justified as a formidable force for ushering a person into the kingdom of God.

Never forget that sin is designed to grab you and hold you real tight so you will not be able to come to Jesus. It is God's power that forces sin to release you. It is the anointing of the Holy Spirit that ushers you into the arms of Jesus. We can only run from sin because the Holy Spirit pulls us. The Holy Bible says, "No person can come to Jesus except God first draws him or her" (John 6:44–45). Listen to what the apostle Paul says in 1 Corinthians 12:3: "No man speaking by the Spirit of God calleth Jesus accursed: and that no man can say Jesus is the Lord, but by the Holy Ghost."

To make sure you never become a liability to the kingdom of God, I challenge you to always respond to the service of God with obedience, vigor, humility, enthusiasm, reverence, love, hope, trust, compassion, and the understanding it is all about Jesus and not about you. Responding to God with urgency shows Him you respect and value His ability to operate and manage the world and creation He brought into existence. When we submit to God's will, it sends a positive signal to heaven that you are on board with His plans. When you surrender to the call of God, it sends a strong message to the enemies of God that you are a warrior for Jesus with commitment, and if need be, you are willing to die for the love of the gospel of Jesus Christ.

When we think of an asset, it is something that enhances or adds to something in a positive and powerful way. Whereas a liability causes things to weaken, diminish, and even become a burden rather than a blessing. When tactical soldiers sit and do nothing while the battle is raging, and the mission dictates for them to render firepower, the question arises whether these soldiers are faithful and loyal to the mission or cause.

Do we make heroes and heroines of men and women who refuse to fight and protect their nation when it is under attack by an enemy force? No, these soldiers failed to carry out their wartime mission of protecting and defending their nation's interests. Will you allow the Enemy to make you run from a battle God sent you to fight and stand in the gap for Him so that others can receive the salvation of Jesus? When we accept Jesus as our Lord, it is a binding agreement with great expectations for the disciple.

Here is a very important "newsflash" women of the clergy must never forget. Women ministers who have been called to the gospel ministry and are still contemplating whether to come out of their foxhole or continue to stay buried underground are in the same predicament as the soldiers who refused to join and support their units and nations. People who refuse to stand and fight for justice will probably never fully understand or appreciate justice in the same sense as someone who may have gotten scared on the battlefield while fighting for justice. A soldier who will not stand and fight to preserve his or her nation and freedoms (blessings) becomes a disgrace to the integrity of the unit and nation.

Maybe the young, rich ruler Jesus met in Luke 18:18–24 was also afraid and turned into a coward because he feared the thought of losing everything. Following the calling of Jesus sometimes demands you may have to lose something or everything in order to gain Jesus. When some people understand what they have to give up to follow Jesus, they sometimes become fearful of letting loose of the things that give them identity, recognition, and comfort. The young, rich ruler may have been able to discern the weather forecast and storms as a potential disciple of Jesus and came to the conclusion he did not want to endure the rocky storms in life that Jesus was offering him by selling all his earthly possessions, and giving the profits to the poor.

People who refuse to stand and preach the Word of God will have less of an appreciation for the kingdom of God than the ones who stand in obedience to the calling of God. Just think about this for a minute. When someone sits down on God or tells Him no, it is not like talking to your best friends, siblings, parents, or strangers. You are talking about God! I believe each time we reject God's personal invitation, there is a wall of separation that hardens to the point that future attempts for submission become easier to reject. Please do not allow the fear of man or woman to become the cause God uses to harden your heart.

Remember, it was Pharaoh who failed to listen to God's requests through the voice of His servant Moses, and because of Pharaoh's continued disobedience to God, He hardened Pharaoh's heart so much he could no longer hear the voice of God (Exodus 3:10–4:23). Fear has a way of tormenting a person to the point that the individual loses his or her bearings and zeal to move forward with assurance. Even if the person intended or wanted to do right, he or she becomes too paralyzed to move in the right direction. The thought of doing right is there, but fear stands between the thought and the response to do the right thing.

In Matthew 22:1–14, Jesus tells the parable about a king preparing a wedding banquet for his son. He sent his servant to invite people to the banquet, but the invitees refused to come. By the act of his love, grace, and mercy, the king sent some more of his servants to invite the guests because the banquet was prepared and the celebration could not wait any longer. Again they refused to come to the wedding banquet. Instead, they went off and did their own things, which pleased them after they had mistreated the king's servants, killing some. Does this sound familiar? Finally, the king sent his army to kill the murderers and burned their city. Afterward, the king was determined to have his wedding banquet for his son and told his servants to go to the street corners and invite people—good and bad—to come to his son's banquet, and the wedding banquet was filled with people.

The moral to the story is when the invited guests do not do what the king demands of them, he will call those who are both bad and good to do his work for him. If God can use a pagan king like Cyrus the Great to bring an end to Babylonian captivity, restore the city of Jerusalem, and rebuild His temple in Jerusalem, surely He can use women to preach His Word (Isaiah 45:1–9). God will call the willing and unwilling to preach His divine gospel if those He has invited refuse to obey Him. This one particular guest in the banquet room was only there to start trouble by bringing division and corruption at the wedding and wedding banquet, which demonic spirits are designed to do. The uninvited guest was easily recognizable by the king because he did not have on the right uniform or clothes as the other wedding guests.

When people enter your life and do not mean you any good, you have to quickly recognize the fact they are out of place and immediately remove them from your presence, like the illustration Jesus gives in the parable in Matthew 22. Please do not waste time with people who are only in your life to harm you or kill your dreams by leading you in the wrong direction. Any direction God does not send you is the wrong direction. If God has called you into the gospel ministry, do not allow anyone to lead you out.

Do we pin awards on men and women who continue to sit in the foxholes when the situation on the battlefield demands their immediate support and service? The kingdom of God needs women ministers who will stand up and take their places of leadership in the clergy ranks more now today than ever before in the history of the church movement. If women ministers continue to sit on their callings from God and allow the egos of prideful men to dictate their roles at the dinner table with Jesus, they stand the chance of losing their seats at the table. When Jesus has invited you to preach the gospel, you do not need a middleman or anyone else to give his or her approval. When it comes to fulfilling God's plan, the Holy Spirit is the only negotiator. My sisters, it is time to answer the roll-call and give an account for your absence if you have been AWOL from your duties as a minister of the gospel.

Some women ministers want to remain a fan in the stands or just live life as a spectator on the sidelines because they fear the crowd and the enormous task at hand that goes along with the territory of preaching God's Word. As an afterthought, when one really considers who is in the crowd, in all truthfulness, it is fair to say the crowd could consist of anyone who is not God. No crowd is ever larger or could make a more powerful or greater sound than God. No crowd is ever more awesome and powerful than Jesus. No crowd is ever greater in action than the Holy Spirit. No crowd has ever raised the dead or gave life to the living. No crowd has ever volunteered to die for your sins and the sins of the world. No crowd has taken your place in the grave and resurrected itself.

For these reasons, women who refuse to step into their calling for fear of the crowd should always consider the wonderful things God has done in their lives. Whenever a person truly reflects on the compassion of Jesus, truth will help propel the person in the direction most pleasing to God. When a person understands the essence of life, it is only then that he or she begins to understand his or her purpose for living is to provide a service for the kingdom of God in a way that is pleasing in the eyes of God!

Some women who have been called into the gospel ministry of Jesus Christ often give the crowd more respect and attention than the Holy One of Israel calling them into the ministry. When we allow fear and people in the crowd to dictate our actions, it is usually a response with disobedient consequences toward God. We are asking for trouble from a power that we have no chance at winning. When we allow outsiders to encourage us to walk away from God's divine mission, we have given the crowd more authority than God. Yes, crowds can be brutal and fearless at times, especially when something goes against the wishes or the grain of the crowd. Yet the crowd is limited by its sheer numbers and strength when it comes to standing against the plans and move of God.

A crowd is like a two-edge sword; it can cut you and render you unable to fulfill your mission, or it can help encourage you to accomplish your intended goal in life. A crowd was never designed to prevent people from fulfilling the calling of God on their lives. In Matthew 21:1–11, look at the life and ministry of Jesus and how on one day the crowd celebrated him shouting, "Hosanna, thy Son of David," and few days later, this same crowd was pleading "Crucify him and let his blood be on us and on our children … Let Barabbas go free, but *Crucify* this Jesus, which we do not know" (Matthew 27:15–26).

Some people only want to remain fans in the fight to proclaim the gospel message because they understand what is involved and what is at stake when they switch from spectator to player. Example, prior to my sister being called into the ministry, she envisioned herself coming in the arena and taking a seat and cheering as a spectator. Now that the calling of God is on her life, she has to exemplify the best she has to offer under the eyes of the all-wise and all-seeing lights of God. No longer can she hide and move at her own pace. She has switched the roles from observer-evaluator to participant. As I often say to others, when death comes upon our lives, we do not make the call whether we should live or die; only God has the authority and power to make such a call. The same principle applies when a person is called into the gospel ministry. God makes the call, and He does not ask you for your advice during the process.

Can you see the picture? The once faithful spectator has to step into the realm of fulfilling the role of a star that is willing to live and shine for Jesus. The call to the ministry demands the discipline of a player who now must put her skills, talents, and gifts on public display for the entire world to see and for critique of the glory of God. The former spectator now knows she falls under the scrutiny of the public, press (media), management, and the crowd. Prior to the call into Christian ministry, all she had to do was be a fan, without any obligation or exposure to personal shame, guilt, or hurt.

But as God would have it, she must step up to the plate and exert the discipline and commitment of Jesus in order to succeed with the most important message and mission in her entire life. To tell the wonderful story about Jesus Christ is what we were given a place in life to do, and we should be excited about boasting about Jesus as we spread God's love. As the Holy Bible says, "Many are called, but only a few are chosen" (Matthew 22:14). Count yourself blessed if you have been chosen to carry and preach the words of the Most High God!

After spending over thirty years in the US Army, and over twenty years in the local pastorate and military chaplaincy, I learned when people are hurting, they do not care about the color of the skin or gender of the person helping them. Sick and dying people do not care about the gender of the person providing them with life-sustaining medical care to help them get or stay well. When people are in need of life-sustaining aid, they do not care about the looks, gender, nationality, or religion of the person who can save their lives.

People are dying in sin, and those seeking a life preserver while drowning do not care whether a man or woman is throwing them the lifeline that will pull them to safety. People within the church community should not be concerned about the gender of the leader of the flock, as long as the flock and leader are going in the right direction. We need to be more concerned about heaven bound as the principal thing and not the gender of the vessel being used to get people to the salvation of Jesus.

I am so amazed how male ministers are in a bad place about female ministers. When I think about the very important role women play in the entire circle of life, I say to myself, "Something is just missing in the equation that espouses the view that women are not allowed to serve as preaching ministers in many churches and denominations across America. She brings all of us into the world and nurtures us through the infant stage, adolescent years, and beyond. Yet when we reach adulthood, only then do we say she is no longer worthy to provide for us the most important meal in life." There is something wrong with this picture. Wake up, people! How long must we sleep before we recognize and realize the game Satan is playing on us?

Furthermore, all humanity should support the efforts of women ministers because any effort to build God's kingdom is a positive response to a negative action that is trying to do everything within the wicked power to prevent women from preaching the gospel of Jesus Christ. Imagine this scene in your mind. A group of children is playing and swimming in a body of water that they do not know is infested with alligators. All the children's fathers are across the lake, fishing. The fathers are totally oblivious to what is happening in the water because the competition for the largest catch has their undivided attention, like a crucial play during a football game. This one play, and the call by the referee, will determine the outcome of the game, and the men drawn to the television set. Everything else in their lives is tuned out.

The mothers and other women see the alligators coming toward the children. By instinct, they spring into action to get the children out of the water and carry them to safety. Were the women and mothers out of their lanes for saving the children's lives during this life-or-death situation, even though all the women were not the mothers of the children? Is it not the natural order of preservation in life to save one's self? But for the mothers and the women with motherly instincts, the first order of business was to save the children whenever danger threatened. They could not wait for the men to come across the body of water, because it would have been too late. Therefore, the women had to do what was necessary and answer to the call of safety as danger threatened the lives of their offspring.

In all truthfulness, when there is a situation that involves life or death, it does not matter who is being used to sustain life or lead a person or people to safety. Once the women and mothers saw the children in danger, I do not believe they had time to stop and call over to the men and debate with them about who should enter the dangerous water to save the children's lives. If the mothers and women had not acted when noticing the terrifying alarm, more than likely the children would have died at the powerful and ruthless jaws of the alligators.

Men need to stop pushing women aside and blowing them off as some rebellious servants when a vicious and deadly enemy ambushes and destroys our children. Mothers are tired of seeing their children being destroyed in the murky waters of gang violence and drugs, while men stand on the banks, fishing. Men and women need to accept the fact that God put us here on earth to serve as co-laborers in His kingdom.

Mothers and women are sick and tired of seeing their children being lost to crime and drugs, while men continue to stand on the banks, fishing! Women are tired of seeing their children being ravaged by poverty, homelessness, domestic abuse, bullying, and other demonic strongholds, while men continue to stand fishing on the banks of life! Women are tired of being disrespected in the workplace by their supervisors and those employed by the same agency. The time has come that the church as a whole must accept its daughters as preaching ministers!

Moreover, I am amazed how we allow a machine like GPS (global positioning systems) to lead us places and sometimes causes us to end up getting lost. We seem to have a bad habit of putting our faith and trust in things made by the hands and minds of humans rather than into the hands of God. How can we put more trust and faith in mechanical instruments than in the God and Creator, who has allowed humanity to make the machines and instruments we trust? It seems we would rather take instruction from machines, such as traffic signals, computers, and automated telephone answering systems, than from God.

Also, we have become so complacent with modern technology that we allow automatic teller machines to disburse and manage our money and finances on a daily basis. More people are reading the stock market results and reading and posting to Facebook, Twitter, Instagram, LinkedIn, and other Internet sites than reading the Holy Bible or other religious materials. Social media is probably the most central thing people have in common across the globe other than oxygen, water, food, and life.

Believe it or not, we seem to depend on machines and other technology as a natural instinct, but find it difficult to listen to the preaching coming from women ministers. To add insult to injury, some of us fight with vigorous intensity against the idea the Holy Spirit uses women ministers in leadership roles to take us to the Promised Land. Thank God for the Holy Bible because it has always highlighted how God has used women in different facets of the ministry to help build His kingdom on earth. Men need to wake up if they think women will continue to sit silently in churches, while their babies lie dying in our streets, incarcerated in our prisons, and buried daily as a result of youth-on-youth crime and failure to be mentored by men and women with a strong and wholesome sense of ethical integrity and law-abiding citizenship.

I continue to ask about the real motive behind the rejection of women ministers by male ministers, especially pastors. It is also quite disturbing to me why other females would fight against women ministers, knowing the struggles they have to endure daily from a male-dominate industry. Women ministers have a place in the clergy like they have a place in the U.S. Labor Force; not only as laborers but as managers and supervisors as well. According to the U.S. Department of Labor in 2010, women comprised 47 percent of the U.S. labor force. The U.S. Bureau of Labor Statistics reported in May 2014 via www.bls.gov that 57.7 percent of the U.S. population was female. Also, in 2013 the U.S. Bureau of Labor Statistics found that among all industries tracked, women made up 27 percent of chief executive positions by an article written by Mark Jurkowitz. Finally, a report from *Catalyst*, a nonprofit focusing on women in the workplace, found that women account for about 15 percent of executive positions in the Fortune 500 companies. If the secular world can accept women as bonified leaders, why cannot the church do the same for its female leaders in the ministry with all of its love?

It is amazing how on one end we hold women in high esteem and on the other end of the spectrum we put them down. For example, I would be safe to say most boys and girls love their mothers and believes no one else on the earth is greater than their mother. When certain special holidays like birthdays, Valentines Day, Christmas, Mothers' Day, etc. rolls around, we make sure we do not forget about mother. We give our mothers a sort of divine respect and love. But somewhere along the way with our personal religious journey to the church, some of us have seemed to have lost that agape love and respect for women to include our mothers. Disrespecting a woman's desire to do the will and please the Almighty God is probably the ultimate disrespect we can demonstrate towards a woman.

Furthermore, many of us grew up and were taught in school about these wonderful fairy godmothers we loved. Some will deny it today, but we believe in fairy godmothers in stories and movies, and still teach our children by reading the stories to them. We refuse to allow women to preach to our congregations but allow them to serve on search committees to help select qualified candidates to present to the church as future pastors.

If women have enough professionalism, wisdom, knowledge, and spirit to help guide congregations with the necessary pools of qualified candidates for the pastorate, what makes people turn the other way when women break the news they have been called into the gospel ministry? It is sad that some of us put more trust and emphasis in the opinions of men and women who believe God did *not* call women into the ministry than in the evidence taken from Holy Scriptures that God uses women in ministry to proclaim His gospel by the preaching of His Word.

It is my most sincere prayer this scroll is used to help unlock the doors of opportunities for women to exercise their God-given gifts, talents, and rights to preach God's Word in local churches that profess to be congregations of Jesus. If women ministers make *Preach, My Sister, Preach* part of their daily devotions, they will receive the nurturing insight about how to stand boldly in the ministry God has called or ordained them to fulfill. This book is to serve as the trampoline that encourages and allows women to leap above and beyond man-made shackles and barriers that have crippled their progress in local churches for so many years.

If women do not stand up for Jesus now, God will raise another to take their place. Who knows? You who are willing to stand boldly and preach God's Holy Word might be the next Esther. The question is who is willing to stand in the gap and help save our society from destruction by a chauvinistic dictator spirit that is out to control and eventually destroy the cohesive fellowship within the body of Christ (Esther 4:13–16). The spirit of Haman is still alive and well in many of today's churches, and we must never bow or surrender to it.

If you as a woman minster never submit with faith to the power of the Holy Spirit, it is possible you are saying to God, "I give up!" Always remember there is no problem too hard for God. We know God has the power to change the hearts of evil men, like He did with the Pharaoh of Egypt, Haman, Saul of Tarsus, and King Nebuchadnezzar; the list goes on and on. All these wicked men fought the move of God in their own ways. Each thought he was right in his own eyes, but he either knowingly or unknowingly fought against the move of God.

Furthermore, I have never seen God back up or change direction when someone or something tried to stand in His way. History has proven when He got ready to move in the lives of His people, places, or things, no one was able or powerful enough to hinder or stop Almighty God. When God got ready to liberate His people from slavery in Babylon and build His temple and city, He raised up a pagan king from Persia by the name of Cyrus to the do the job (Isaiah 45:1–9). God is not limited in power; neither can He be controlled by humanity.

God can do the same for you as He did with the enemies of the Israelites that were bent on stopping them from glorifying their God. God can make those who fight against you stepping stones to your success. As women ministers, do not allow anyone to stop you from receiving the blessings God is about to bestow upon you for your obedience as you fulfill your divine calling. As we continue to fast and pray against the ministers, people, and nations fighting against you for accepting your call into the gospel, stay strong in the power of the Holy Ghost. The Devil has his men and women in key positions and high places to fight against you about your calling into the ministry by refusing to allow you to grow in the grace of God's vineyard as commissioned ministers of the gospel of Jesus. Yet they will never win, because God has already determined Jesus is the winner.

I recommend you find a pastor who will provide a spiritual covering and format for you as you seek the will of God for your life and ministry. Every minister should be covered by some other ministry, minister, pastor, or group of ministers, so he or she will never lose touch with the fact God is still making us and saving us from sin daily, even as we live and labor in His kingdom. Every minister needs someone whereby he or she will have accountability. Ministers without accountability are sitting ducks for the Enemy and bombs waiting to explode. Ministers who feel as though they have everything under control and accountable to no one except God, Jesus, and the Holy Spirit are disasters waiting to happen. Every great soldier or warrior needs help while in battle!

The story of Esther shows how God used a young woman to save a blessed nation of God-fearing people from destruction by an evil force.

It is also the story about a woman willing to forsake all else for God's mission and purpose. God gave her life and put her in the position for His glory to be revealed, and she did not let Him down, even if it meant she had to tell her husband what thus saith the Lord of host.

Sometimes the tides of events or circumstances force you out of your comfort zone before expected. Esther had to move in God's time and not in her desired time. God will put the urgency of the moment into your spirit, heart, mind, and soul, and on receiving His beckoning call: "the chicks must come home to roost."

We sometimes need to be reminded that God will use someone else to take our place if we refuse to stand up for His justice and holiness. Uncle Mordecai commanded Esther not to become complacent with the luxuries of the king's palace. He reminded her she was not put in the king's palace for her benefit but to become a blessing to the kingdom of God by being the vessel through which God would work his plan. God has allowed many of us to position ourselves in places not just for our own benefit but so we can share His glory and blessings with others. God gives to us, so we can help pass it on to someone else.

On the other hand, this is not to say you are not allowed to experience and enjoy your blessings from God, but it is to say exercise kingdom sharing when you get yours. Always be willing to reach down and pull others up and even beyond where you stand. Hopefully they will do the same for someone else. Words of wisdom I leave with you: Make greed and selfishness your enemies, and prosperity will be your friend for life.

In retrospect, Esther was allowed to win her way into the palace by the intervening grace of God. Esther's work did not get her into the king's palace. Rather, it was the hand of God, guiding her from the beginning to the end of the process and beyond. God placed Esther in the king's bedroom, so she could become the beacon of hope that would save the Hebrews from destruction. God put Esther in the palace so she would have a place in the king's heart because every decision in life is pondered in the hearts of men and women (Proverbs 4:23; Matthew 12:34–35; Luke 6:45). God placed Esther in the palace so there would be a divine presence in the midst of an empire where evil plots vibrated against God's people like a destructive earthquake. God put Esther in the king's palace to become a great basin of water to protect the Hebrew people from the lava of hate that spewed from the diabolical volcanic eruptions within a culture that abhorred the Jewish people. She served as the sacrificial lamb that would be used to help set the Israelites free from a wicked man's plot to destroy the entire Hebrew nation. Yes, God chose a woman for this monumental task and great act in history.

It was imperative that Esther stayed on task and remained true to her calling in the kingdom of God. Mordecai, the prophet of God, gave Esther an ultimatum to either speak up for God or die a horrible death. Do you feel like you are caught in the position that Esther found herself? If so, obey God, and speak up and live for Jesus. It is better to have so-called friends walk out of your life than to have God angry with you. It is better to have the peace of God in your life than it is to be fixated on the complacency of living by the standards and dreams of others. Tell me what fun or pleasure in life is granted without purpose? It is better to face rejection here on earth than to have God chastise you for disobeying a direct order. You must make the call; the choice is yours to make.

Once someone has been summoned into God's gospel ministry, he or she has the most serious decision in life: obey God and live, or disobey God and die. It is really this simple because rejecting a directive from God, like the seriousness of preaching His divine Word, is a deadly fate, to say the least. God's calling to preach His Holy Word is not negotiable. There are some things in life God does not allow us the opportunity to negotiate, such as choosing our parents, our gender, our ethnicity, or our siblings.

From personal experience, there is no joy going home, to work, or to school knowing you have failed God by rejecting His voice. On the other hand, pleasing God is the most gratifying thing a person can do in this life. Remember, the first order of business in life is to first seek the kingdom of God and His righteousness. Other things will then fall into place for you. When we acknowledge God in all our ways and trust Him at His Word, I am a living witness that God will indeed direct your path through life (Matthew 6:33; Proverbs 3:5–6). If I were you, I would preach, my sister, preach.

4

Women in the Ministry

Who Told Women to Deny Their Calling from God?

The issue of women in ministry (women ministers/preachers/pastors) has created much discussion throughout church history and its share of debates and arguments over the years within various cultures and nations. Women in the preaching ministry have sparked a lot of controversy in many churches across America. Some churches ended up splitting their membership over the issue of whether God has truly called women to serve as preachers. It seems like women are allowed to serve in any capacity within church ministry except the preaching or pastoral leadership one.

Why has no one ever brought up the issue that the Bible says a woman cannot serve as the minister of music, choir director, or usher board president like they do with women being in the preaching ministry? People fight and fuss and will even leave the church over the issue of women in ministry, but they will sit and often take part in actions God is clearly against without saying a word. Is there a bias against women within the church community? Are male ministers allowed to get away with things in the eyes of the people in the congregation that females dare to think of and definitely must not attempt?

In some congregations, the women preaching issue has ignited so much controversy among church members that members have divided into various factions and often end up embracing separation as the best solution to their differences. Some people even argue the issue has caused a great deal of dissention between male and female ministers in local churches/congregations. It was recently brought to my attention that the rejection of women into the gospel ministry has spilled over into some of our renowned Bible colleges and theological training institutions throughout America.

Also, some of these well-known theological seminaries forbid women to pursue a master of divinity in pastoral care vocation but will allow them to obtain a master of divinity in pastoral counseling. Some denominations endorse their female ministers to become chaplains in institutions but not to serve as pastors or preachers in churches. They will allow their female ministers to be licensed as evangelists, missionaries, and chaplains but not allow them to wear the cloak of preacher/pastor.

When I first came into the ministry in the 1980s, a denomination allowed female ministers to speak before large audiences but not to use the term "preaching." You were strongly encouraged to use the word "speaking" to describe the proclamation of female vessels but never "preaching" as the stated act. Today, because of the relentlessness of the women's movement in the local churches, this denomination's national headquarters had to move in the favor of allowing women to step into the pulpit as preachers and pastors, not just missionaries and evangelists. Without the presence of the women in their churches and meetings, the denomination would have experienced a financial catastrophe, and many of its church doors would have closed.

I have witnessed male and female churchgoers walk out of sanctuaries while mumbling under their breath with anger, "God didn't call a woman to preach." I wanted to ask them to tell me when and where they spoke with God about who He calls or does not call into the gospel ministry? Would not God let the person claiming the ministry calling know if she or he has not been hired, since the person is the one who has to be accountable? Or maybe God will skip the employee and consult only with you as a member of the board of directors for heaven's approval whether to allow the person the right to preach. I wish people would let God be the Master and do His job as God, and everyone else fulfill their own roles as human servants for the Lord. I am appalled we now live in an era when servants dictate to God who He should or should not allow into heaven's kingdom as ministers.

When we allow God the opportunity to use us with the humility of the Holy Spirit rather than by the influence of our knowledge, other people, education, or pride, everyone in the faith community is blessed by the awesome miracles we witness daily. Think about all the energy, time, and resources we invest fighting women as well as each other over women ministers, one of the oldest issues in the local church. Rather than fighting over whether God has called women into the ministry, we could be doing something more productive, valuable, and beneficial for the kingdom of God. We need to focus our fight on helping to feed the hungry, clothe the naked, provide shelter for the homeless, and provide afterschool tutorial programs and activities for our youth that will bring glory and honor to Jesus.

As saints of God, our focus seems to be off as to who the real enemy is. It seems like the Devil—the real Enemy—is enjoying this battle because we have inflicted injuries and casualties on our own, while he sits back, waiting on the body count. When people fight over battles where there are no victors or about things that have nothing to do with Jesus' salvation, only the Enemy can claim victory.

When the people look at us fighting over such trivial things, like whether God called women ministers, the Affordable Care Act, and biracial marriages among Christians, some can easily wonder why they should become part of an already divided church. If the church cannot reflect a definite sense of light and love among its kind, why should sinners look for true love among Christians? The church must be willing to recognize its obligation to bring peace on the earth and not war within its own ranks over issues that do not control a person's salvation. Do you love Jesus enough to forgive, even if you think your brother or sister is wrong? How is it that we can work together and get along with sinners in every facet of our lives that we disagree with but cannot get along with brothers and sisters in the church over issues that are not earth shattering or cause us to become hell bound?

I have seen churches ready to declare the battle of Armageddon when female ministers grazed their pulpits. It did not matter whether they approached the throne of grace by mistake or on purpose. The response from the congregation was the same: scolding and rebuking.

It was as though the person had blasphemed sacred ground with the intention of going into the Holy of Holies. Yet over time, I have also seen some of the persons who were against female preachers experience a paradigm shift—a change of heart for the better—and grow to love the idea that God was using women in the gospel ministry.

I truly believe a large part of people accepting women ministers will be determined by how women present themselves to God and humanity as humble, obedient, and professional ministers of the gospel of Jesus. I continue to echo throughout this book how important it is for women to remain ladies as Christian servants, and not try to mimic the preaching gestures and styles of men as they preach, teach, and serve in gospel ministry in churches across America and throughout the world. Since there are not enough laborers to work in the vineyard, what is the point of rejecting workers God has sent to help and take some of the load off their male counterparts? We all must be mindful and never forget the preaching ministry does not belong to mankind. It is a calling God created, designed, and employs.

Since God made us male and female, I encourage women ministers under my leadership to display femininity in and out of the pulpit. I urge men to continue to showcase their masculinity as humble servants of the Most High God. During my thirty-year experience in the ministry, I have noticed when women ministers stand before the people of God and hack and grab their crotches, like some of their male counterparts, the audience or congregation are completely turned off.

I even go as far as to recommend to women ministers to stay away from the whooping and hollering that symbolizes some male preachers. As women ministers of the gospel of Jesus Christ, you have to pray God will give you a preaching and ministering style that is both approved by God and encouraging for kingdom building here on earth. Women ministers must always remember they serve under a different microscope than their male counterparts.

Like it or not, this is the reality of the process. This is the time to be wise as a serpent but harmless (innocent or pure) as a dove, as Jesus instructed His disciples (Matthew 10:16). Women will get in the door and sit at the table of brotherhood and sisterhood by how they submit and handle the gospel message of Jesus Christ. When your ways are pleasing to God, the Holy Spirit will fight your battles for you. It is much better to allow the Spirit of God to fight for you than try to do so yourself or with someone else.

As I have stated before, some people are not going to like you simply because you are a woman minister. Do not allow the feelings of others affect how you fulfill your calling from God. Some people you meet in these churches are not angry with you because you are a woman minister. Remember, the church is a type of hospital, where people come to get healed. We really have some sick people in our churches that refuse to allow God to heal their various social ills and personal issues.

Some who come to church are sick in more ways than one. Some people in churches are angry with the world and will not allow God to change them. People in many of our congregations are angry about their lives and hate the day they were born. They will strike out at you with deadly hostility. They are ready to displace their anger onto anyone or anything that gets in their way. They seem to blame everyone but themselves for their misery in life.

On the other hand, there are some people in various denominations who are angry and do not have a clue why or with whom they are angry. Please try not to take their dislike of women ministers as a personal attack. Their oppression and bondage have them so confused that it is very difficult for them to see the light, even though it is shining in their faces. Yes, they have eyes, but they are still blind. Yes, they have vision, but "they see men walking as tall trees as the man saw before Jesus completely restored his sight" (Mark 8:24).

Here is the bottom line. It is more than likely the angry people in churches probably dislike ministers in general, whether male or female. My recommendation is for us to continue to love and pray for those who seem filled with anger and hate toward others. Our prayers should focus on God filling their hearts and eyes with the unconditional love that the apostle Paul talks about in 1 Corinthians Chapter 13. We need to pray God will open their eyes, so they can see His grace.

There are others in congregations for whom we pray they, too, do not allow themselves to become blind and stagnated by their self-righteous laws and man-made traditions. Here lies the place where people get caught up in the women minister issue. We must pray God will open their ears to hear His divine Word and not give in to the criticism and opinions of doubters and critics, who will refuse to believe no matter what God says or shows them about the women minister issue. My prayer for the entire Christian community is God will open our hearts to live holy, continue to extend mercy, and follow peace with all men and women. Without holiness, no one will see the Lord in His glory (Hebrews 12:14).

I also want to point out disagreement and division about women ministers exists in the ranks of the male ministerial leadership in many churches. To this day, the argument many male pastors make for why women should not be allowed to be preaching ministers does not constitute or justify God's approval or disapproval. Biblical history teaches us men have rendered verdicts they thought were the will of God but later found their rulings overturned by the Supreme Judge. Humanity has the ability to make unjust rules, ordinances, and laws, and God has the power to overturn them whenever He wants.

The life of Saul in Acts Chapter 8 is a good example of how God will turn the tables on a situation, even when the person is convinced he or she is doing God's will. Just because people think they are right in their hearts it does not make them right in the eyes of God. This is why the prophet Jeremiah reminds us that "the heart is deceitful above all things, and desperately wicked" (Jeremiah 17:9). Following the whims of our hearts has gotten some of us in lots of trouble over the years.

A person must be careful in interpreting whether what he or she feels within the heart is the perfect will of God. Many people every day are motivated by their own emotions to render certain actions. They believed it is the voice or will of God guiding them, only to find out later their emotions were playing tricks on them. You see, Saul was convinced in his heart he was doing God's will by crushing a religious sect (the Church of Jesus Christ) that was a threat to his religious beliefs and upbringing. The box Saul lived in restricted and limited his worldview about what God was doing beyond the walls of his homeland and his traditions and religious beliefs back in Jerusalem.

I believe the majority of parishioners in local churches who say they are against women ministers cannot give a definitive biblical reason why. They probably have taken the lyrics or idea from a broken record of past traditions. Although God is always God and does not change, He is always doing new things in the lives of His people. Our God is not a boring God. Nor does He play games or assign tasks and missions based on race, creed, color, sex, or age when it comes to promoting and proclaiming His divine Word to people dying in droves by the lethal venom called sin. Under the era of grace, the rules and major players have changed to give everyone a fair shot at making heaven's team. Each player is given the same fair opportunity to produce fruit by the gifting of the Holy Spirit, without discrimination or separation based on ethnicity, sex, color, or Christian denomination.

As you ponder what I say about traditions, please do not think I am denouncing traditions. I am not saying religious traditions are bad. What I am asking is do you believe our religious traditions are greater than God's grace? Just think of it this way; any tradition without the gospel of Jesus being carried out in the lives of the disenfranchised is without power and a destiny without hope. In the past, many religious leaders have used traditions to ostracize people. Some have even used them as a protective wall to hide behind while they conducted ungodly acts in the name of religion and God.

Jesus tore down the wall of religious tradition that kept people from becoming all God wanted them to become. This is one of the main reasons Jesus went to the cross and God tore the veil of the temple, so people would no longer be imprisoned by humankinds' traditions. We live under grace, so we would no longer be bound under the law of tradition. Grace offers us freedom and joy whereas the law kept us bound and miserable.

But if traditions strip people of the opportunity to serve God in the fullness of their potential and in the beauty of holiness, these traditions are lifeless and should be unplugged from the incubator that has nurtured them through the ages. If there are traditions that dehumanize people, imprison innocent lives and souls with the shackles of bondage, and degrade people because of ethnicity, sex, skin color, or physical status (i.e., short or tall, fat or skinny, or the physically challenged), they should be challenged and questioned to change their navigational courses. Sooner or later, channeled traditions will eventually end up shipwrecked either by a protest from within or deterioration of the body due to years of neglect and abuse.

We must never forget God always has the last word in all matters, especially those involving the destiny of His people and church. If you lined up all the male pastors and ministers in a city and asked them to agree on the various Scriptures in the Holy Bible, you will probably get nothing but a group of people saying some of the same things, but also disagreeing on many things about the Bible. Some ministers and denominations believe Jesus ate the Passover Meal and conducted feet washing with His disciples on Maundy Thursday while others believe these events took place on Good Friday, including the execution of Jesus.

Did you know that many preachers and pastors—black and white—and churches disagreed with Dr. Martin Luther King Jr. and the Civil Rights Movement? They thought within their hearts he and the movement approached social justice issues in America using the wrong method. One of Dr. King's letters, which became the book, *Letter from Birmingham Jail,* addressed some of the religious leaders in direct opposition of him coming to Birmingham, Alabama, with civil rights demonstrations. The majority of local black ministers led the bandwagon against King's visit to Birmingham to protest Jim Crow laws.

Like Saul in the book of Acts, while a person can fight for something he or she thinks is right within the heart, it can end up being totally wrong in God's eyes. Many people in local churches and denominations across the world fight from the side of traditions, not from the side of the righteousness and holiness of God. If people would stand up and fight for God's grace like they do for the traditions of men and women, the world would be a much better place for all people. When we stand up for what is right in the eyes of God, the Holy Spirit will always fight for you and defend the righteousness of God, regardless of the opponent. Never become afraid to stand up for the truth of God regardless of rejection or consequences, because God's justice always prevails.

Furthermore, if pastors, ministers, and preachers disagree about basic things, such as whether ministers pay taxes or be exempt from paying employment and Social Security taxes, how do we expect them to agree on more complicated things? Ministers and people in churches have a difficult time agreeing on whether biracial marriages are acceptable or if integration, desegregation, or segregation is right or wrong. Is the death penalty right or wrong in the eyes of God? Should sovereign nations have the right to go to war without the interference from other nations?

If ministers, pastors, and faith groups have problems agreeing on the previous issues, it should be no surprise that we find it hard for them to agree about a heart-changing issue like accepting women into the ministry. For many male pastors and ministers to accept women ministers as counterparts requires them to be intentionally forced out of their box of security and into a world beyond their comfort zone or understanding. When you have been told repeatedly something is wrong for so long, you begin to believe it.

Finally, some of the individuals discussed above will also disagree on the role of the church in politics and the party or candidate who is best for the kingdom of God. Pastors and ministers do not agree on which political party best serves the people of God by helping them arrive where God desires to meet them. Some pastors see voting as a basic democratic right while others see it as an essential necessity to help protect their freedoms from oppression and slavery. And some pastors/ministers only see voting as a worldly fashion of politics the church should have no association with.

I refuse to believe the Devil should possess all the political power and influence over God's people. "When the righteous remain silent, the wicked rule with an evil vengeance" (Proverbs 29:2). There is no happiness for the righteous when the wicked are in leadership positions. The wicked will never cater to the righteous; they will do their best to torment the righteous every opportunity they get.

During my research, I came to the conclusion there are no biblical mandates or directives from God that bar women from the gospel ministry. We must ask ourselves a few questions. Is the rejection of women ministers a fear being fueled by male ministers so they can keep a monopoly and dominance on the ministry vocation? Is there a call from God to purge the field because so many male ministers have taken God's grace and mercy for granted by yielding to the enticements of the Devil? Or is the struggle between the two sexes a weapon Satan uses to divide the leadership of the church, so he can slip in and devour the precious pearls of God? Whichever is the case, it is not a good scenario for the congregations of God to be at odds with each other at the same time we are fighting the most ruthless and evil Enemy in the world and throughout the universe.

I am convinced pastors and ministers have taken a few Scriptures and used them out of context for many years. They have made mockery of the ministry by trying to prove God does not commission women with the authority to preach or pastor in His kingdom. They have fought long and hard to defend this position without conducting thorough research on the issue. Many of these ministers seem to be driven by the advice and instructions of mentors who are self-centered and have the answers to solving the world's problems but cannot conquer their personal problems.

Over the years, it also seems like the church has dealt with the issue in passing, swatted it off like some aggravating gnat, or swept it under the rug and dared anyone to remove it. Sometimes people tend to want to only eat the sweet part of the scroll and refuse to eat the bitter words of wisdom that always produce a sweet ending. Never forget humility and devoted worship will perfect our praise to the Lord. Therefore, if we are to become mature men and women of Jesus, we must be willing to eat both the sweet and bitter parts of the scroll (Ezekiel 3:1).

For example, take a look at Exodus 20:13: "Thou shalt not kill." I can run off in a totally different direction from which the Scripture was meant. I could argue it should be taken verbatim, without any interpretation or dialogue for a better understanding. I could promote the text as if it is saying that needs no explanation or interpretation, and leave the reader hanging in limbo and confusion, even in a situation of killing in self-defense. When ministers failed to admit they erroneously interpreted the Holy Scriptures as it relates to women in the gospel ministry, it became a battle of pride to insinuate the minster was wrongly dividing the Word of God. Sometimes ministers can make drug addicts and alcoholics look like amateurs when it comes to living in denial.

Even in the text that is our topic of discussion, there is more to the story that needs some interpretation, so people can have the opportunity to serve in their nation's military or law enforcement, and so on without fearing some great, negative retribution by God. Sometimes people take bits and pieces of information and tell it to others as though it is the entire story. They either purposely leave out some of the details, or out of ignorance, omit pertinent information that could offer a different assessment about the story or issue at hand. Many Scriptures need interpretation and explanations in order for the audience to grasp hold of the message God is conveying to His people.

Case in point, 1 Samuel 15:3–7. God tells King Saul and the Israelites to kill and utterly destroy the Amalekites (men, women, children, livestock, and so on). God intended for nothing to remain alive during this holy war campaign.

These illustrations all came about after the writing of the Ten Commandments, which were given in Exodus Chapter 20. God published them on His own printing press and wrote a sacred law in Exodus 20:13 that must be followed by all inhabitants of the earth. God instructs the Israelites not to kill. But after writing the book of Exodus, He gives some of His leaders permission to kill. God orders Joshua, Saul, David, and Jehoshaphat to go to war and kill their enemies.

This is not to say God was contradicting Himself. God has never told and will never tell a lie. As it is written in the Holy Bible, "God is not a man that he should lie" (Numbers 23:19). We need to recognize God is in charge, and He can change the rules to fit His supreme purpose. We need to know God does not have to answer to us or anyone else, but we have to answer to Him. As finite beings, we feel as though we have the right to know nearly everything God is doing. But when we activate the word "trust," we are saying we know everything is all right, even though we may not know the details about what is going on. Our friend that is named 'Trust' knows God has everything under His control, although it may sometimes feel like your world is falling to pieces.

Trust knows everything is going to be all right, even though things may not feel or look all right from your perspective. Trust encourages you to ride and without knowing where you are going. Trust says go to sleep tonight, and I will watch over you through the night. When morning comes, I will wake up with replenished energy to make it through another day.

King Saul had a difficult time understanding God's purpose/will was greater than his personal desires and goals. Somewhere along the way, King Saul underestimated that God's grace and mercy would take priority over Saul's wicked quest for greed and power. Saul neglected to understand the basic fact that no matter how much God loves someone, He can never be purchased, especially with something that has no value to the spiritual Savior and King of the universe. King Saul missed the boat by not understanding the difference between having a genuine relationship and a bribe. God cannot be bought by the cheap things we offer Him.

Believe it or not, God is more concerned about having a relationship with us than what we think we are bringing to the table as a gift for Him. If the relationship is genuine, authentic, and trustworthy, there is no need to use a bribe. A person can never walk in God's favor with a disobedient heart. Disobedience does not bring in a harvest of blessings from God. In fact, disobedience is the poison that chokes the life out of vessels that can be used to usher in a harvest for the kingdom of God. Disobedience is like when a gallbladder tears to the point human waste starts leaking from the bladder into the human body and begins to poison the entire person. Disobedience can cause us to go into a comatose state and could eventually lead to physical and spiritual death.

In retrospect, Saul either disobeyed God out of greed and power, or because he thought God would allow him to exercise the special powers act, since he was the leader of the pack. Regardless of the reason, the bottom line is King Saul disobeyed God. I believe God was trying to use Saul as the commander in chief, who would inflict divine retribution on the Amalekites for their past actions against the Israelites. God had not forgotten how the Amalekites laid in wait and ambushed the Israelites when they came out of slavery from Egypt and were on their way to the Promised Land (1 Samuel 15:2–10). God purposed in His mind to repay the Amalekites for their evil deeds against the Israelites during a very vulnerable time in Israel's history.

In Joshua chapters 6 and 7, God instructs Joshua to kill the citizens of Jericho and Achan, along with his entire family, because they disobeyed God's orders and compromised the integrity and progress of an entire nation. God would not allow the nation of Israel to move forward to the

Promised Land until the culprits who disobeyed His Word were exposed and brought to justice by death. God has a very high standard for His people to follow and He will not compromise His integrity for anyone.

Regardless of the argument, a true Christian cannot and will not deny these events happened exactly like the Holy Bible claims. How does one begin to explain the many accounts where God commanded His leaders and people to kill or destroy a person or group of people without hesitation or mercy? These biblical accounts, along with other examples, should encourage people to think, research, and pray for interpretation and revelation before trying to reach a verdict or come to a conclusion. Such cases often end up as mistrials in a court of law, and very little, if anything, gets settled. Only in this case, the perpetrators never get off the hook; they have to pay the piper for their disobedience, and the stakes could be as high as their loved ones' lives as well as their own.

Here is another situation that will baffle your mind and spirit if you try to confine God in the narrow box of your mind and world. God is much larger and greater than our tiny theologies, denominations, worlds, and minds. Although some people may think they have arrived and accumulated great measures in life, to God, it is still small and nothing to boast about. In Deuteronomy 23:17–21, the Holy Scriptures talks about "there shall not be a whore from the daughters of Israel," yet when you examine the lineage of Jesus, one would have to come to the conclusion God's grace and mercy had to make provisions for this rule.

In Matthew Chapter 1, the writer is talking about Bathsheba, King David's wife, but he never mentions her name as he did with Mary and Ruth. Maybe the writer was told not to mention Bathsheba's name as part of the lineage of Jesus because of the shame associated with it or for some other reason. For whatever reason, the queen's name was left off the 'roll of distinction' and not mentioned, though other royal ladies were recognized for their roles in the royal birth of Jesus. Why these women were not given the same recognition courtesy as others remains a mystery to many. We can only speculate because the Holy Bible gives no definitive answer as to why their names were not part of the roll call of the great women in the lineage of the Savior of the world. We can only speculate for now as to why Bathsheba's name is not mentioned in the lineage hall of fame with Mary and Ruth.

On the other hand, let us not forget when David and Bathsheba started their courtship and adulterous relationship, they were both married to someone else. Was Bathsheba not inducted into the hall of fame because she met the criterion in Deuteronomy 23:17–21? Even among the turmoil that surrounded David and Bathsheba's marriage, it was God's grace that allowed this particular marriage to produce one of the wisest and greatest kings to rule Israel, King Solomon (1 Kings 1:11–35; 3:4–28). Even though we live under the period of God's grace and mercy, which is extended to all creation, we can never take God's love for granted and start trying to play the Lord like people play the lottery or slot machines. One thing gamblers know is sooner or later their winning streak runs out, and hard times can be brutal and unforgiving, to say the least.

Furthermore, I would like to refocus your minds to 1 Samuel 23:2. It is a time when David inquired of the Lord through prayer whether he should kill the Philistines who were looting and robbing the people of Keilah. Keilah was a town located in the territory of the Promised Land, when Joshua divided the lots among the Israelites (Joshua 15:44). God's response to David's prayer was an affirmation of capital punishment for the Philistines. God told David to destroy the Philistines in the territory of Keilah but to save city of Keilah. In other words, God told David not to burn or destroy the city. David prayed to God for His divine direction, and shortly afterward received his answer from God to not only make war with the Philistines but not to utterly destroy them.

The way God answered King David's prayer would probably leave many of us scratching our heads in disbelief, discontent, or confusion because it does not fit the classic model of Ten Commandment teachings. As people of God, we must always keep in mind that we are not called to judge people, like the critics who brought to Jesus the woman they said was involved in an adulterous relationship. The perpetrators hoped to set up Jesus and deny the woman of God's grace and mercy. They were more bent on putting the law above life at the expense of denying love to a sinner in need of God's grace and mercy.

Over the years, I have learned when people are more concerned about the systematic and ritualistic rules of religion than the souls of people, they tend to miss out on the move of God in some way. They miss communion with God because they are too focused on the fundamentals and not people's lives. They get lost in the belief the rules are designed to produce a desired or expected outcome. When this does not happen the way they think it should, they either allow persecution or execution to take control and drive their motives.

When people cannot see and recognize the creativity of the Creator in others, some great ingenuity and learning opportunities are denied. When men and women refuse to believe the Holy Bible expresses the entire creative process of God's Holy Word by way of His creation (man, woman, animal, and angel), then denial of the total creativity process of God is in jeopardy to be recognized and obtained by humanity.

Finally, in Chapter 6 of the book of Joshua, God tells His holy people to rescue the prostitute (whore/harlot) Rahab from the city and allow her and her family to dwell in the Promised Land among the congregation of God. Joshua 6:17 reads, "only Rahab the harlot shall live, she and all that was with her in the house." Some might argue the reason God gave a lifeline to Rahab and her family is because of the courage, faith, and trust she demonstrated when she risked her life, as well as the lives of her family, to help the people of God conquer the land of Jericho. Yes, I would definitely agree there is probably some truth to this supposition. But I believe the real matter to the story is for us not to focus on Rahab or the spies but on the grace and mercy of God the Father. It is the same grace and mercy He so graciously extends to all of us on a daily basis.

One of the beautiful things about the story of Rahab is that in all reality, it was just a matter of time before destiny caught up with her and the deadly lifestyle she lived. As I examine the story of Rahab and the Hebrew spies, I can witness the unconditional love of God, sending grace into the home and life of Rahab the sinner, and giving her the greatest opportunity of her life. When God extends salvation to us like He did with Rahab, this is the greatest opportunity we will ever receive on this side of the Jordan River. Rahab's story represents us being dead in our sins, but when we cooperate and surrender to God's will, the opportunity of everlasting life is offered to us through our obedience to the commands of God.

Furthermore, we must understand that our life on earth is not greater than demands that we walk in obedience to the desires of God. The kingdom of God is much greater than our personal ambitions or goals for happiness and success. Rahab the harlot was willing to turn from her wicked ways and submit to God's plan. It was in Rahab's obedience to God that she and her entire family were blessed with life in the Promised Land of God on the earth.

Also, life is not so much about what we do to achieve great milestones or what we do to fail various tests. Life is really all about what God does for us and what He allows us to do for ourselves and others. The bottom line is no one can achieve anything without God's blessings. A person cannot even get out of bed without the blessings of God. Airplanes could not take off or land without the blessings of God. Ships could not sail on the waters without the blessings of God. The psalmist says in Psalms 127:1, "Except the Lord builds the house, they that labor build in vain." If we really want true success in life, we must line up with the will of God to experience authentic success in the eyes of God.

If any of us did not have the Lord cheering and rooting for us on a daily basis, what would happen to us? When you sleep through the night, who watches over you and your loved ones? When you failed to follow God's instructions, who protected you and led you back to the arch of safety, like a shepherd does with sheep? So if you ever find yourself feeling self-righteous, like you have all the answers, or you bear the retainer rights as if you are God's attorney, I encourage you to think about who speaks for God while you are sleeping or sick and cannot get out of your bed, or before you were ever born? Who will you leave in charge to speak for God when you die? Have you made these kinds of plans and decisions for God?

Moreover, without the right evidence, tools, or instruments, a person will draw a conclusion or form an opinion based on only the tools or equipment he or she has to work with. The writing of this book was mainly inspired because there seemed to be some disconnect with people having enough biblical evidence or information concerning the issue of women in the ministry. It is my most sincere desire that through this book, people will have an extra tool to make a decision based strictly on biblical facts and not just on tradition of humanity.

For years, I have heard the debates and arguments why women could not preach, pastor, or lead men in the church arena with very little scriptural evidence to support this position. I have yet to hear the argument or defense why women should not preach the gospel of Jesus Christ. It is my desire, under the lead of the Holy Spirit, to give the necessary biblical information so people can make an assessment by the leading of the Spirit of God, not just because some man or woman has told them it is wrong for a woman to preach God's Holy Word.

I am willing to go where many have dared not go because of fear or rejection, or persecution from their denominations, bishops, pastors, colleagues, friends, family members, church members, associations, and yes, even their enemies. I have decided I would rather suffer the consequences by humanity than miss out on the rewards from God. As a newly called minister in the 1980s, I learned very quickly that the issue surrounding women ministers was a very sensitive and touchy one that could cause a person trouble if he or she advocated such an idea in many churches. I made my decision early on that I was willing to endure the pain of rejection and isolation rather than deny the truth about God's Holy Word. I am willing to be used by God to put the pieces of the puzzle together without intimidation or fear of rejection or criticism. I echo the words of the prophet Isaiah as he responded to a request by the Lord: "Here am I, send me" (Isaiah 6:8). God needs people willing to stand for His righteousness and if need be, die for His truth. Are you willing to go all the way for Jesus?

Many worshippers are perplexed about how to interpret the Holy Scriptures when it comes to women ministers operating as pundits of the gospel. They are equally unsure about women who emphatically claim they have been called by God to preach His divine gospel. Some of these women have been accused of having an overbearing approach to demanding their rightful place at the table with other clergy. I encourage women ministers to stay focused on the fact God called you to preach the gospel for His kingdom and not to depend on approval from men and women (humanity).

When the "big ball" drops out of the sky for the new era for the people of God, the Lord is not going to look to anyone except you to give an answer for your service as one of His preachers. If you know you have been called by God to preach His most Holy Word, what will be your answer if you fail to preach? Who can you blame when the Master has told you to drive on and preach? There are times the blame game will not work, no matter how you try to manipulate the process. Like a court summons, when you do not show up for court, the judge sends out a warrant for your arrest on contempt of court. When we disobey God, we, too, are held in contempt by the kingdom of God, and Jesus is the only lawyer good enough to defend you when we have to stand before the Almighty Father.

It is my recommendation that you prepare yourself to handle rejection and persecution, as well as know you do not have to defend your calling when you are among friends and family members who truly love you unconditionally. Some people fight so hard to prove their point that they miss golden opportunities to build a trusting and authentic relationship. We have to be sensitive enough to know when the door is open, as well as when the door is closed. Do not become distracted by the Devil, with sidebar arguments about your legitimacy as a minister of the gospel of Jesus Christ.

As always, the approval for God's divine calling on the minister's life is evident in the wholesome and holy life the person presents to Jesus and exemplifies to others. Your actions will prove God's calling in your life, not the agreement or disagreement of men and women, and not the ability or gift men and women can preach or teach, because the Devil can do the same and probably better. Sisters, trusting God and obedience to the Holy Spirit are the greatest advocates a person can have in the midst of this constantly changing world we live in.

More importantly, once women accept the idea their authority comes from God and not from the endorsement of men and women, they will not concern themselves with the opinions of others when it comes to demonstrating their devotion to God. If God truly called you to preach, then preach His Holy Word, and let the critics continue to analyze your good deeds as God continues to give you the proclamation of His Word. Women, as you endure hardship as good soldiers of the gospel, I want to refresh your memory and ask you to look at the ministry of Jesus, and see how He stood against the rejection of a culture full of disbelief. Jesus was heavily challenged and criticized by those with a good understanding of God's Word, yet they missed the move of God through Jesus.

The religious leaders of Jesus' day had knowledge but lacked the wisdom to discern when the move of God was in their presence. I believe we can safely say the religious leaders who fought the move of God through Jesus were like King Saul. They allowed their pride to grandstand on the wrong stand. The religious leaders who fought the move of God thought they were the only translators for God. They seemed to have missed all the signs that told them to submit to Jesus, the Son of God. When people are so desperate to fight against something based on their own ideas, moral beliefs, traditions, or cultures, they can become entangled by pride, greed, and a superiority complex that shows no mercy or grace for those they believe violate their laws, guidelines, rules, traditions, sops, constitutions, or bylaws.

Many of the Pharisees, Sadducees, and Scribes never accepted the idea God ordained Jesus as the Messiah and sent Him to the earth to become the innocent Lamb that would be slain for the sins of the world. Many leaders in the religious circle did not respect the fact Jesus was the only Lamb that had the complete holiness to fulfill God's mission of the earth—the liberation of humanity from the sinful shackles of the Devil. Jesus stayed focused and kept working His divine plan of salvation in the lives of those who believed He was the Savior of the world and the only hope for our salvation.

Jesus never let rejection, persecution, betrayal, or fame deter Him from the mission of spreading His gospel. As you follow the examples of Jesus, do not allow the stumbling blocks *Satan* will put in your path by the way of other people get in the way of fulfilling your mission in Christ Jesus. The Devil is the great accuser of the family of God, and he will never let you rest from persecution. So buckle your seatbelt, and get ready for the rough and joyous ride for Jesus (Revelation 12:10).

Believe it or not, some pastors are too afraid to address the issue of whether to allow women into the pulpit in their local churches. There are pastors who believe women ministers are being treated unfairly in many churches, but they are too timid to stand up for fear their own heads may end up on a golden platter by members of their own congregations or their national bodies. I believe it is time for more male pastors and ministers to raise the bar to a higher level than some of our colleagues. I challenge pastors to open their hearts and doors, and allow women ministers opportunities to exercise their godly gifts in the houses of God across the land for the sake of keeping the church unified in Jesus.

Strange as it may sound, I had an encounter whereby an elderly pastor emphatically told me if he intentionally denied the possibility something exists, the likelihood of it ever becoming an issue is slim to none. He believes if you never teach people about demons, they will never become afraid of them. Of course, when the gentleman made the comments, he was referring to women being called into the ministry by God. This pastor does not allow the issue of women minister to ever come up during any type of discussion in the church where he serves as the pastor. It is an issue that is completely off-limits for his congregation for now. When individuals or groups try to use various mechanisms or schemes to suppress or bury an idea, belief, or movement, the objection becomes the fuel that gives those in the struggle the power to press on for victory.

Some pastors would even say they know it is wrong for them to try and bar women from the ministry, but they just have go with the traditions of the past and what people are accustomed to. For these pastors, it is more about keeping peace within their sanctuaries rather than being radical for Jesus and following the Spirit of God to operate in the lives of His people. These pastors will tell you, why should they rock the boat when there is no need to rock it? They will tell you smooth sailing is their aim, and they are determined not to pick up an issue that is too hot for them.

Some pastors believe they are not called into the ministry to deal with controversial subjects. So, they stay away from anything that looks, smells, or acts controversial. Then there are those ministers who have purposely created segregated platforms with a strong wall of defense in their sanctuaries to prevent the slightest possibility that a female might in some way enter the pulpit by mistake, or out of ignorance, or out of of disobedience. Everyone in the congregation knows there are invisible signs that read, "Stay out! Women not allowed in the pulpit!"

There are also ministers who have made the decision not to discuss the issue about women ministers as their method of rejecting the notion that God gives His approval for women in the ministry as preachers of the gospel. Some pastors believe the women ministers' debate is a dead issue from their perspective. Therefore, the best medicine for the issue is a silent tongue. These pastors and ministers rule their congregations with fear and iron fists and dare anyone to challenge their authority in the "lord," so they say. These pastors are modern-day church godfathers, and if pushed, they will respond like many of the godfathers on the big screen in Hollywood.

Finally, you have those shepherds who are being led by their sheep, which is an indication that we have entire congregational flocks heading in the wrong direction. When you see airliner passengers flying a passenger plane without any training, licenses, or instructions, you are more than likely about to witness a deadly crash. When sheep begin to lead the shepherd, this methodology is not consistent with the teachings of Jesus. Nor is it compatible with Holy Scriptures. These are the congregations where the majority rules due to a set of written rules or guidelines that has nothing to do with the Holy Bible, the kingdom of God, or instructions from God. These religious congregations are doomed by the *Robert's Rules of Order*; because it is a deceitful method that government has control in church affairs.

Many in the congregation will argue the point their decisions and actions are democratic in nature, but when it all boils down, their actions and hidden agendas are dead to the Spirit of God. The members set up their own standards and procedures, which are quoted more times than Bible verses from God's Holy Word. God's Word should become the foundation for our meetings, actions, and conversations. Some of the members are so clever that they use their parliamentary procedures and rules to stagnate and kill the prophets of God, while elevating themselves as saints of their gods. These Pharisees can quote *Robert's Rules of Order* at the drop of a dime but have problems yielding to the words of God as recorded in the Holy Bible. Whenever a pastor and preacher refuses to follow the instructions from the lead sheep in the congregation, the lead sheep assembles his or her decisive flock together with a so-called democratic procedure to remove the minister from the church pulpit with a lethal vote of rejection.

One of the biggest mistakes some ministers make is to believe rejection of the issue concerning women ministers will eventually become a lost subject due to a lack of interest. History seems to teach us that when dictators try to suppress equality and liberation, catastrophe results. People do not normally rebel or protest when truth and justice are the norms in a society or environment. Most revolutions and reformations occurred amid corruption, where unjust rules, practices, and laws were exercised against people who deserved fairness and equality.

God has put an innate ability in human beings to discern when wrongness is being practiced. Sooner or later, the oppressed will rise up and demand justice, equality, and fairness across the board. Ministers of the gospel should be willing to endorse and embrace oppressed people with respect. Ministers connected with Jesus know it is a devastating blow to anyone who has been dehumanized by the various customs demands within a culture. For this reason, it is important for ministers of salvation without bondage to be able to share an unbiased ideology geared toward lifting humanity from the dungeons of ignorance. Ministers should know best how the shackles of tradition make people feel less a part of God's creation. Ministers need to be the main catalysts for using the keys of the gospel as opportunities to liberate people from oppression. Ministers should never become part of the problem by encouraging or forcing people to remain in oppressive and dehumanizing conditions, with impossible rules established by sinful people.

If we were to reflect over world history and examine the various cultures and people across the spectrum of time, we would see how people would rather die than give up some of their basic human and God-given rights. The freedom to exercise God's will is a right women will revolt about if churches fail to recognize their calling into the gospel ministry. History has shown us that though women may bear long, once they begin their revival or revolution for fairness, they will stop at nothing short of what they set out to accomplish. I believe women ministers should have the opportunity and freedom to operate in the gospel ministry without the shackles of segregation and the hardship of suppression being inflicted on them by many of their male counterparts.

Whenever selfish and greedy religious rulers try to use Holy Scriptures to promote their own agendas, it leads to chaos and rebellion by the people. This tends to happen simply because God has equipped human beings with the drive and willpower to eventually reason on the side of truth, justice, righteousness, and fairness. Once people have the distinct honor of drinking from the fountains of freedom and joy, they will continuously have the thirst for such life-sustaining drinks. I am more than confident the joys of equality will always defeat the ugly heads of discrimination and bigotry.

Furthermore, Jesus says to us that He did not come to the earth to be served by people; He came to serve others. There seems to be a mix-up with the concept of servants and humility by a large percentage of the leadership, especially by many males serving in the pastorate (Mark 10:42–45). Some of today's ministers and pastors have the opinion that God only called the masculine breed to patrol the pulpit within local churches. If this is the mindset of male pastors, such sexist thinking seems to give some indication that it is going to be very difficult for anyone other than men pastors and ministers to stand a chance of serving in the pulpit. All I can say is God is still on the throne, and He has the last word and action in every conversation and situation. God can crumble mountains just by His divine Word. God has the track record of moving systems, kingdoms, kings, nations, religious leaders, armies, and people for getting in the way or for trying to stop His plan.

It seems as though much of the fear people have concerning the issue of women ministers, and the attitude for rejecting women in the ministry as preachers, is partially based on tradition from long years ago. It seems like many pastors are quite comfortable with staying glued to the idea that women may indeed have a place in ministry, but not in the pulpit as pulpiteers. Why is there such a panic about women ministers serving in the role as preachers? Why do some pastors fight women in ministry but rely on over half of their membership to be filled by women?

It seems like God is using women as an important thread to keep the fabric of His earthly church together. Women continue to give faithfully, serve honorably, and pay temple taxes on the same scale as men. Yet they have little or no representation as ministers of the gospel because many of the gatekeepers in the clergy field continue to practice Jim Crow laws against women ministers. They use a different set of tactics that is coded under a different name. Something is wrong with this picture, especially when women emphatically know they have received a calling from God but are constantly being turned down by their fathers in the ministry.

When it comes to their male counterparts, women are not given a respectable seat at the table of "brotherhood" in the gospel ministry. I say again, something is gravely wrong with this picture and practice. Although things are still difficult for women ministers in many local churches, here is some positive news. Nearly every Christian denomination accepts women in the ministry in some form or fashion, except for a few smaller conservative sects that refuse to accept equality for all worshippers, regardless of gender. Hopefully one day they, too, will see the light. It is my prayer the groups that refuse to allow women ministers to enter their ranks of leadership will one day recognize some of the practices and traditions of yesteryear had to evolve to a belief God uses human beings to promote His kingdom through the preaching ministry, regardless of gender.

The struggle to gain open access into the pulpit in some churches across America might be the final battle for women on the Western frontier. Women ministers and those who support women in the ministry must never abandon their fight to obtain total liberation within local churches. Women need to write about the discriminatory practices in magazines and news articles, and work together to try to force denominations to debate the issue and make the necessary adjustments to cordially welcome women ministers to come all the way into God's upper room and break bread at the Lord's Table with male ministers.

Women seem to be respected in nearly every aspect of American life (sports, politics, entertainment, education, medicine, military, and so on) except the pastorate or clergy in local churches and national denominations. There is a double standard for the way women ministers are accepted and treated versus how male ministers are treated and accepted. The thing I find most interesting is some of the same people who have been affected by the stings of racism and segregation seem to practice a similar caste system in their churches when it comes to recognizing women as preaching ministers. I am amazed how some people forget where they came from when others are being mistreated by similar unjust rules at the hands of those who endured the pain and shame of unjust rules that robbed people of their personal dignity.

The hypocrisy of rejecting women ministers is intensified when ministers involve themselves and their congregations in fighting for the civil rights of disadvantaged people. Then they themselves turn around and go to their own congregations and discriminate against women in the preaching ministry. It's like a man who publicly fights against the abuse of women and then goes home to abuse his wife and family. Nothing has changed about the man's actions; he just moves from public abuse to personal/private abuse at home.

Also, I have gone as far as to witness a female elected official stand and say she was against women ministers in her local church but campaigned as an equal rights politician. She would argue for women's rights but be the first to protest against women ministers in her local church. This is why it is important to never allow religion and politics to become separated from each other. Religion and politics need to hold each other accountable.

Remember when you do not hold people accountable for their actions, they will develop the attitude they are invincible and above correction. If you allow a person to selfishly take over the dance floor all by him or herself while other people are desiring to dance or when the dance floor is designed for others to dance as well, then the one on the dance floor by him or herself will eventually develop the attitude to dominate the dance floor. He or she will become oblivious to others wanting to get on the dance floor to enjoy dancing to the music. This is what happens when people develop the prideful and selfish attitude that it is all about them and less about what the Holy Spirit wants to do in their lives and the lives of other people. Like the Devil, his demons want all of the attention focused on them so they can get the praise that belongs to God.

5

The Separation of Church and State, But Protection Under the Law for All

The First Amendment of the U.S. Constitution says, "Congress will make no laws respecting an establishment of religion, prohibiting the free exercise thereof ..." These hollow words illustrate the deep concern the Founding Fathers had for protecting the religious rights of individuals. The patriarchs of America and this great republic wanted to limit the powers of government from crippling, disabling, or controlling the religious affairs of people. God knew men would come up with the various baseless arguments to try and use to forbid women from preaching the gospel of Jesus. For this reason, God has plainly laid out in the Holy Bible the necessary Scriptures to demonstrate His endorsement of women ministers. The opponents of women in ministry may not want to recognize it, but God's endorsement is the writings of the Holy Bible even if the protestors are bent on denying it.

The writers of the U.S. Constitution never intended for there to be a complete and total separation of church and state. They were well aware of the fact the church and state must always share power in order to serve as a check and balance for each other. Whenever the government begins to move in the wrong direction with its policies and practices, it becomes the duty of the church to sound the alarm and challenge the government to steer itself back in the right direction for the good of the people. However, without the consciousness of God in the lives of the people, we would care less about the right way to live and doing things as pilgrims of this earth. Without the consciousness of God, humanity would not have the morality or understanding to know the difference between right or wrong as prescribed by the great Creator of the universe.

Likewise, whenever the church or religious community becomes too overzealous and out of control with its beliefs and practices, like what we witnessed with David Koresh in Waco, Texas, and Jim Jones in Guyana, South America, it becomes the government's duty to protect the lives and rights of citizens from such fanatical and destructive religious leaders and organizations. In America, the Bill of Rights is designed to protect the rights of every U.S. citizen and people living within freedom's borders. It is like the Founding Fathers knew if individuals were ever going to have the liberty to practice religion freely, there needed to be systems in place to prohibit interference from the government. Religious freedoms for all citizens and people within the shores of America must be protected and respected as a way of life and not just another hobby.

Sooner or later, I am convinced if these preachers/pastors continue to discriminate against women minsters in churches across America, "big brother" will rise up and defend the people within its shores. I know what you are probably thinking right now. I know you are thinking the U.S. Constitution forbids the government from interfering in affairs of religious organizations. If you believe this, where have you been for the past fifty years? Even the U.S. Constitution will change within the next fifty years. Just take a look around our society and see some of the sweeping changes that would not have been an issue thirty years ago but are center stage today. Any document or country that tries to create an image of what is right and good without seriously acknowledging and recognizing God as the supreme foundation for its existence is bound to fail. History has proven this from the great dynasties to the great kingdoms.

In America, we say religious freedom is protected by two clauses in the amendment: the establishment clause and the free exercise clause. The establishment clause prohibits the government from setting up a state religion. It also forbids the government from preferring one religion over another or from passing laws that aid, promote, or restrict religion. Yet it never says government will in no way or fashion tell religious institutions how to manage their financial affairs.

On the other hand, I am curious as to why churches and religious institutions have to receive a 501(c)(3) tax-exempt recognition letter from the federal government or a tax exempt form from respective state offices in order to receive tax-exempt status? Why is the U.S. government in the business of telling churches how to operate its financial affairs? Without the 501(c)(3) status from the Internal Revenue Service, churches and religious organizations are locked out of applying for government grants as well as other grants, even from private venues. All I am saying is the government is very much involved within the framework of helping to establish religion. Within the near future, we probably will see the government taking a more aggressive and leading role with the shaping and making religion within America. What does the term separation of church and state really mean in the broad sense? By the time you finish reading this chapter, you will become versatile about the religion and the U.S. Constitution and the Separation and Church and State topic.

The free exercise clause protects individuals' right to worship or believe as they choose. Taken together, the establishment and free clauses require the government to be neutral toward religion. This is one of the reasons why women ministers are unable to use the court systems to achieve justice in many of the religious halls across America. However, this may change, depending on what the Supreme Court looks like over the next ten to twenty years. As I write this manuscript, a pressing court case is in the federal court to change the housing allowance given to minsters from being tax exempt to earned income. If this rule is changed, who has made the decision? Either way it goes, it will be a decision made solely by the federal government.

According to the U.S. Constitution, the government should not endorse or disapprove of a religion unless the government can prove its practices are a danger to individuals as well as to the public. The Bill of Rights was mainly designed to protect the rights of Americans against the federal government, but after the Civil War, the U.S. Supreme Court extended most Bill of Rights protection to the states. The Women's Suffrage Movement was instrumental in bringing about the Fourteenth Amendment, which requires equal protection under the law for all citizens and no state can deprive any citizen of "life, liberty, or property without due process of the law." The U.S. Constitution usually restricts Congress or states from taking away the basic rights of individuals.

Why is this information important to women ministers and churches? Technically, if a church organization is operating with a 501(c)(3), that church or religious organization should not discriminate based on a person's ethnicity or sexual orientation. If any church disagrees with this mandate, it should relinquish its 501(c)(3) status and pay the necessary taxes as other businesses. As I stated earlier, if churches and religious organizations continue to deny women equal access, I believe we might see the day of court battles concerning this issue. If the stubbornness of men and women continues to rule conscientiousness and actions, we are most definitely headed to court. It was in 1878 that the Supreme Court interpreted the extent of the free exercise clause in Reynolds v. United States, when it said, "laws are made for the government of actions, and while they cannot interfere with mere religious beliefs and opinions, they may with practices."

During the past fifty years, courts have ruled unfavorably against churches and religion in America, starting with the famous Murray v. Curlett lawsuit in 1963, a landmark Supreme Court ruling, ending official Bible reading in American Public Schools. The case came just one year after the Supreme Court banned officially sponsored prayer in schools in the Engel v. Vitale ruling according to Wikipedia, the free encyclopedia by Goeringer, Conrad F., 2006, 'About American Atheists,' http://www.athesists.org/about. I am appalled that one woman can cripple nearly an entire nation's religious system simply because of her disbelief in God. If one woman has this kind of power to do evil for the Devil then I believe God has one woman with greater powers to do righteous for the kingdom of Heaven. Who knows? You might be the woman God is preparing for the mission.

Over the years, I have become somewhat baffled by many opponents of women in the ministry and their stalwart fight to ensure women have no place in pulpits. I am even more alarmed by political officials who espouse the idea of discriminating against women preachers behind closed doors, yet some of the women they oppose helped put them in office. Why vote for a person who does not respect and consider you to be equal to him or her? Why attend a church where the pastor refuses to see and respect you as a human being and possessing the same rights, qualities, and gifts he does in the kingdom of God? Why do we continue to perpetuate a mentality that continues to oppress the people of God by restricting their services to God? Who has given any of us the right to say women are not allowed to preach in God's pulpits?

When you know God has called you, let no one hinder you by suppressing your ability to make good on a divine calling. Once the calling of God has gone out, you have to wait on and trust the Holy Spirit to open the doors for you while you to continue to work in God's vineyard. Although the journey might be a difficult pilgrimage, do not give up. Keep on fighting for justice in the kingdom of God. There is no room for intimidation or cowardness while on the battlefield for the Lord. If you are truly a soldier in the army of the Lord, then you must fight for God's righteousness and justice until Jesus' return or until He calls you home to glory.

For example, if God has called you to do mission work in Africa, but at the time of your calling, you do not have the money or the passport to get to Africa. It does not mean you are never going to go to Africa to fulfill your calling from God. If God has truly called you to do mission work in Africa, He will make the way for you to travel to Africa to minister to His people. Amen. God wants to keep the responsibility of making His calling come to life for you and not for you to have the burden of the responsibility on your shoulders. Whenever God wills anything, He always fulfills it through His power and might.

Furthermore, if God has truly called you into Christian ministry as a preacher, He will open the doors for you to minister or preach in a pulpit. When we allow the Holy Spirit the opportunity to operate in our lives, we can witness things beyond human influence and comprehension. God will do things for you that you probably thought were impossible. When God is on your side, He will open doors for you that probably were sealed. God will make the impossible become a ladder of opportunities for your greatness in Jesus. Keep the faith that every stone someone throws at you, Jesus will turn into stepping stones for you to climb higher in His kingdom.

All you have to do is keep the faith and hope alive, and the assurance that God is always in charge. Trusting God must become your GPS because it is your trust that will lead you into the presence of the Holy Spirit. The Lord will place you on the fertile ground so you may serve Him without any stumbling blocks in your way. God has the power to allow you to serve in the same field(s) where you were once denied access. God has a humorous way of reversing the actions or decisions of humankind that interfere with His purpose. Always remember, if you commit your ways to the Lord, your destiny is linked to God and not to the decisions of men, women, or any other thing.

As far as some of our politicians, I do not believe those who denounce women in ministry ever broadcast their religious views as it relates to degrading the role of women in church. Politicians who hold discriminatory views based on gender need to be singled out and exposed for what they really stand for, especially if they espouse discriminatory views about women who have answered their calling into the gospel ministry. People need to challenge politicians to discuss their views as they relate to women across society.

Do not allow them to espouse only those political views they feel should be discussed in the public. Most politicians will try to evade questions about their religious views, ideas, and affiliations. We often allow them to get by without disclosing who they really are as it relates to their commitments to the kingdom of God. I believe there is a great danger by allowing politicians to avoid or refuse to answer questions about their religious views. How someone sees God has a lot to do with how he or she treats others. How a person loves God has a lot to do with how he or she feels about other people.

Some people are adamant about denying women the right to exercise their God-given gifts and talent as their male counterparts. I am appalled by the large number of educated people who hold onto outdated theological views, traditional practices, and culturally bankrupted checks from yesteryear. Today, we have a better understanding of Holy Scriptures and knowledge is not as limited as it was hundreds and thousands years ago. With all of the biblical resources we have today, understanding has reached its mature potential; pastors have the proper tools and training to make the necessary paradigm shift needed to abandon wicked acts of gender discrimination. Under grace, we now have the Spirit of God dwelling with us and leading us to the fountain of truth about God's words where we can bring divine changes in the churches of God across America and throughout the world.

Yet many ministers and pastors refuse to come out of the box of ancient thinking, which has no relevance in ministering to congregations in this modern era. Regardless of the century in which we live, we know the Word of God remains the same, regardless of the changes in culture over time. However, the methodology by which we promote God's Word to people is constantly changing. God's holy words remain the same whether spoken five thousand years ago or yesterday. The power and influence of the Holy Spirit is on the alert and monitoring the souls of men and women in order to offer an appeal that addresses the needs and conditions of those it seeks and calls.

The crux of the gospel message is not only to bring about positive changes in people's lives. Its foundational mission is to restore humanity to God the Father through Jesus Christ. Without authentic and proven evidence by the believer of a divine experience with Jesus, positive changes that occur in people's lives are no different than the positive changes that are experienced by any other religious affiliation claiming to bring about positive changes in the lives of its followers. Christian actions must be more than just positive changes. They must present themselves in such a powerful way that the onlooker is compelled to take note of the presence of God in the life of the disciple of Jesus.

To a certain degree materially, socially and economically, nearly every sector of our society has moved on to the more prosperous territory of the Promised Land. The Promised Land experience has been accomplished by extending freedoms and equality in areas that were forbidden in the past. In times past, we witnessed examples of segregation and discrimination as the norm for American society. At one time in America, only certain people were allowed to advance.

Their potential for success was based on gender and/or the color of their skin. The prosperity of the Promised Land was only available to certain people.

Under the grace of God, the Promised Land is open to whomever wishes to come and serve Jesus. Jesus only allows the Holy Spirit to give out the personal assignment for each servant willing to serve in His kingdom. Coming into the Promised Land is an experience like nothing else in the world. The Promised Land experience is greater than all the world's tourist attractions put together.

Some people want to return to the way things used to be mainly because they are afraid of stepping into the future. For many fighting change, moving forward brings out the great fear of going to a place where they will not be recognized, and their personal needs will not be met. They are afraid of entering a world that will no longer cater to their selfish agendas and needs. They are afraid of the thought or idea of someone taking their space and forcing them into a world where they will have no supervision or connection.

People who seek power, control, and attention will often have a meltdown if they are disconnected from the source that makes them feel needed, important, and invincible. Some men need a structure in place that makes them feel superior to women. They build empires and place themselves at the top of the pecking order, so anything they disapprove will never threaten their domains or kingdoms. These insecure leaders are masters at training men and women to think and behave like them. They value no ideas, philosophies, thoughts, or dreams apart from their own. They only encourage others mainly when it is of value to their own success and not necessarily to the kingdom of God.

It is amazing how some of the same people God liberated from the shackles of oppression argued to stay in Egypt as the enslaved and shackled population. The oppressed people had grown up in a world that offered them a limited view for seeing and interpreting the world from a global perspective. Like some of the Hebrews, they were only allowed to eat what Pharaoh fed them! Their troubled minds could only grasp what Pharaoh wanted them to learn. They were very loyal to the traditions Pharaoh placed in their psyche for over four hundred years of bondage. Keep in mind some people's liberation can only come by a forced hand of God. In other words, if God does not come down and speak to them in an audible voice, they will never hear the voice of God. Even then, sometimes God has to thrust them into situations that give them no other choice but to live or die.

The oppressor knows in order to perpetuate his vision and increase the longevity of his oppressive regime; he must ensure the oppressed never gain access to his throne. In the oppressor's mind, the pulpit is the lighthouse for his power dynasty, influence, and decision making. This tactic is one of the greatest tools used throughout centuries by political dictators. Now we see some pastors employing the same method of control in pulpits across America.

Some pastors use some of the schemes and tactics they learned from their own oppressors. They will grab one or two Scriptures from the Holy Bible to justify their position of refusing to allow women into their pulpits, rather than examine the entire Holy Bible, from Genesis through Revelation. These pastors researched and exegeted the following biblical text with great intensity for a clear understanding, yet reject the idea the apostle Paul is sanctioning slavery: Slaves obey your masters (Ephesians 6:5-9; Colossians 3:22; 1 Peter 2:18).

On the other hand, these same pastors readily and aggressively accept the Scripture where Paul says he will not suffer a woman who tries to usurp authority over a man" (Ephesians 6:5–9; Colossians 3:22–24; 1 Peter 2:18–22; 1 Timothy 2:12). The former text is interpreted as figurative speaking, while the latter text is explained as having the dialogue of literal interpretation by the reader. I often share with the congregation that I currently serve as the pastor that there are about four main things God looks at when we move into action: 1. The will of God is most important; 2. Your Purpose; 3. Your Motive and 4. Your Intent for doing whatever you do.

From my understanding of the Old Testament, God told Eve to help Adam till the grounds and keep the garden. The mantle of supervision was given to both Adam and Eve, male and female, regardless of management position. The responsibility of keeping the garden was given to the male and female. God mentioned to Adam and Eve that a certain section of the garden was off-limits for the male as well as for the female. Where Adam stood, Eve was allowed to stand. There was no distinction between where Adam worked and where Eve worked. Their jobs were the same: to keep and dress the Garden of Eden for the Lord. God never looked at Eve as a second-class citizen in the Garden of Eden. Eve's work in the garden was just as important as Adam's work in the Garden of Eden.

Furthermore, God gave Eve the same respect and responsibilities He gave Adam. One can easily get a glimpse of the level of responsibility and accountability Eve received from God by observing the punishment issued to Eve after she and Adam sinned against God (Genesis 1:26–28; 3:16–17). When it was time to receive punishment, Eve stood in the same place of judgment as Adam to accept her chastisement in the same fashion as Adam did during the great fall of humanity. Responsibility and accountability make a person liable for successes as well as the failures, regardless of personal involvement.

Within the pages of this book, it is my most sincere desire to outline what I believe the Word of God says about the positions and roles of women in ministry, especially as preachers serving in pulpits and not just teachers of the gospel of Jesus. I am convinced some people will probably read this book and their positions will remain locked in the traps of the traditions of the past. They either offer a limited voice for accepting change or stand firmly on their chauvinistic views and offer no hope for experiencing a paradigm shift for the present and future. Hopefully this book will help liberate some ministers' minds and hearts from the religious shackles of legalism and dogma that minimize and restrict women in their God-given roles as pastors/preachers in the kingdom of God.

Religious legalism is deadly because it is when church folk feel as though they have been empowered by God to police and/or interpret God's Holy Scriptures based on their traditional upbringing or educational training. Religious slave masters have the mindset they are doing God a favor by policing and enforcing traditional mandates God cannot handle on His own. Within the legal system and law enforcement world, this kind of tactic would be called either abuse of power or obstruction of justice.

Yet like Saul in Acts Chapter 8, religious legalists feel and think they are doing God a big favor by protecting His pulpit from those who have gone astray in the work of the Lord. When females inform their male pastors God has called them into the ministry, and the pastor either immediately gives them their pink slip of dis-fellowship, this is a problem within Christendom. When a woman comes to her pastor to discuss her calling into the ministry, and he tells her maybe she has been called by God but cannot fulfill her calling in that church, it is a problem within Christendom that many women are facing. Some male pastors will not even discuss the issue with women coming to them with the most important message or news of their lives. Every person who feels and knows he or she is being called into the ministry deserves the respect as a human being to either get or not get the pastor's blessing before going into the world as sheep among wolves.

Many pastors and clergy who believe God does not call woman to preach seem to be of the opinion they have to protect God from women and men who have gotten out of line. They adopt the attitude there is a need for women to be put back into their respective lanes. It's like when a person of authority steps out of line and needs to be reminded of his or her place in society. Whenever God gets to the point that He becomes so weak He needs humanity's protection, then the entire universe is in trouble. God does not need our help when it comes to protecting Him or His ministry. We need God's help.

Whenever it comes to God's ministry, the Holy Bible has already told us that God has no respect of person (Romans 2:11). Yet humanity has created a system of protocol and respect based on gender. If this practice is not segregation and discrimination then I have no clue about race relations and equal opportunity.

The religious security guards and church bouncers who are trying to patrol God's traffic do not have the police powers or the authority to do so. To put it quite bluntly, these people have deputized themselves to become the modern-day Pharisees, with no intention of allowing God to speak to their hearts. It is not uncommon for men pastors to get a whiff of their own pride and have to be broken down by God. Here is my response to those battling the deadly disease of pride: "An ounce of humility is greater than all your tons of pride." Proverbs 12:15 reads, "The way of a fool is right in his own eyes, but a wise man or woman listen to advice."

In Acts, God had to have a face-to-face talk with the apostle Peter for lifting himself up too high on a rooftop while the church was expanding beyond the boundaries of human perception and control (Acts 10:9–22). When the apostle Peter thought he had it right concerning whom God calls into His kingdom, God had to have a personal conference with him. Just because Jesus and the Holy Spirit installed apostle Peter as the pastor of the earthly church does not mean he had the right to make the call to those God calls or those He forbids into His preaching ministry.

During the meeting between God and Peter, God rebuked Peter and set the record straight about Peter's sexist and racist stance against the Gentiles. Peter refused to eat because there were some items and people he considered to be common or unclean. God reminded Peter it is He who determines what is clean and unclean, and no decision of this nature is left up to a pastor. When pastors and church members get into the business of determining who God has called to preach the gospel of Jesus, segregation and discrimination become the ringleaders, not grace.

Peter was determined to keep his faith from contamination. His limited knowledge of God's compassion persuaded him to think he was acting in the right manner according to the Scriptures and Hebrew tradition he was taught from childhood. However, God looked at Peter's selfish and pompous behavior concerning salvation and grace for all and immediately intervened, corrected him, and challenged him to experience a paradigm shift from his traditional way of thinking and interpreting Scriptures. God told Peter that from that day forward, he was never to call anything unclean that God has cleansed.

On the other hand, to tell a person he or she is restricted or denied because of a permanent physical characteristic they have no control over is insane, to say the least. This classifies and segregates people based on physical characteristics or makeup. Let the truth be told, Peter—as well as all our past, present, and future—are unclean until the blood of Jesus washes us and the Holy Ghost purifies us from all sin and unrighteousness. There is nothing that can wash away our sins except the precious blood of Jesus.

Think about this scenario. When a building catches fire, the entire building is on fire, and everything associated with the building that is on fire can be lost. Yet if an immediate water supply and firefighting equipment and personnel are available, the building has a greater chance of being saved. What if there are no men in the area to respond to the burning building and only women to respond to the building that is being devastated by fire? Do you restrict women from delivering water because they are women? The answer is probably no because you deem it to be a serious emergency. You want to save your building as well as lives because we never know for sure who is inside the burning building. Why restrict women from bringing water to the fire when God's buildings are burning down? Yes, people are burning in sin and on their way to hell, and we lack the manpower to handle the problems all by our masculine selves. The kingdom of God, like the garden of Eden, is enriched by us working together and serving cooperatively in the same vineyard, without fighting and arguing about who is not called to preach God's Holy Word.

Peter's experience is important to mention in this book because I have heard many pastors and preachers say the reason they do not allow women in their pulpits is because certain times of the month women are considered unclean (when menstruating). Some of these men feel as though since they do not know the exact time of the month women have their menstrual periods, it is best to bar them from the pulpit altogether. The pastors based their position on an Old Testament law in Leviticus 15:19 and 18:19, which made the woman unclean during a certain time of the month.

My curiosity is why these same antiwomen ministers never expound on the fact that under the Leviticus's laws, they would not be able to serve as priests if they had not become circumcised. Also, they would have to classify themselves as unclean to serve in the priesthood if they have any kind of skin condition, or skin disease like boils, pimples, skin colorations, physical deformities, any running fluids protruding out of their flesh such as pus or blood, any type tattoos or markings drawn, carved or branded in their flesh. All were grounds to bar males from the ministry under Mosaic Law. Please read the book of Leviticus, chapters 10 through 21 for more information.

Under the law, if a male child was not circumcised within eight days after his birth, he was considered unclean. Not only would the child be unclean according to Holy Scriptures, it would also have been an act of disobedience to God on the part of the parents and could result in the death of the parent(s) (Genesis 17:9–14; Exodus 4:24–30). Many male ministers who espouse the idea women are unclean have probably not been circumcised. Yet God allows them to serve as shepherds over His sheep without any retribution. This is because we are now the tenants of grace and no longer live under bondage of the law. God understands our situations yesterday, today, and tomorrow. He knows all about the times during the years of Jim Crow and segregation when many African Americans, especially those born in the South, were not afforded the pleasures and luxuries of being born in a hospital, unless they were born in cities with an African American hospital.

Many pastors who adamantly oppose the idea of women in the ministry fail to recognize that God has given all of us a reprieve from the curse of the law. Now that we are under grace through the blood of Jesus, we should always remain mindful of how God saved us from society's hang-ups and from the Devil. It is amazing how soon many people forget that yesterday they, too, were entangled by some of the same vices of sin, and God had to step in to free them from some of the same things for which they reject others.

In Galatians 3:13, the apostle Paul puts it this way: "Christ has redeemed us from the curse of the law, being made a curse for us: for it is written, Cursed is every one that hangs on a tree." Paul argues that under faith in Jesus, the Holy Spirit brought us grace, so we will no longer have to live under the bondage of the law. Paul says we have been baptized into Jesus through the Holy Spirit, which makes us put on Christ and become one with Him. Becoming one with Jesus gives us a different identification because according to Holy Scriptures, "there is neither Jew nor Greek, there is neither bond nor free, there is neither male nor female: for we all are one in Christ Jesus" (Galatians 3:28).

If we are neither male nor female, but all are one in Christ Jesus, why is there such a strong opinion against women ministers? Please explain how females are left out of the equation as being one in Christ Jesus in the local church as it relates to them exercising their ministerial gifts. I interpret Galatians 3:28 as meaning God does not look at our differences—physical limitations, age, or gender—when it comes to kingdom work, and how

He is going to use those with a calling to become a blessing in the lives of other people. Since God is an equal opportunity employer of men and women, boys and girls, animals and beasts, who are we to tell God that He cannot hire a particular section, part, or person in His creation? All the Lord needs is a vessel who is willing to submit and obey Him. Whenever we are talking about God, please keep in mind that all His vessels except Jesus will have shortcomings and limitations in His kingdom-building service here on earth.

The blemishes we bring to God are often used as opportunities to demonstrate the awesome powers of an unchangeable and almighty God. We serve a God who is constantly changing the lives of people in miraculous ways, releasing them to do even greater things in life and for His kingdom. The Lord consistently changes us in positive ways for the good of His kingdom and to keep us from self-destructing. When God changes us to do a great work for His kingdom, everyone in the family becomes benefactors of God's marvelous blessings and works. We are blessed by Jesus to become greater blessings to others. God never intends to bless us so that we become a curse or a stumbling block for other people. When people are in the church and become stumbling blocks for those reaching out to Jesus, I seriously think they need to check and see whose jersey they are wearing. People in the church cause others to go astray through some divisive act. I recommend they seriously check the tower they are receiving their order or commands from (John 10:1–18).

Furthermore, when God looks at us, He should no longer be able to see us as separate people with human and physical limitations. As newborn Christians, God should be able to see only the Mediator (Holy Spirit) operating in our weaknesses and shortcomings. As children of God, the Lord sees all of us through His eyes, which are filled with grace, hope, and mercy. God knows and understands better than anyone that we are sinners, struggling with sinful issues daily. Yet God chooses to use us by the hands of grace and with the touch of faith and hope that one day we will bring a harvest of righteousness to His holy marketplace. God sees us as the greatest investment on the earth and possibly in the universe. Once the working of the Holy Spirit matures in us the faith of Jesus Christ, we become a work that is wonderfully made by the hands of God.

When God observes a person under grace, He should be able to see only the Jesus in the person. When a person is truly covered by the blood of Jesus, he or she can no longer remain the same. The blood of Jesus is so powerful that it brings about a sweeping change wherever it goes and in whomever it touches. If God still sees you as the old you, I challenge you to allow Jesus to overwhelm you to the point that you no longer exist as the person you once were.

Moreover, Jesus never treated women as second-class citizens. To Jesus, it did not matter whether the women were part of the kingdom of God, He never devalued or dehumanized women based on their gender. Think about the woman at the well in John Chapter 4, who told Jesus He could not get anything to drink because He did not have a bucket or rope to draw the water from the well. She also told Him the well was too deep for Him to be able to draw water. This illustration of agape love on the part of Jesus should serve notice to all of us that it is not our place to ever tell God what He can or cannot do or who He can use or cannot use in His kingdom. If God is God, let Him be God. Even after the woman at the well had gotten somewhat verbally combative with Jesus, He kept His composure and stuck to His goal of winning her over to His team by the grace of God, the Father of us all.

In spite of the woman's condescending dialogue, Jesus took the time to converse with her, when others probably would have shunned her. After the woman finished giving a history lesson about her Samarian people, she told Jesus He needed her help to draw water from the well because she possessed the necessary tools. In all honesty, she was the one in need of Jesus' help and His saving water.

Finally, Jesus summed up the meeting by extending to her the opportunity to drink His living water. Jesus informed the woman His living water would restore her life and offered her the opportunity to change her life. Jesus was allowing the woman to reestablish herself in society through the lens of a God who continuously extends the olive branch of forgiveness to all of us who have done wrong in life. Jesus was giving her the chance to embrace Christian respect in the community in which she was a resident (John 4:7–30).

Think about it this way. The woman at the well was able to do something many men were not able to do. God gave her the chance to have a personal, uninterrupted conversation with Jesus in the natural as well as the spiritual. She was able to see Jesus in the natural but left the meeting clearly seeing the kingdom of God from a spiritual perspective. She was able to draw her natural water but was granted the opportunity to taste the living water of God.

The woman at the well was able to stand in the presence of the Son of God and be given the floor to discuss and debate her theological views concerning the coming of the Messiah. She also received an intelligence briefing from the Messiah. What an awesome gift this woman was granted by God. I am sure she left this meeting with Jesus feeling greater than she ever felt in life.

I believe this woman left the meeting feeling accepted and respected by Jesus and God. I believe this woman left the meeting with Jesus feeling uplifted and no longer downtrodden because of traditions and people's opinions. I am more than confident this woman left the meeting with Jesus feeling vindicated of her sins and redeemed by the Messiah of the world.

Last but not least, the woman at the well with Jesus was given a firsthand glimpse of the dignity by which Jesus relates to people, regardless of their sex, ethnicity, gender, or spiritual status. She embraced and respected Jesus because He first respected and embraced her. The woman came to draw water from the well yet left with a spring of living water in her soul. Jesus gave this woman the opportunity to express herself in His presence, while she was living in sin with a man who was not her husband. Jesus never pulled out His "hold card" that says, "Because you are a sinner, you cannot talk to Me, the Messiah." Jesus never said to the woman, "Because you are a woman, I will not allow you to address me."

Also, Jesus did not remove Himself from the woman because of physical or spiritual turmoil she may have been dealing with at the time. He saw the woman as a lost soul who, with the right opportunity, could end up being a great blessing to His kingdom. To Jesus, the woman at the well was another opportunity to spread God's love and demonstrate the miraculous power of the Holy Ghost on the earth. Jesus exercised His grace and mercy over the laws of men and women as they relate to the compassion God has for His creation.

6

The Deadly Force of Religious Legalism

Legalistic raiders move across the horizon like insensitive law enforcement officers with badges, handcuffs, blackjacks, stun guns, and so on, searching for people who do not believe like their 'gangs.' Once they find the so-called brothers or sisters who are in error according to their interpretations of the Scriptures, they brand the person or persons and exclude them from their fellowship, like gang members excommunicating a former member from their clan. This gang is very intelligent, social media savvy, computer literate, and financially equipped to make every attempt to ruin your life through the avenues of social media, and its members are ruthless and very lethal. The group is well connected in the communities which they live and operate. The group disguises itself very well and you will need the guidance of the Holy Spirit to reveal their activities and ring leaders.

You must do everything within your power to avoid these religious bandits by yourself, because they specialize in covert operations that are designed to set you up, and then sabbatoge your ability to minister. Their purpose is to scandalize your name in mud so you can never recover. They are heavily armed with secret agents that are known for smiling in your face, while behind your back they are planning your spiritual assassination. They will attack your calling, crush your self-esteem, and destroy your walk in the ministry if you do not have complete assurance of your calling into Christian ministry. They will go as far as to kill you, like the anti-Jesus groups banded together to murder Jesus on a wooden cross. Modern-day religious assassins have been highly trained to destroy the reputations and lives of those who deviate from what they teach, believe, and practice.

Trust me on this one thing, if you ever meet a religious raider, he or she has been trained to shred you to pieces if you do not know how to stand firmly about your calling from God. The religious bandits are very astute in the Word that they often use the deception of witchcraft like the Jehovah Witness or Mormans and other cult leaders to convince people of a different plan of salvation other than what the Holy Bible offers us through Jesus Christ. They will service you with their own menus, similar to how some restaurants serve you as you dine with them. They let you choose your own meal and eat as much as you want, but you have to select from the specialized menu they offer you. They will always want to be in control or in charge of the conversation and if they cannot be the dominate teacher, then they will break dialogue and move on to another fish in the frying pan.

Throughout the ministry of the apostle Paul, he had to deal with a lot of religious 'thugs' that proselytized their way as being the best and only way. You see this especially when you explore the various confrontations he encountered with the legalists in the book of Galatians. These religious gang members run around claiming turf, and if you do not believe exactly like they believe, you either have to leave their so-called turf, or they will do their best to terminate your presence as a meaningful entity among the clan. These religious assassins will make every attempt to prohibit you and your ministry from going forward, deploying the wicked tactic of character assassination.

Once the religious "super-clan" has deemed you a threat to their male dominance, they quickly disassociate themselves from you, as though you have just betrayed the Messiah or been infected with an incurable or contagious disease. They tend to have no compassion for reconciliation. To them, the only solution is to decimate you from the ranks of the ministry. These groups will label you an outcast in many religious circles in your community, across your state, and even across the nation. With such groups, your only chance for mercy is in your ability to publically recant your claim that God has called you for the preaching of the gospel ministry. This is why it is so important every woman of God knows without any doubt or hesitation that she has been called into the gospel ministry by God and not by the authority of humanity.

Religious legalism is deadly because it allows no room for God's grace and mercy to mediate a disagreement. A religious legalist has established the mindset that it is his way or the highway. There is no room for bargaining or negotiating with people who have spirits and attitudes like the Pharisees and Sadducees. The rules are set in stone and will not change for anyone violating the rules of the game.

Religious legalists are so-called perfect and astute students of theological philosophy. They master the letter but miss out on the tenets and compassion of grace and the mercy of God's Holy Spirit. Some of them are good and likable people, but never stand in their way when it comes to them living out the law as they view it.

If religious legalists are challenged on their actions or beliefs, they will not hear a word you say, even if they surmise God is using you. If you do not believe as religious legalists do and become an outcast, they have no problem with marking you as a renegade or menace to society. Religious legalists feel strongly that part of their job is to protect the ideology of their society lest others cause it to become contaminated with ungodly beliefs and practices.

Thank God for grace and mercy. They create the atmosphere that allows people to agree to disagree in love, respect, and with understanding. Religious legalism is lethal because it takes the letter of law and excommunicates brothers and sisters from its fellowship without any compassion for reconciliation, unless he or she forsakes his or her views, ways, and practices, and submits to the legalist traditions, which ultimately turn out to be traditional bondage. It is good to know the grace and mercy Jesus died for dissolves us from the bondage of traditional legalism that judges men and women based on their gender, ethnic group, or nationality.

When Jesus died for the sins of the world, He opened the playing field for all of us male and female to have equal access to the various callings and vocational offices in the kingdom of God. God sent Jesus into the world to make us full partners in His kingdom. Men are not superior to women neither are women superior to men. Yet everyone and everything is inferior to God. In the eyes of God we all are partners in His vineyard of service. God would love to have all of His creation to serve as His servants at His disposal.

Finally, as long as the religious legalist party thinks it is in charge of God's vineyard, there will never be any peace in the valley. I guess you are probably wondering who or what is the religious legalist party. It is the mentality of people that carry the same self-righteous spirit as the Pharisees, Sadducees, and Scribes of Jesus' day. In your church or religious organization they may go by a different name, but I would like to go on record by saying nearly all churches have this particular group of members who think they are more saved than others in the church. If there is sin in your church, then you have card carrying members of the religious legalist party within the ranks of your church.

Moreover, the religious legalist party members will continue to fuel wars with their self-righteous agendas and conflicts that are not beneficial for anyone, especially for the kingdom of God. When men and women think their way is the only way and their position is right and everyone else's is wrong, you have just entered the world of perfection. This is a make believe world where the religious legalist life is so perfect with great fantasies, but with deadly human errors that even Jesus would not be welcome if He came into the building. These people have set themselves as little gods on their earthly thrones. Regardless of what you do, you cannot please them unless you surrender to their rules and regulations.

Keep in mind that the perfect Pharisees, Sadducees, and Scribes never accepted Jesus. Only people who were striving for perfection through God's grace would listen to Jesus and follow Him as Lord and Savior of their lives. The same principle holds true today. Only people striving for a perfect life in the kingdom of God are willing to listen to the voice of Jesus. Jesus made this point clear in Matthew 13:10–15, when He pointed out there will be those who think they have it all together but really have nothing.

I encourage you to become the person God intends you to become and do whatever God has called you to do. Do not allow the diabolical strings of chauvinistic theology to disrupt your lives by becoming a stumbling block of discouragement. It is amazing how many of my African American colleagues in ministry use similar self-righteous patterns and tactics to suppress women ministers as some of our Caucasian clergy and denominations used to discourage and break the will and hope of our god-fearing African American ancestors during slavery and Reconstruction. Years following American slavery, many of our white brothers refused to believe and accept the notion that God had called their former slaves into the gospel ministry as preachers and pastors. Servants, yes, but not as religious leaders of the gospel of Jesus, where whiteness was divine, and blackness was the opposite of divine. Being born black meant a person was more of a servant than the leader. You see, the gospel of Jesus is a message of hope, freedom, prosperity, and peace that continues to perpetuate the African American fight for freedom in America.

As children of God, we must never forget God's agenda will be fulfilled regardless of who is standing in the way. Like the War of Independence between British and Americans, the Civil War, and the Civil Rights Movement, the will of God will always prevail. God is determined to rule with or without your vote of confidence. It behooves anyone to think his or her actions are so powerful that he or she can sway God's plan. Just think about why we refer to Him as the Almighty! God does not need anything, including society's bounty hunters, who go after female ministers, like slave catchers pursued runaway slaves with the hope of preventing them from living out their dreams in freedom. When a person is fulfilling the will of God, it is the greatest freedom he or she will experience on this side of Jordan (heaven). There is no better plan in life than to be in God's will; this is true freedom.

The status of women ministers in America is a travesty of injustice in the halls of our great congregations. Women ministers are treated unfairly by many of the churches across America. Some women have lost hope and faith in the churches that gave them birth. Women ministers beg and plead with church leadership to allow them to take their rightful places in the ranks of ministry as devoted and professional clergy members. Local congregations (earthly churches) cannot move out of bondage without godly leaders. These godly leaders must be willing to hear the voice of God and follow the guidance of the Holy Spirit on the issue of embracing women ministers in the gospel ministry. I try to encourage some of my pastor friends who are struggling with the woman preaching issue by letting them know it is better to take the small step of action than to always dream big about the giant leap of nothing.

Our God-fearing patriarchs were more assured of their calling from God than life itself. If American slavery taught us nothing else, it taught us you cannot break the spirit of a unified people when Almighty God is their source of strength and hope. For someone who has made the decision to die for Jesus, turning his or her back on the commitment is not an option; it is worse than committing suicide. When someone has the uncompromising drive that he or she has received a mandate from God, it is useless for anyone to try to stand in the way.

Women ministers who have received their callings from God will not back down on their commitments to fulfill the mission and ministry God has ordained them to fulfill in His ministry. These preachers are just as determined to obey and please God as the evangelist Stephen was when he preached Jesus. Stephen was determined to proclaim and promote the kingdom of God to people who refused to accept the idea God was establishing His kingdom on earth with a group of disciples. This kingdom was separate from the traditional, mainstream denominations that had called the shots for years about the direction of religion for the nation (See Acts Chapters 6 and 7).

I would rather die trying to complete God's mission for my life than to be found in a discouraging place because I allowed someone to deny me the opportunity to fulfill God's plan in my life. Only God knows what is best for all of us. We must never forget that divine assignments come only from God and not humankind.

Therefore, who has the authority to tell someone what he or she can or cannot do while serving in the kingdom of God except God the Almighty Father? Never allow anyone to push you around when it comes to completing the assignment God has given you. Remember, the mission was not given to those who oppose you; it was given to you. You are the one God holds responsible for completing the mission. You will have no excuses when you stand in the presence of God. As you stand before the almighty throne of God, He will reward or chastise you based on whether you obeyed His commandments and guidance.

Which evil is worse, sexism or racism? From a historical point of view, some of you have firsthand knowledge of how the oppressor refuses to see or even admit his faults or the wrong he inflicts on his helpless victims. The perpetrator abuses mainly because it makes him feel powerful and superior over his victims. He controls people with his power and authority because he feels it guarantees him an advantage over his victims for things he wishes to obtain.

The religious dictator who refuses to accept women preachers is relentless in his quest to control and dominate by any means necessary. If his or her rules are not obeyed at all times, the oppressed receives a suspension or expulsion. It is just the rules when you deal with the spirits of sexism and racism.

The oppressor constantly looks for ways that will give him the upper hand or edge that will allow him to remain a step ahead of those he feels the need to oppress, control, or dominate. He oppresses others because he has low self-esteem and lacks the ability to give genuine compassion to others. This person hides in a shadow because real transparency exposes him for the person he is within. He refuses to accept truth. He shuns the truth by putting on his blinders, which forces him to experience and see things only from his limited worldview, from the inside of his own box.

Moreover, he seeks superior power and control because he is self-centered and selfish, which are the things that stroke his ego. He refuses to let go of his prideful spirit of dominance and give in totally to God. His heart becomes so callous that it experiences no joy in doing right in the eyes of God. These are the attitudes of many men in ministry leadership positions who are fighting against women preachers in America and across the world.

Always remember the calling of God for you to serve in the ministry does not come from men or women. It is a calling from the bosom of God only you have the ability to answer. Over the years, problems have come when those the Lord called have allowed the opinions of ruthless theological dictators to control their destinies with God. A word to the wise is to never allow anyone to control or attempt to control your destiny or your relationship with God. If you or I allow other people to have this kind of control over our lives, then where would God fit in? How could God and Jesus fit in when you have given the reins of your heart to someone else to control? Since our God is a jealous God, if He cannot have total control of our lives, then He has no control at all (Exodus 20:5; 34:14).

For over twenty years I have believed how unstable and unfair it is for men to be so adamant about denying women the right to enter the pulpit and preach the gospel message in churches. I believe the Holy Bible supports four compelling reasons why women should accept their callings into the Christian ministry and preach the gospel of Jesus Christ:

1. God promotes women in ministry.
2. Jesus Christ endorses women in ministry.
3. The Holy Spirit empowers women in ministry.
4. New Testament church equips women for ministry.

If we accepted the premise that God does not call women into the ministry because of their physical makeup, it is safe to say men who are not circumcised are not called into the ministry because they have not been circumcised. I know, I know. Now you want to play the saved by grace card and say the works of faith have nothing to do with the works of the flesh as recorded in Galatians 2:7–10, 16–21; 3:10–14. Think about it. The driving force used to keep women out of the pulpit is all physical in nature. It is a fight that focuses on the physical attributes of the woman and not her spiritual qualities and gifts. We put the emphasis on woman rather than the vessel God is using to feed His people.

When you really get down to where the rubber meets the road, rejecting women ministers from preaching is all about the outward appearance, rather than the inward spiritual blessing she can bring to the kingdom of God through preaching the gospel of Jesus Christ. This world needs light, just like it needed light when Jesus came into the world through a woman's womb over two thousand years ago. If God uses women to bring light to people who are dying in darkness, why reject this notion or fight against this move of God?

If we can get off the physical qualifications of the instrument God uses, perhaps we can start using the term "vessel" for what God is using. When we say "vessel," it does not specify gender, ethnicity, or whether we are from the human or animal kingdom. You see, once we remove the physical piece of the puzzle, then we can see God more clearly in the spiritual realm and recognize the fact that as leaders and disciples of Jesus, we should be more concerned about our spiritual state of mind and attitude rather than our physical looks and abilities.

Women can argue the Holy Scriptures say, "There is neither Jew nor Greek, there is neither bond nor free, there is neither male nor female: for ye are all one in Christ Jesus (Galatians 3:28; Colossians 3:10–11). According to scriptural references from the book of Galatians and Colossians, God does not limit His spectrum to race, social status, physical abilities, or gender when determining someone's call into ministry. When God goes fishing on the earth, He is looking for the fish willing to bite His bait and stay on His line of righteousness until He can bring it in. When a hungry angler throws his or her line into the water, he or she is thankful for whatever fish can be used to prepare a meal for the family. Although the angler may have a certain fish in mind, he or she is grateful for the blessing from God.

We should not focus on what type of fish God has sent us. As long as the fish fulfills the intended purpose of providing a healthy and delicious meal. Why fight over the type of fish, unless it is one that is forbidden to eat, because it has been classified as a health risk? Women preachers/ministers are no more of a health risk than male preachers/ministers.

When the apostle Paul said, "I suffer a woman not to teach or usurp authority over a man and if a woman desires to learn and acquire an understanding concerning church matters, then she should wait until she gets home and ask her husband in the privacy of their home," was he really saying to Christians that according to the Bible, women are forbidden to preach God's Holy Word (1Timothy 2:11–15; 1 Corinthians 14:34–35)? What if the woman does not have a husband or is a widow, then who does she ask? It is clear Paul was speaking from his male-dominated experiences and not according to the mandates of God. He never says the Lord or the Holy Spirit told him to give the church such a biased directive. In 1 Corinthians 14:34–35, Paul's directive seems to espouse his personal opinion about the procedural tenets of the law rather than the freedom grace brought to the church through the blood of Jesus.

It seems very clear the apostle Paul is dealing with the issues concerning women minsters from inside the box of his cultural traditions rather than from the perspective of grace and mercy. I see a preacher operating out of the tradition of the law rather under the grace and hope of the Holy Ghost. It is evident that over the life of his ministry, the apostle Paul had to reach a point like those of us who have come to Jesus, whereby each of us is challenged to grow and mature as a seasoned saint under the tutelage of grace and mercy rather than hold onto the bondage of the law.

Even the great apostle Peter had to pass through this tunnel of great spiritual growth in life. In the gospel of Mark, we witnessed Peter sticking his feet in his mouth when he called himself, rebuking the Messiah and telling Him how the plan of God was going to work in the Messiah's life (Mark 8:31–33). When men and woman refuse to accept women ministers after they have told you God has called them into the preaching ministry, it is similar to the distained act of Peter when he called himself rebuking Jesus in the gospel of Mark Chapter 8. How dare a grain of dust attempt to rebuke or refuse to accept anything God has blessed and given His mantle of approval?

In addition, it seems like the apostle Paul never met the prophetess Anna, who labored in the temple of God and spoke about the redemptive salvation of Jesus to everyone that would listen to her (Luke 2:36–38). On the other hand, the apostle Paul did have the privilege of meeting Philip, the evangelist, and his four preaching daughters, but Holy Scriptures show no evidence of the man of God rejecting the notion of women in the preaching ministry (Acts 21:8–9). This is why I lean strongly on the side that says the apostle Paul was dealing with a localized situational issue in 1 Corinthians 14, rather than a universal policy for all New Testament churches.

It is apparent the saints in Corinthians were having a serious problem dealing with the variety of talents that came with spiritual gifts. It seems things had gotten so bad the apostle Paul had to come into the community and bring order to the congregation to keep the house from falling to pieces. The saints were in a tug-of-war about which spiritual gift carried the greatest value. The apostle Paul understood the church was being split right down the seam over the issues of speaking in tongues, prophesying, and other gifts manifested by the Holy Spirit. This is why he enters the conversation at the beginning of chapter 14 of 1 Corinthians by letting his audience know love is the greatest and most essential gift. He goes on to say the reason love is so essential is because without it, gifts become self-centered toys that can bring division and confusion among the saints of God if not used correctly.

If we are honest with ourselves, we, too, can remember a time when we operated out of our culture values and not by the Holy Spirit. Even today, some of the things we do within the congregations of God are cultural habits or things we have picked up from our society. For example, we allow women to wear hats or headpieces indoors but tell men it is a sign of disrespect to wear a hat indoors. Some people in our congregations continue to frown on women who wear pants to church.

In some churches, women are not allowed to enter the pulpit area. With men, however, whether saved or sinner, the question of salvation does not come up before he enters the pulpit. The apostle Paul lets his readers know he is the person requesting for women to wait until they get home to have a personal dialogue about church matters with their husbands. Many have speculated on why he made this statement, but no one other than God and Paul really knows the truth. Whenever in questions about anything the apostles have said, always turn to the acts and words of Jesus. Somewhere in the life and ministry of Jesus lies the solution and answer to all of our questions, problems, concerns and issues.

The apostle Paul makes it clear to his audience that he is vocalizing his personal thoughts and beliefs as one operating still under the law. Look at what he says in 1 Corinthians 14:34: "let your women keep silent in the churches ... they are commanded to be obedient as saith the law." He never says this is the policy of the God, Jesus, or the Holy

Ghost. He points to the source (the law) from where he received his directive. Since we know God delivered us from the law by the blood of Jesus, do we allow others to put us back under the bondage of the law? God gave neither the apostle Paul nor any other apostle the right to put His New Testament church under the bondage of the law.

Although the apostle Peter spent precious time in the presence of the Messiah, there was still a lot he needed to learn about Jesus from the Holy Ghost. The apostle Peter argued male Gentiles needed to be circumcised in the flesh to receive all rights as a full-fledged citizen in God's kingdom. The apostle Paul, however, argued they did not need to be circumcised in the flesh to have complete union with God. The apostle Paul argued that since we live under grace, the Gentiles only needed to accept Jesus as Lord and Savior. According to the letters of the apostle Paul by way of the Holy Spirit, he argued that once a Gentile accepts Jesus as Lord and Savior, he or she did not have to go through the tenets of the law, as would someone living under the rule of the law, to become united as one with the Son of God (Galatians 2:1–21; 3:11–29). Only those that were bound by the law by birth or conversion under the law needed to follow the practices of the law according to the apostle Paul.

Keep in mind the love of God will use people regardless of their levels of commitment and personal struggles. God is the only force I know in the world that will stick with a person regardless of his or her conditions, successes, or dysfunctions. As long as you have life and strength to make it to the altar of grace, you can come in at the last hour or second and still catch the train to heaven. When God drafts a person for His team, He has already taken into account all the good and bad things about the person (you). God already knows our pitfalls and shortcomings, yet He still makes the investment to rescue us from sin, with all the potential to become something much greater than what we had when we started life.

For example, God knows where people come from, where they are at the present moment, and where they are going in life. He has the ability to use information from His scouting report to keep us motivated and to remind us from where He has brought us. We must never forget God is the Master Craftsman, the Master Potter, the Master

Tool Maker, the Master Steel Maker, the Master Builder, the Master Carpenter, and the Maker and Sustainer of Life. It is God who signs off which airline you decide to travel in life. Believe it or not, you and I have traveled some airlines (such as pride, drugs, alcohol, power, money, sex, fame, sin, and selfish ambitions) that would have crashed a long time ago had it not been for the power of God watching over our lives.

It is awesome and unique how God has a way of allowing the Holy Spirit to purge us while we serve Him. When God starts moving and operating in our lives, we usually do not know what is going on in the spiritual realm until the surgery is over. Then one day we wake up and notice the struggle is over, or the stronghold that used to hold us down no longer exists. God has removed it from our lives. It is amazing how God can use an unclean vessel to do wonderful things in the lives of others, while shaping and purifying the servant vessel at the same time he or she is being used by the Holy Savior.

The apostle Paul's experiences in life are comparable to some of the experiences some of you reading this book have gone through. You see, the apostle Paul was a Jew, and his ethnic group was oppressed by the Roman government for years. He lived in a world and environment where his group was not part of the political decision-making structure for the region. As usual, you have to get in wherever you can fit in without losing your principles or denying your God and Creator.

Some of you reading this book recognize you are not part of the political clout or decision makers in your own churches. Decisions about your future are being discussed and made without your input or concerns. Like in the Roman territory of Palestine, you pay taxes for nearly everything the ministry is doing, but you do not have a vote on your future outlook in ministry within the church. All I can tell you is continue to pray, hope and believe. I believe the answer is already set in motion. In the words of a gospel song, "Put Your Time In Because Payday Is Coming after While!"

Apostle Paul was in an environment where he had to learn to adapt for survival. Paul knew he either had to fit in with the rules or face the rigor of torture, discipline, or beating, or be imprisoned or even put to death by the rules he one time enforced across the region. Let's not forget that the apostle Paul, as Saul, was one of the main mob enforcers for the priestly ruling class in Roman Palestine. One of Saul's duties was to keep peace in the temples and region so the Roman government would not to get involved in temple affairs.

Understanding someone like Paul's life, especially his or her upbringing, helps you better understand a portion of his or her thought process and actions. Knowing such valuable information concerning the personality traits about your enemy or friend is a very important thing to know while in ministry. Such pertinent information teaches you how to make necessary adjustments when the writer, director, or layperson decides to throw you an unexpected curveball from left field. The Holy Spirit prepares God's servants for the unexpected. God's Angels and His Holy Spirit watch over God's people so the Devil and his staff cannot destroy us or stop us from doing whatever God has commissioned us to do on earth.

The more we understand a person's cultural beliefs are deeply connected to his or her theology, the better understanding we can have about the individual's actions. How people feel about themselves and various things in life are usually more than likely connected to the force they see as supreme in their lives. Some call this great force God, religion, self, spirits, or some other name. Yet it all boils down to the God who inspires our belief system.

The thing that has the greatest impact on a person's actions is not his or her mind, heart, family, or society. It is the force and energy that controls the person's mind. The source that controls someone's mind will control the person's actions, regardless of any medication he or she is taking. According to the teachings of the Holy Bible, when people believe and trust in the God they serve, they will be influenced by the authority they submit themselves to. People's religious beliefs inspire their cultural practices and family values. This is why knowing religious affiliations or associations is essential to understanding how people think and act.

There is always an engine driving every train down the railroad tracks. The engine within a mechanical vehicle is like the brain for the apparatus. A person's religious belief's system acts as the engine that drives the person like the engine drives the train or vehicle. Nearly everything you need to know about the vehicle is found mainly in the engine, and nearly everything you need to know about a person, you can find it in whatever source that reign as supreme in the person's life. I challenge you to examine his or her religious beliefs or afflilliation. The person's religious beliefs and the engine oil tell you a lot about what is going on internally with the person or the engine. Believe it or not, all people are driven by a religious belief, even the atheist. This is why I started off this section by saying there is an engine that drives every train down the railroad tracks.

It is important for us to understand that when we interpret some of the writings in the Bible, we must pray to God that we do not allow our culture and life experiences to hinder the message the Holy Spirit is trying to teach us. If we are not careful, we can become influenced by our culture's ways and completely miss out on what God is trying to teach us. Many modern-era theologians have worn blinders when interpreting and writing about some important social issues. I believe when the Holy Spirit was trying to teach them a different message about the cross and kingdom value, they learned from the political currents in society rather than the wind of the Holy Spirit.

A good example of the picture I am trying to paint can be seen as an illustration in the Women's Suffrage Movement, American Slavery, and the Civil Rights Movement that swept across America. If the men and women of God had stood boldly for God's righteousness, there would never have been any reason for the existence for any of these three movements. When the people of God stand together for God's righteousness and His justice, the entire earth and universe become better. The word of God says when the righteous rule, the people rejoice; but when the wicked rules, the people mourn (Proverbs 29:2, 11:10).

Throughout the course of American history, I believe there were many good hearted preachers and theologians who probably thought there was nothing wrong with their racist or sexist views or practices. Some of these pundits probably believed it was God's will for America to have a caste system that degraded and dehumanized certain groups of people simply because they were born inferior, at least according to the oppressors. We must never forget there will always be those who disagree with God in their minds and hearts or with their actions. Cannot you just hear them say, "Yes, I believe in God, but ..."

Believe it or not, people are more likely to admit susceptibility to contaminating the interpretation of Scriptures if they do not totally submit their motives, thinking, and actions to the Holy Spirit. Racism and sexism in American is a clear example of how we can allow our total existence to become contaminated by our inability to connect with the Spirit of God. As the Holy Ghost begins to moves over a place or in the lives of people, it illuminates and reflects the ill and good within an environment and people. It is very important for us to be mindful of how much of our own interpretation is revealed to us by the moving and operating of the Holy Spirit. Whenever we truly allow the Holy Spirit of God to manage our lives, we can see how much of our own thought process is a result of our culture, religion, family beliefs, dynamics, and so on. The better we understand the truth about our inability to manage a holy force that is under the control of God, the more we can protect ourselves from interfering or getting in the way of God's business.

Have you ever made a statement about someone or an issue that was driven by your emotions? Have you ever given an opinion concerning a person or topic when you know you probably should have kept quiet? For some reason, your mind or heart did not set off an alarm, reminding you it was better if you did not weigh in on the discussion because of the limited knowledge you possessed about a subject, person, or issue.

The apostle Paul is a great biblical hero, but we have no biblical evidence he ever consulted with God concerning the use of women in the ministry. Yet in Luke 2:21–38, the Holy Bible gives us a very clear picture of God's approval for women to speak in the church, temple, sanctuary, or congregation where the Holy Spirit is active in the lives of the people of God. The authentic people of God allow the Holy Spirit to take full control of their lives. There is never a doubt or you do not have to guess when the Lord is in charge of the person's life. Some people attempt to cloud this very clear episode with their own opinions, misfires, and Scripture interpretation to justify their chauvinistic views and actions. God never meant to put women in an environment where they would be abused, denigrated, or shackled by traditions set forth by religious slave masters.

Under the law, it was common practice for a woman to be accompanied to the temple by her husband to offer a sacrifice for their child. The child's gender determined when the woman was allowed to go to the temple and offer her gifts. If the child was male, the woman could offer her sacrifice not before the seventh day and no later than the eighth day after birth because all male babies had to be circumcised by the eighth day under Jewish law. Yet the directive was fourteen days for a female child (Leviticus 12:2–8).

According to Old Testament Scriptures, a woman was unclean for seven days after she bore a male child and fourteen days unclean after she had given birth to a female child. The complete purification process for a male child was forty days, and eighty days if the woman gave birth to a female child (Leviticus 12:2–8). This process under the law is one of the ways sin separates us from total equality in God's blessing plan. It is a clear example of the gender discrepancy under bondage of the law. Yet grace through Jesus restores humanity the equality it lost with God under the leadership of Adam and Eve. Jesus was brought to the temple to be circumcised after His mother's purification process, according to the Law of Moses (Leviticus 12:2–8).

After the birth of Jesus, Mary and Joseph demonstrated obedience to the law by coming to the temple to offer Him to God. Remember, Mary and Joseph did not have the authority to change the law. Their mission, like any other Jewish family, was to obey the law without question. Only Jesus had the power and authority to fulfill such a divine task as changing the law. In Matthew Chapter 5, we witness Jesus changing some of the principles and rules of the law. Please keep in the mind that although Jesus is the Messiah, He was still born under the law, and as a Jewish citizen, was bound to observe its tenets until He decided a change was needed. Jesus submitted Himself to the law by choice and not by force. Jesus respected the law but did not worship it. Jesus only worshipped God, His Father in heaven.

You see, it did not matter that Mary and Joseph were the parents of Jesus. Their relationship to Jesus did not exclude them from obeying God's laws. Jesus understood the plan of His heavenly Father and was committed to doing whatever it took to follow God's plan to completion. So Jesus' parents offered the same sacrifices any other persons offered under the law. For example, a pair of turtledoves or two young pigeons (Leviticus 12:6–8). Even today, under grace and mercy, we respect the law, but we celebrate and worship Jesus.

Luke 2:21–38 illustrates how Mary and Joseph went to the temple to present Jesus. While in the temple, Jesus was handed over to a devout and just man by the name of Simeon. It was the priest Simeon who performed the ceremony according to the customs of the law. Simeon was a prophet of the Most High God. The Holy Ghost revealed to him that he would not see death until after he had personally seen Jesus Christ (Luke 2:26). When Mary and Joseph entered the temple, Simeon took the baby into his arms and blessed God for sending us Jesus. Simeon was overwhelmed with great joy that God allowed him to live long enough to witness the birth of the Savior of the world. Simeon knew salvation had come to all humankind through the birth of Jesus. Simeon is just another example of what God will do when we trust and wait on the Holy Spirit to move on our behalf.

After Simeon finished ministering to Jesus, Mary, and Joseph, a well-seasoned prophetess of God named Anna entered. Prophetess Anna was allowed to play a divine role in the ministry of Jesus as a promoter of the gospel through the preaching ministry. According to Holy Scriptures, the prophetess Anna was advanced in age (around eighty-four years old), and the wisdom of God was very strong in her life. On the death of her husband, she refused to leave the temple and devoted the rest of her life serving in the temple with fasting and praying both day and night. The Holy Bible says Anna departed not from the temple (Luke 2:37). Anna was in the temple when Jesus arrived with his mother and father. She must have entered the room as Simeon was finishing his dedication ceremony for Jesus.

Simeon may have conducted the dedication of Jesus, but Anna gave the benediction during this historic moment in the temple. As the Word of God proclaims, not only was Anna in the temple, she spoke in the temple, giving words of exaltation to everyone who looked for redemption in Jerusalem (Luke 2:37–38). What is the only source in life that can give people redemption from sin and death? God used prophetess Anna mightily in the temple, where she brought forth God's holy and revelatory message of inspiration to the ears and hearts of those seeking truth and life. Prophetess Anna was used by God to deliver a message of hope for a stagnate world that was suffering in the shame of misery and sin.

I am baffled how people are willing to believe with a totally different mind-set when the word "prophesy" is associated with a man versus how the same word is interpreted and discussed when referring to a woman. It seems like most people in sanctuaries have no questions about the gift that is being used in its genuine state as long as the vessel is a male figure. On the other hand, when used as an active verb under the umbrella of a woman, the authenticity and definition of the word seem to take on a different meaning. When the word "prophesy" is associated with a woman, it seems to get devalued in a sense, rather than held in reverence like it is when used to describe a male minister.

For example, in Luke 1:67–79, it is espoused that Zacharias was filled with the Holy Ghost and prophesied. As you investigate the text closely, it is not hard to come to the conclusion that Zacharias preached a sermon about the coming of Jesus, who is to bring Salvation to the world. Yet in Luke 2:37–38, when the prophetess Anna preached a similar sermon about the blessing of Jesus to the world, the term "prophesy" seems to get overlooked or minimized as not having the same meaningful impact as when associated with a male minister, prophet, or preacher. It is time out for us within the kingdom of God to stop overlooking the contributions women are making in the ministry of the gospel of Jesus. They are leaders and will remain leaders not because we accept them; but because God has ordained them to preach His divine words!

I understand the rules were different under the law but now since we are all under grace, many of the rules that separated vocations and duties based on gender have changed. Grace changed a lot of things for the way we worship and serve the Lord. Grace changed the way we submit our sins to the altar of God. God changed the sacrifice we place on the altar for repentance. Grace changed the way we can approach the Holy of Holies. Grace even changed the way God looks at you and I. So I ask the question, why keep the shackles of bondage on women ministers? What is the rationale behind not giving women ministers the same respect and opportunities as their male counterparts?

As you peruse the pages of the Holy Bible, you will discover when God called on women to fulfill divine missions—like He did with Deborah, the judge; Esther, the liberator; Ruth, the faithful friend; Elisabeth, the mother of John the Baptist; and Mary, the mother of Jesus—for His kingdom campaign, God did not seek approval from men. God always knows what is best for any situation. He chooses to use whomever He desires to use for His glory. The same rules apply to the gospel ministry; it belongs to God, and He can recruit and sign any player for His team He deems worthy. I need to see where in the Holy Bible that Jesus told women not to preach His gospel.

As a matter of fact, God silenced Zachariah, so he would not interfere with the naming of his son by his wife, Elisabeth. Does this sound like God telling a woman not to preach or speak in His name? Within the culture of Zachariah and Elisabeth, it had its rules; but God suspended the rules like you do in the Robert's Rules of Order. He overruled the rules of nature and humanity and allowed Elisabeth to take center stage for His glory. Also, God told Joseph to hold his peace and do nothing to shame Mary, the mother of Jesus. God made His message very clear to Joseph that Mary had become impregnated by the Holy Ghost.

I have learned over the years that willful ignorance and hate will never be friends with truth. Choosing to be willfully ignorant is a direct attack on enlightenment and truth. Ignorance has a drive to want to fight and destroy knowledge and justice with fierce blows, accompanied with pride and arrogance. The Holy Bible sums up the act of ignorance like this: "My people are destroyed for lack of knowledge: because thy has rejected knowledge, I will also reject thee, that thou shalt be no priest to me, seeing thou has forgotten the law of thy God, I will also forget thou children" (Hosea 4:6).

Therefore, when God calls a woman into the gospel ministry, He does not consult with humanity for its approval. Women need to allow God to speak to them, follow His lead, and not become distracted by some of the cynical traditions of men. Women must stop allowing themselves to buy into the hype in the local churches about how some people feel about women ministers. When women ministers stop allowing hype and gossip to discourage them, they can hear God with a clear conscience and accept their callings into the gospel ministry with great confidence and assurance. As long as women allow men to manipulate their minds and thinking, they will never stand up and become what God intends them to become. As long as someone remains in slavery, he or she can never be free to achieve the great milestones God has in store.

Here are some of the ways pastors manipulate and suppress the dreams and callings of women ministers: they work you, yet they do not respect you; they take your money, but they offer you no return on your investment; they consult you for your ideas, but they do not allow you at the roundtable, where decision are made, and they personally benefit from your many talents and gifts. Yet when it is time to feast at the Lord's Table, they tell you the table is sacred, and it is forbidden for women to be seated there. If this is not a true replica of a slave and master relationship, I have to be missing something. I can find no evidence that Jesus responded to women who surrounded Him during His earthly ministry with such demeaning rejections or insensitivities.

In churches across America, women ministers are being cast down and pushed aside simply because they expressed their desires to answer a calling from God. Many of these sisters are being ignored because their pastors are adamant about the idea that God does not call women to preach. This reminds me of when I was a little boy and used to hear the older matriarch and patriarch say if God wanted us to fly and go to the moon, He would have given us wings. For whatever reason, my ancestors were threatened and intimidated by a world outside their little box. Out of ignorance or fear, they seem to reject the transformation that was occurring in the new era.

Some of the women waiting in the wings can probably do a better job preaching and pastoring than some of the pastors who refuse to give them the opportunity to accept their calling and preach. Some of these women will not leave their home church simply because it is the church they have known from childhood. Even in the midst of rejection and abuse, they still refuse to fight or leave their home church.

Alvin E. Miller, Sr., D. Min.

Women have such a profound nature to be great caregivers. Many have an angelic and sensitive intuition that is second to none. Women also possess a unique quality and drive to nurture other women, while at the same time, assisting them to excel in their live's endeavors. These are some of the foundational reasons women have become effective communicators. Women are gifted by God to be in tune with the natural order of things and with people in a different way than most men. Men look to see how they can conquer things, whereas women are programmed to see how they can embrace things in life. Men look to see how they can minimize or delete problems, while women look to see how they can solve problems. Men look to take the shortcut while traveling, but women will be patient and travel the longer route, so they will arrive at their respective destinations without getting lost.

7

God Promotes Women in Ministry

The fight to keep female ministers out of the pulpits across America is a ferocious battle that male ministers will not win. God has already determined the winner of the battle. Think about this picture over the course of time. God allowed women to speak to Him in His presence. From the Old through the New Testaments, you can witness women having conversations with God while either standing or sitting in His divine presence. In the Holy Bible, we witness Sarah, Hagar, Elisabeth, and Mary speaking to the Most High while in His presence. If God allowed women the opportunity to enter His presence and talk with Him, why does man try to prevent such an awesome meeting from taking place?

In retrospect, God never questioned the geographical location of the women. God only demanded one thing from the women, which is the same thing He demands from men: "Obedience." God is more concerned about a person's loyalty and commitment to Him in the way of obedience to assist the kingdom of heaven with the mission of carrying out God's divine plan on the earth. When God spoke to Mary or Elisabeth, He did not first ask anyone for approval. God just showed up. When He left the scene, His divine plan had already been put in motion, regardless of whether humanity objected or approved. God only relayed the message to Zacharias and Joseph after He affirmed the women for the mission and journey that was ahead of them. God admonished the men not to interfere in His business because He was about to do a great work in the lives of the women of favor.

I find it amazing that God personally visited Zacharias and Joseph and cautioned each of them about His move in the lives of their wives. I am of the opinion for God to make a personal visit to someone meant the issue was of a very serious matter to Him. God knew if He had not shown up when He did, the men in the women's lives would have probably created chaos and made a holy situation messy, like many men in the Bible did. So God had to order each man to stand down, while the Holy Spirit stood up. Whenever people act out of the will of God, unless the grace of Jesus comes and extends mercy in the situation, it will end up in the river of chaos.

Who is greater than God? What minister feels he has the ability to usurp the authority of God by forbidding women to speak to the people of God? God never muzzled or barred women from proclaiming His marvelous words. Then what are those male ministers doing who are trying to restrict women from preaching in pulpits across America? Are they in denial about how they, as well as their ancestors, had to endure the same kind of disenfranchised treatment? If a woman is special enough to be used by God to carry and present His Holy Word to the world, surely she is worthy enough to speak His words in pulpits.

Much of the confusion and panic surrounding women ministers as they try to establish themselves in various denominations across America has derived from how the words "prophesy," "preach," "teach," and "speak" have been used to define their actions. It is like many of the church leaders are saying to women seeking support for acceptance into the ministry, you can think about the word preaching while you are speaking, or duplicate the results of preaching, but you better not say the word preaching! Some anti-women opponents allow women to speak or teach but not preach, as they would say. Regardless of what it looks or sounds like, it is taboo to call it preaching. As William Shakespeare would say it, "A rose by any other name is still a rose." By any other name, a rose is still beautiful. Call it what you may, but it is still the same thing.

Preaching by any other name is still preaching. You know the old adage, "If it walks like a duck, quacks like a duck, and swims like a duck, it is a duck." Plain and simple, it is a duck! The exaltation or proclamation of God's Word out of the mouth of a donkey is still preaching. The vessel is irrelevant if God wishes to use it because He has the power and authority to make even demons speak His truth against Devil's wishes. The Greek word for "proclaim" (*Kerusso*) has the same translation as the word "preach" in Matthew 10:27; Luke 4:19; and Acts 8:5; 9:20.

The word "prophesy" normally refers to something prophets do as the Spirit of God would inspire them. God allowed King Saul, with his wicked heart, to prophesy in Ramah with the prophets, when he was hunting down David with the intention of killing him (1 Samuel 19:10–24). King Saul had come into the presence of God with the prophets of God and became overwhelmed by the anointing of the Holy Spirit, and began to prophesy like the prophets of God. Some may wonder if this event was a fluke or a demonstration of God's power. All I have to say is the Holy Bible has recorded it as an event that happened, with God holding the whole world in His hand.

I will not question the validity of the event, because the writer has proven how God can take an impossible situation and make it a powerful reality right before your eyes. God has the awesome ability to take what people least expect to be successful and make it a grandstand. God is known throughout history as taking the least and making it the best. God is known for taking a "nobody" and making him or her somebody of greatness in His kingdom. God's power is so awesome that His Holy Spirit overwhelmed some of the most sinful people and made them do the right thing, even when they had no intentions of right. I am a living example of this great and awesome phenomenon.

If God's anointing can take control of a wicked man on a mission to destroy another man's life, surely the Spirit of God can come upon a woman. I am not talking about just any woman. I am talking about a woman who has given her heart, mind, soul, and desire to fulfilling the will of God. I am talking a woman who has submitted to the Holy Ghost in order for the Lord to use her in His service. This could also mean allowing the woman to prophesy. Many women in modern-day churches have been oppressed and misled by many pastors, ministers, and Bible teachers to believe it is not God's will for them to be called into the ministry and definitely not to preach God's words. It is not right for anyone to tell a woman she cannot preach. As long as women are clothed in garments of humility and diligently express the attitude of service for the kingdom of God, they will always have the opportunity to exercise their God-given gift of preaching the gospel of Jesus Christ until the return of the Savior of the world.

Consider the word "prophesy" and the actions associated with it, which God instructed Amos to carry out in Amos 7:12–16. This same word is used to define some of the women of the Bible as they performed their divine duties to the Lord and for the people of the God. Just like the Lord called Amos to be a prophet and told him to prophesy to His people, it is the same God who called women to be prophetesses and to prophesy unto His people. As I often say, man cannot stop whatever God has ordained, and the sooner we learn this basic truth, the better off the entire world will become for all of us.

When men try to fill God's shoes, their walk becomes clumsy, and they constantly fall over things. We can never become God; we can only assist Him as He gives us the power. In all we do, let us never forget there is a name greater than our personal ambitions and this name should never get confused with any other name on the earth. It is the most holy and powerful name in the universe and the reason the church exists today. It is the wonderful name of Jesus! The name of Jesus should be the driving thrust behind all of our reasoning and actions. The name of Jesus is so much about righteousness, fairness, and equality that I am appalled how people have tried to used it to justify their injustices and unfair practices, even in the many church organizations.

Regardless of what name you give something, it is the action that really defines the authenticity of anything. If a product claims to be able to perform a certain service and the results are never proven, the product has failed to live up to its name and the purpose for which it was designed. If Jesus claimed to be the Savior of the world and could not save people from their sins, He could not have held the title as the true Savior of the world. God sent Jesus to save us from our sins and to prove to the Devil the unending power of His majestic throne. Jesus is God's constant force of energy that forever reminds the Devil he has only a limited amount of time before his execution date. To the Devil,

Jesus represents his signed death certificate, with no chance for a stay of execution by heaven's high court.

When you reflect on the creation of humanity and the universe (Genesis Chapters 1 and 2) that were handcrafted by God, please take notice how God created nearly two of its kind—mostly male and female, and a greater and a lesser as a prototype. The same mandates concerning the rules in the Garden of Eden he gave to Adam, God also gave to Eve. The same power of influence He provided for the sun, He also gave to the moon. Each just had different times to take center stage. God may not have given the moon as much light as he gave the sun, but they both had the same purpose of providing light for the earth, one to rule in the day, and one to rule in the night (Genesis 1:3–4, 13–19; 1:26–30; 2:15–25). I share this example so you will be able to read my next paragraph and grasp how the male prophet and female prophetess have the same mission to provide light on the earth to the people of God, similar to the way the sun and moon give light to the earth.

Take the words "prophet" and "prophetess." One refers to a male and the other to a female, in respective order. Yet they both do the same kind of ministry, proclaiming God's Holy Word in the kingdom of God. They both have been called and commissioned by God to speak divine words of wisdom unto the people of God.

The word "prophet" derives from the Greek word that means "to announce or foretell." A prophet or prophetess of the Lord God speaks the words of God while operating under His anointing. If we focus on the physical attributes of the vessel God uses, I believe we will more than likely miss the significance of the message He is conveying. I pray people of God do not allow themselves to become so entangled with the physical that they missed the spiritual. It is in the spiritual realm where God desires to take His people who are willing to follow His leadership.

Many theologians espouse the belief the first church started in the New Testament, either in the book of Acts or with Jesus and His disciples. I believe the first church on earth was started in the Garden of Eden by God Himself. If the "Ecclesia," or the church or body of believers, is where the Spirit of God dwells, then the garden of Eden has to be the first recorded church on earth because according to the Holy Bible, the Spirit of God created the garden, and His Spirit visited

His people (Genesis 1:26–30; 2:1–24). God visited Adam and Eve in the cool of the day and seemed to look forward to the fellowship. A church is a symbolic place of worship and praise, where the Spirit of God dwells in amid God's people. In the Garden of Eden, the people of God fulfilled His orders, and God was present amid Adam and Eve.

Moreover, God created humanity and put His Spirit and life into both the man and woman, a specified purpose to keep the garden. Until the Serpent enticed them to sin, the family (Adam and Eve) was a unified and glorified one that communed with God (Genesis 3:8–10). The reason I am convinced Adam and Eve communed with God on a regular basis is because the day Adam and Eve fell, Adam did something very strange and unusual; he recognized God's voice and tried to hide himself. To recognize a voice assumes you have heard it before, and to recognize it to the point you try to hide from it indicates you know it like none other. To recognize something is to recall a familiarity, and Adam recalled the distinct voice I believe he consulted in the past. Then Adam said he hid because he was naked. Yet he never tried to hide himself the other times he was naked, nor did he ever mention being naked before.

If God would allow a woman to speak to Him in His presence after she and her husband allowed sin to devastate the world, surely God would allow a woman to speak to His people in a building constructed by the hands of sinful people. More than likely, not every carpenter, mason, electrician, drywall installer, heating and air-conditioning technician, roofer, inspector, or other skilled tradesperson who built your house of worship were born-again believers. Yet we allow some of these people who have no relationship with Jesus to build some of the most beautiful and well-structured edifices in the world, while on the other hand, we fight women ministers as though they were our enemies.

I am baffled by the fact some men have the audacity to think women are not called into the ministry as they have been called by God. I am very curious who told men they have a monopoly on what God says to creation and who He calls into His vineyard to labor in order to bring in a harvest for Jesus. The ideology or theology that women are not called into the ministry is a poisonous spiritual chemical that infiltrates the mind and then works itself into the souls of innocent bystanders. Once this happens, people begin to align themselves with the oppressors, thereby believing women should stay in their place, which is out of the pulpit and the gospel ministry. This is a perfect example of how a religious tyrant, who build his foundation on intimidation rather than compassion, can turn misguided leadership into spiritual mayhem.

When I was a little boy, my great-grandfather, Grandpa Proctor, told me stories of how, when white slave owners freed their slaves, some of the African American slaves got angry with the freed slaves for celebrating their freedom. Think about how sad it is for others to wish you were in bondage rather than living in freedom. Religious people who like worshipping traditions rather than Jesus will react in similar fashion. Ministers who desire to lead without the Holy Spirit will become very upset when his slaves become free because he lost his grip on the power base that brings him satisfaction. When religious leaders seek power over compassion and bondage over freedom, there is a serious problem in the camp. This type of leadership environment is rooted in pride and destined for destruction.

Prophetess in the Bible

God's power and anointing is so powerful that whenever it falls upon any person or thing, the entity will succumb to His power with an outward expression of God's supernatural powers, gifts, and son (Luke 1:35–37). We witness the power and anointing of God falling on an animal (ass) and witness it speak the words of God. When the prophet Balaam disobeys God and goes with the wishes of Balak, king of the Moabites, observe how the anointing of God falls on the ass in the text. God's anointing gives the ass the ability to see the move of God in a way the naked eye cannot see (Numbers 22:21–30).

In the story, it is the ass that sees the vision of an angel, trying to give a message to preserve the life of an out-of-control prophet. It was not until God opened Balaam's eyes that he was able to see what God enabled the *ass* to see (Numbers 22:21–35). It is amazing to me how men would believe and accept that God used an ass to speak to one of God's prophets and how he allowed a wicked king like Saul to prophesy when he fell under the spirit while the prophets of God were prophesying (1 Samuel 19:18–24). Yet these same male ministers have problems accepting women as ministers of the gospel of Jesus.

These same pundits refuse to accept the fact God uses women with the same emphasis as He does men. Just look around the churches and communities, and observe the move of God in the lives of women. I would even go as far as to say the New Testament started off with a woman being used by God to prophesy the greatest news in the history of the world. This woman, Elisabeth, was used by God to foretell the birth of Jesus to the entire world (Luke 1:39–56). This must have been a very powerful and encouraging message from God for this woman to carry it to the world. If God meant for women to take the backseat in the proclamation of His gospel, why would He change His plan, especially when He has told us He is God and changes not (Malachi 3:6)?

As stated earlier, one cannot ignore the fact God allowed King Saul the opportunity to get a whiff of the beauty of the awesome power of God, which is used to transform the lives of the wicked. Even while King Saul was hunting down David to kill him, God allowed Saul to come into His presence from among the prophets and to prophesy in their company. Even with King Saul's sinful intention of killing a man, God was still willing to give someone the opportunity to be used by His anointing, probably with the hope that King Saul would experience a change of heart against David. This shows God has the power to use unclean vessels to do great things under the power of the Holy Spirit. For humanity, this is out of the ordinary, but God will continuously blow your mind with acts that do not synchronize with the traditional pattern of the human psyche or behavior (1 Samuel 19:18–24).

In Exodus 15:20, we see the word "prophetess" used to identify Moses and Aaron's sister, Miriam. At the beginning of Exodus Chapter 15, Moses gives God praise and honor for triumphantly leading the Israelites across the Red Sea and giving them victory over the Egyptians. The song of praise Moses led as the Israelites crossed the Red Sea was such a magnificent act of worship that it moved God so much He turned bitter water into sweet water. How can God tell His servant Moses to take a piece of wood, cast it into water, and the water becomes sweet enough the people of God can drink it? When the anointing is prevalent in a life—male or female, human or animal—it is such an awesome testament of faith that it demands an immediate response from the true worshipper of God.

So in this particular situation, prophetess Miriam wasted no time in responding to Moses' call to worship. She knew this was a special move of God and was determined not to be left out. Miriam made up her mind to get her praise on for the Lord. It seems like Miriam was determined to share a testimony of praise to the Lord, and no one was going to stop her from praising the God who delivered the Hebrews from the hands of death. The Holy Bible says Miriam took a timbrel in her hand and started praising God. The women followed her with their timbrels, and they began to make music for the Lord as they danced with joy unto the God of their salvation and the great I Am that I Am, who delivered them from the hands of the Egyptians (Exodus 15:1–21).

When God delivers people from the dungeons of hell, and the people have any inclination about what God has done for them, the appreciation of the Lord should evoke praise without anyone having to say a word. According to Judges Chapter 4, the Holy Bible says Deborah was a prophetess. As a prophetess of God, part of her daily responsibilities was to judge the affairs of the Israelites, males as well as females. Within daily administration, she had the duties of giving counsel and judgment to men and women. Deborah's ability to judge God's people meant she had to be astute in the Word of God, so she could judge His people fairly and righteously in the ways of the Lord (Judges 4:4–5). Women's role in ministry is to do more than just teach dance lessons for our youth and provide wholesome music for the fellowship. It is evident God also gave women the ability and authority to proclaim the gospel through preaching.

On another note, we not only have the opportunity to witness Deborah's legal skills and her ability to be fair and just when ruling on issues concerning God's people, we also observe her prophetic gifts as well. In one case, we see Deborah being led by the Spirit of God with divine knowledge to be able to see His Vision and to speak with the voice of God as she addresses Barak, son of Abinoam. It is amazing how God uses this powerful woman of God to encourage the man God intended to send on a dangerous tactical mission. Barak had God on his side and the support of a brave leader named Deborah. It was clear God was sending him on a mission where he would use lethal force against the enemy of Israel to accomplish the mission. Not only does Deborah deliver God's words to Barak, she gives him a powerful and convincing pep talk to help him overcome some of his fears and doubts concerning his success on the assigned mission.

Prophetess Deborah was clear about her calling to serve in a support role for King Barak. She was ready to serve Barak by helping him obey the Word of God, but he had to take the lead in the battle as God had intended. At the conclusion of consulting with prophetess Deborah, Barak understood his task from God with concise clarity. Yet he had only one request of Deborah and that was for her to go to battle with him. Deborah agreed to do so for the sake of the nation of Israel. Deborah knew God was with her all the way to the depths of the battlefield (Judges 4:4–24). If God truly wanted women to have no part in the leadership of His gospel, why would He allow this story to be told and written about in His Holy Bible?

In 2 Kings Chapter 22, we watched while construction workers (carpenters, builders, and masons) repaired the temple of God. The workers found the *Book of the Laws* and presented it to Hil-ki'ah, the high priest, who presented it to King Josiah. King Josiah commanded Hil-ki'ah to go to Israel and inquire of Huldah, the prophetess of God, for the interpretation of the *Book of the Laws* (2 Kings 22:2–14, 18). Please take note of the king's instructions: "Go ye, inquire of the Lord for me, and for the people, and for all of Judah, concerning the words of this book that is found" (2 Kings 22:13).

Keep in mind the *Word of the Lord* did not come from prophetess Huldah. Instead, the Word of God came from God through prophetess Huldah. This is normally the process of how God's words are revealed to the person or people of God by way of His prophet or prophetess. Some people are confused or get it twisted as to how prophetic words come about. The earthly vessel is only an instrument God uses to convey His most divine words. The human vessel is never the originator of prophetic expression. This process is one of the methods God uses to keep humanity and animals humble and loyal to His commands. It seems like when people and creation get their hands on the realm of unlimited power or control, they tend to attempt to try and takeover God's throne. Lucifer, who was one of God's angels, is proof of this overbearing attitude of covetousness and jealousy (Revelation 12:3–10; Isaiah 14:12–19; Ezekiel 28:1–19).

I am amazed how out of all the men throughout Judah, including the high priest and other male ministers, the interpretation of the *Book of the Laws* was given to a woman minister named prophetess Huldah to interpret. It seemed as though no one played the gender card in this particular situation. There were no questions or issues about whether a woman was called to handle God's sacred Word (2 Kings 22:15–20). Thank God that King Josiah was not intimidated by godly gifts in a female minister and had enough sense to call on a woman prophetess to help the nation of Israel get a word from the Lord. There may have been other prophets and prophetess in the land, but the king was confident in prophetess Huldah's relationship with God, and the Lord would use her to interpret His divine words, which the people of God needed to hear.

That story alone should be enough evidence to make church members, denominations, and others within the Christian community think twice about discriminating against women ministers, especially when it comes to the preaching of God's holy words. His message of hope came through Huldah, the prophetess of God, and not by the high priest or some other male prophet. It should be very clear to us that God puts His prophetic words in women like He does with men.

In the book of Isaiah, we see the prophet Isaiah going to see a prophetess who had given birth to a son. God sent Isaiah to the prophetess to name her son and to bless her (Isaiah 8:1–6). Whenever God sends His prophet or prophetess to bless a person or situation, this is usually a good sign of God's approval of the calling and mission He has given you. It was not uncommon in the Old Testament for God to send His prophet or prophetess to demonstrate His approval or disapproval about a person, place, thing, subject, or an issue.

One of the most sophisticated ways of rejecting truth is to deny its face value by creating in your mind that it does not exist. Many people employ this skill by using the clever process of elimination by analyzing a text with a "closed-fist." What I mean by this is the person comes to the text with his or her mind made up and will not accept anything other than what the person believes to be true. This never allows growth or enlightenment the opportunity to present its case as the truth. This is a good defense mechanism because if the text is not written the way someone supposes it to be written, or if there is any attempt to exegete the passage with words other than what is in the person's Bible, he or she cries foul. It is an easy way out because the person cannot justify the ability to reject truth that demonstrates no wrong or error within its concepts.

Once a person has convinced himself or herself to believe in only the things in his or her box or world, that person only has to paint the picture the way he or she thinks it should look. Once this has been accomplished, the individual discards the paint and paintbrushes so no one else can change the imagery of the pictures. These people make it very difficult to get your point across because they try to force you into situations where you either mix in or cover up the original painter's artwork to create one of your own. According to them, once you have tampered with the original, you have blasphemed the text, and now they can classify you as a heretic. I believe this is what the apostle Paul was referring to in Galatians 5:1–18, when the leadership in Galatia was using issues of flesh to keep certain people out of fellowship with people God had already cleared by grace through the blood of Jesus.

Furthermore, in Galatians 3:1, the apostle Paul goes so far as to ask the congregation in Galatia who the world bewitched them to believe in something totally different from the truth of Jesus. According to Paul, he is convinced whenever people allow others to use witchcraft or any other deceitful method to change their minds and hearts from the truth of the gospel, they become foolish and walk away from the truth of the gospel of Jesus Christ, who died on the cross for the sins of the world. This is why the apostle Paul opens Galatians chapter three with 'O Foolish Galations, who has bewitched you, that you should not obey the truth . . .' The apostle Paul had to constantly fight the battle for us by reminding us that we no longer need to live by the rules of the law, but Jesus redeemed us from the curse of the law. Yet there is a group that continues to try to keep women ministers under the curse of the law by denying them the right to preach in pulpits across the land (Galatians 3:13).

When people read the Holy Bible, they often tend to read into the Scriptures or deny some important, powerful concepts and principles the Holy Spirit would have us learn. Or we refuse to see things the way God would have us envision them. Some of us like discipline or strict, enforced rules until they apply to us. When others break the rules by speeding or failing to yield at a stop sign and the violator ends up getting a traffic ticket, we are quick to say they should not have been speeding or should have made a complete stop at the stop sign. It is like we become desensitized to others until it comes to us. It is like we want grace and mercy for us, but when it comes to others, we become very hard and stubborn about releasing God's compassion to other people in the manner God has released it to us.

It is amazing how when we are the ones in violation, we do everything to plead our case that we were not speeding or we did stop at the stop sign. Some even beg the officers not to give them a ticket for a moving traffic violation, explaining how the ticket will increase their auto insurance premium and subtract points off their driving licenses.

Believe it or not, people react to the Holy Spirit in a similar way as they do when they get caught for speeding or running a red light or stop sign. Some ministers, theologians, and students of the Holy Bible will deny a portion of Scripture when it conflicts or goes against their religious, denominational, or traditional belief system. We can see our needs clearly, but not the needs of other people when we find ourselves in trouble.

They often try and exegete a text by leaving out its original meaning. The Holy Bible cannot be read and interpreted like your daily newspaper. There are things in the newspaper you can look over and never have to hear about them again. You can even pick the things that apply to you, and discard the stories and things that do not interest you. Yet with the Word of God, everything the Holy Spirit says applies to you. There is nothing about God's righteousness you can avoid, and He is constantly watching you as you read and live out His words in your daily lives.

For example, in Joel Chapter 2, the Lord God of Israel talks to the Israelites through the prophet Joel. God explains to the Israelites all of the wonderful things He will do for them in the future. He will restore them in His divine grace, like He did many times in the past. God reminds the people of Israel He is the Lord, their God, and there is none like Him. God goes on to tell Israel that the day will come when He will do a new thing in the land. He says they will know when this new plan of action is upon the earth because He says, "I will pour out my spirit upon all flesh, and your sons and your daughters shall prophesy; your old men shall dream dreams, and your young men shall see vision (Joel 2:28).

I am amazed that I have never heard anyone arguing about whether young men see visions or old men dream dreams. For some strange reason, we tend to get this concept without reservation or conflict. I believe it is safe to say Christians believe the day has come whereby the Spirit of God has come to all (flesh) human beings of the earth who are willing to accept Jesus as Lord and Savior of their lives. Yet there are reservations and rejections when it comes to the part, "I will pour out my spirit upon all flesh and your sons and daughters shall prophesy."

I believe the outpouring of the Spirit of God has occurred more than once.

1. The birth of Jesus, when the angels descended on the shepherds with good tiding for all people (Luke 2:8–10).
2. On the day of Pentecost, when the Holy Spirit fell in Jerusalem as a sign God had sent His Holy Spirit to lead humanity to victory in Jesus.

The bombshell that has caused the church to become stagnate for centuries hinges on whether God calls women into the ministry like He does men. I encourage you to examine, study, and analyze the Holy Bible, and see how God has used women in the life of His congregation from the origin of humanity to the New Testament church. If your answer is culturally, emotionally, or traditionally driven, you may lose out on the opportunity to hear God for who He is when it comes to this very important issue.

Earlier we talked about how people like to try and change the landscape of the Holy Bible if they do not agree with what they read, what God said, or if the verbiage does not jive with their traditional, denominational, or cultural beliefs. Here is the big thing one needs to consider in his or her decision-making process. According to the Word of God, the Holy Bible says our sons and daughters will prophesy (Joel 2:28). This statement cannot be denied or taken from the original pages of the Holy Scriptures, because God meant for it to stand the test of time. Women ministers are not doing something God told them not to do. Women ministers are only doing what God instructed them to do for His divine plan on the earth. This is God's endorsement of women ministers.

I have heard male ministers say the word "prophesy" has a different meaning when it relates to a prophetess. I guess the word "adultery" would have a different meaning for women and men. The men who brought to Jesus the woman they said committed adultery refused to bring the man involved because they had a different interpretation for adultery when it applied to the man. According to the men, only the woman was caught in the act of committing adultery. The man was allowed to go free in a one-sided, male-dominated society (John 8:1–10). You see, these ministers of the law were trying to change the landscape of the Holy Bible and the words of God to fit their tradition and comfort zone.

When God tells His congregation our sons and daughters shall prophesy, He is letting us know they both will serve in His ministry and not the ministry of humanity. When people call people into their ministries, they then set the ground rules. But when God calls a person into His service, God sets the rules, criteria, qualifications, and so on.

I am so glad God does not call a person based on gender, race, weight, height, skin color, religious affiliation, nationality, physical stature, or family origin. Through Jesus, God has made it possible for all of us to be used in His kingdom as He chooses to employ us. Once God has called a person into ministry, no one has the power or authority to take it away.

Think about the awesome scene when heaven sent the good news concerning the birth of John the Baptist. Zechariah, his father, was so overwhelmed by the joy of the anointing of the Holy Spirit, he prophesied the Word of God about the coming of the Messiah (Luke 1:67–79). Zechariah was excited about the news of his own son, but he was filled with jubilation about the forthcoming birth of Jesus. It is interesting how the word "prophesy" never changes its meaning from prophetess Huldah to Zechariah, the priest. Both the prophetess and priest were used by God to deliver a message to His people for the good of God's kingdom. The man priest and the woman prophetess were vessels God chose to use to deliver a message. When you need a word from the Lord, are you going to tell God, "Yes, I need to hear from you, but make sure it comes in the form of a man and not a woman."

Finally, if the word "prophesy" means to announce, proclaim, or foretell, it all goes back to the fact God is using the person to deliver a message to someone with a connection to Him, which usually involves His people in some way or another. Moses went and prophesied to Pharaoh that God said, "Let My people go" (Exodus 3:10; 4:23; 5:1–2).

If women are not supposed to preach, teach, or speak in the church, why did God allow Ruth and Esther to have books in the Holy Bible? The books of Ruth and Esther speak to the life of the congregation of God, including priests and ministers, for hundreds of years. For years, ministers, preachers, and pastors have been using the books of Esther and Ruth to teach awesome lessons and preach some of the world's greatest sermons. If God has a caste system for women, please explain why He honors such great matriarchs of the faith by allowing them to have pages in the world's greatest book ever?

Prophetess Anna (Luke 2:36–38)

According to Holy Scriptures, Anna was a prophetess who lived and worked in the temple of God. Prophetess Anna was known for her great love for and service to God. After the death of her husband, she committed her life to fasting and praying night and day. She was married to her husband for seven years, yet, she never lost love or sight for her first love—God.

Holy Scriptures share that Anna was present in the temple when Simeon met the baby Jesus and His parents. The Holy Bible goes on and tells how Anna shared the good news about Jesus' salvation to anyone in Jerusalem who would listen. The prophet Simeon may have conducted Jesus' dedication ceremony, but prophetess Anna came into the temple room just in time to give the benediction.

Prophetess Anna understood her source of life, inspiration, and salvation came from her faith and obedience to God. She refused to allow human-made customs make her lose focus on her mission for the kingdom of God. She knew she had been called and appointed by God, and during the appointed time, she exercised her gifts for the glory of God. The Holy Ghost placed prophetess Anna on center stage during one of the most crucial periods in human history, and she passed the test by speaking in the temple whatever God put in her heart to say to the world about His Son, Jesus the Christ.

It is amazing that we have so many quotes and illustrations where women are recorded in the Holy Bible as speaking to us today in such a profound and divine manner. The messages they give are for both men and women, yet there are still those who argue that God did not call a woman to preach or pastor within Christendom. Women ministers cannot be left out because God has placed them in His kingdom as preachers too!

The Word of God tells how prophetess Anna praised God for the birth of the Messiah and gave thanks unto Jesus. In all honesty, prophetess Anna preached a sermon about the saving grace of Jesus Christ, who came to the earth to redeem humanity from sin. According to the Holy Bible, prophetess Anna shared the Word of God concerning Jesus to anyone who would listen to her. The Holy Bible does not insinuate or emphatically state she only shared the good news about Jesus with women.

The Holy Bible says Anna shared the word of salvation with all those seeking redemption in Jerusalem (Luke 2:38). This is important to note because some pastors isolate their women ministers and allow them to minister only to women in the congregation. I could understand if this were a feet-washing service, but to segregate the women because you believe they should only preach to other women is one that is beyond me. Some would try and convince others it is better than nothing, and by doing it this way, the women are at least getting something they would not ordinarily receive.

When people are hurting, dying, and in dire need of lifesaving care, they do not care who or what provided the service that save their lives; they just need help. People throughout the world are dying in the graves of sin and need to hear the Word of the Lord for their salvation. Therefore, the gender of the person who brings you water to save your life when you are dying of thirst in a desert is irrelevant. People are drowning and need a lifeline to pull them out of the deep and overwhelming waters of life.

When men become self-centered, impractical, and spend time debating and fighting things and issues that have nothing to do with someone's salvation, time has been wasted that could have been spent on evangelizing lost souls for Jesus. Women have always played major roles in the establishing the congregation of God in the Old Testament and the church of Jesus Christ in the New Testament. Throughout history, some men have tried to destroy the Word of God by desecrating or hiding Bibles and denying women their rightful places in the preaching ministry, including the pulpit.

Even today, there are some women with the same zeal and spirit of the prophetess Anna in many of the churches throughout America, but they are afraid to stand up and step out on faith for Jesus, fearing the spirit of the Pharisees in the local church leadership will crush their efforts. Sisters, I charge and challenged you that if God has called you to preach His Word, you must not allow anyone to get in the way of you and God. It is imperative for you to obey God rather than adhere to the limited and frail advice of humanity. Whenever God calls a person into His ministry, He never asks the individual to get approval from anyone else. God only tells the person to go and do!

Women of God, stand boldly against the deceit of the Enemy, and always stay true to the calling and message God has birthed in you? Or will you let the Devil abort the fertile message of life God has planted in you through His anointed words? Do not allow men or any other creature to intimidate you from carrying out the purpose and mission God has given to you to preach His divine word. Remember, as you examine biblical history, the advice of men somehow ends up contradicting what God commands and moves us further away from His presence. Obey God, and preach His Holy Word. Be led by the Holy Spirit, and preach the words of God! Surrender to the voice of God, and preach the gospel of Jesus Christ.

More important, I beg you to never allow another person to hear and answer your calling from God for you. Answering God's calling is not like answering a telephone call, where you take a message for the person or tell God to hold on until the person comes to take God's call. When He calls you, it is the most ultimate emergency you will ever have. Therefore, I urge you to answer His call before the line goes dead or the call drops. Beware many of the times when God calls, the Devil will also place a call to you while God is on the line to distract you or to make you forget that God is on the other line. This is why we should never answer any other lines when God is on the phone talking.

All I can say to you is preach, my sister, preach because if you do not preach God's Word, what man will stand in your defense and tell God He is wrong for calling a woman to preach? I do not believe there is a man or woman big enough to chastise God for calling women into His ministry. Yes, there are those who will call themselves challenging and rebuking God on the issue of women in the ministry like when Peter calls himself rebuking Jesus for telling of His cruxifiction and death on the Cross in Jerusalm by the chief priest and scribes (Matthew 16:21-23; Mark 8:30-33).

However, I am reminded in Psalm 14:1, "The fool says in his heart there is no God." Only a foolish person would attempt to rebuke God for calling women into the ministry. Only a foolish man or woman would try to chastise the God that creates and gives breathe and life to all. Only a fool will tell God He is wrong for orchestrating the destiny of men and women on the earth. And by now we all should know the Devil is the greatest fool in the universe.

8

Jesus Endorses Women in Ministry

The greatest story ever told, the best sermon ever preached, the most awesome lessoned ever taught, and the best news ever proclaimed is Jesus Christ's resurrection. There is no greater news in the history of humanity than the resurrection of Jesus. Without the resurrection of Jesus, the Holy Bible would be just another good history book for encouragement, enlightenment, and motivation. It would have some great points but would be unable to offer life to all in dire need of salvation and life beyond this old world. Without validation of the resurrection story, the Holy Bible would just be another book of philosophy, proverbs, and good and wise sayings. Without the resurrection of Jesus being validated, we would still be dead in our personal sins.

Without the resurrection of Jesus, the pages of the Holy Bible would not have a true foundation on which to validate the authenticity of the author's writings and claims. Without the resurrection, there would not be an everlasting hope for those of the past, present, and future generations. Without Jesus' resurrection, the gospel would be incomplete. The gospel of Jesus would only be a possibility rather than an emphatic truth. The resurrection of Jesus Christ is proof God is who He claims to be and does whatever He wants to do. It validates that God is unstoppable, invincible, unmovable, believable, and awesome, to say the least.

News so wonderful, so powerful, and so gracious was first given to women by the angel of God to deliver to the church of Jesus Christ. The news was so powerful men could not believe it, so they had to find the truth of the matter for themselves. When they got to the empty tomb, they realized the women had their own conversation with the angel of God and one with Jesus after His resurrection. Jesus validated the women's story, when He commanded them to tell His apostles to meet Him in Galilee (Matthew 28:1–7, 9–10; Luke 24:1–12). There is no greater gospel message than the wonderful news the Messiah has been resurrected from the dead. Yes, it was first given to the women of Jesus by Jesus and the angel of God.

It is amazing how God strategically positioned the women at the tomb the very hour He raised Jesus from the dead. It is interesting none of the male disciples were at the tomb or in the vicinity during His resurrection. Peter, James, and John were the disciples who usually accompanied Jesus during very special events, such as the Mount of Transfiguration, during times of prayer, and when Jesus went into various homes to pray for the sick (Mark 5:37; 9:2–7; 13:3; 14:33; Luke 9:28). Yet they were not at the tomb during the resurrection or thereafter. God handpicked the women to be there for such a special time in the history of the church and humankind.

Neither the resurrection nor the women's presence at the tomb after the resurrection happened by chance. Jesus' resurrection was prophesied and discussed hundreds of years prior to His birth. It was an appointment with destiny that allowed women to have front-row seats and witness the evidence of the most powerful events and forces in heaven and earth at work (Psalm16:10).

On the day of Jesus' resurrection, women received the baton of great joy and passed it on to the men. The women who followed Jesus' ministry with devoted service while He was alive came to His tomb very early in the morning during the first part of the week, possibly to prepare His body for burial with special spices and oil. However, when they arrived at the gravesite, they noticed the stone that barricaded His tomb was rolled away from its entrance. The women did not know what happened, and they looked for answers. Little did they know, God had already invaded the scene with an awesome miracle that even stunned the sting of death by stripping it of its power to keep Jesus in the land of the dead by the way of a borrowed tomb. God allowed Jesus to make mockery of death and the Devil when Jesus rose from the dead and the grave. Jesus got up out of the grave and handcuffed death by the Spirit of God as a way to start the second half of His earthly ministry, which includes everything after His death and resurrection from the dead. This super bowl ended with Jesus being the victor and the Devil being the defeated once again like he did when he lost the battle in Heaven according to Revelation Chapter 12.

By the time the women realized what was going on, the angel of God told the women Jesus was no longer in the tomb but had risen from the dead. After the angel instructed the women to go and spread the good news to the disciples of Jesus, the women ran with great joy to tell the other saints about the miracle heaven had performed. The women delivered the message to the eleven disciples and anyone else who would listen to the greatest news in the world. The disciples refused to believe the women when they told them Jesus had risen from the dead (Luke 24:1-12).

Faith is the ability to believe without actually seeing. Doubt has the crippling effect of making a person doubt the truth because he or she can no longer relate and connect in the natural or physical. Faith is a spiritual phenomenon that produces powerful and supernatural results that can witness the physically manifestation of faith. Faith is the "real deal." All you have to do is believe without doubt, and faith will work for you. As Jesus told Thomas, "The miracle is to believe without seeing, and blessed is the person that can believe without seeing" (John 20:24-29).

For a while, it seemed the women would be overshadowed by the shackles of social traditions that restricted them from delivering the gospel message. However, this time, instead of Peter, James, and John being the first responders, it would was Mary Magdalene, Joanna, and Mary (the mother of James and Salome), and the other women who were first to witness the completion of the world's greatest event (Mark 16:1, 5–9; Luke 24:1–10, 24–27). Men and women may want to deny the significant role women played during the delivery of God's words after the resurrection of Jesus, but the Holy Bible has already spoken the truth. We know what the Holy Spirit has said about damnation on anyone who tries to take away or add to the Word of God (Revelation 22:18–19).

The resurrection episode and everything surrounding the event should be enough to send a clear message that God uses whomever He wishes, the way He wants to, and whenever He chooses. God is too big and awesome to allow human beings to define His nature and dictate who in creation He can use to deliver His divine words or provide a service for His kingdom. God does not have to answer to our denominational associations, our ecclesiastical jurisdictions, our religious districts, our boards of bishops, and so on. God is God all by Himself! God does not need our help with anything. He is so kind and loving that we are allowed by the Holy Spirit to assist Him by His grace and mercy. We are nothing more than God's servant-assistants, who should be willing to do whatever the Master demands or requires us to do in His kingdom.

Moreover, Jesus never told a woman she could not come into His presence or before His mighty throne of grace. So why do some men think they have the right or authority to bar women from pulpits in local churches? These ecclesiastical tyrants contaminate the minds of parishioners by preaching and teaching that women were not called to preach the wonderful and awesome message of the gospel. Other than the work of the Devil using people to fight against women ministers, I am curious to know the real reason women are denied access to the pulpits within churches. Men pastors who advocate for women ministers are attacked by evil spirits unlike before. Yet we must continue to fight the good fight of faith for the liberation of women ministers. If bold men and women of God do not fight for the rights of women ministers, cowardly men and women surely will not fight for them.

Romans 10:5 says, "How beautiful are feet of them that preach the gospel of peace, and that brings glad tidings of good things!" The Holy Bible does not make any distinction between the feet of men and women. Neither does the Holy Bible say the feet of *men* who preach the gospel. It only says 'how beautiful are the feet of those who preach the gospel of peace.' Yet again, someone who refuses to believe in women ministers will try to justify his or her position by explaining this passage totally different from what the Holy Spirit is saying to the church (the true disciples of Jesus). They would read into the text and argue that God is only talking about the feet of men; because God does not allow women to preach the Gospel of Jesus. This passage is shared with you so you can see the cleverness and the extent some will go in order to prevent women ministers from preaching the Gospel of Jesus Christ.

Here is something to consider. When Martha invited Jesus into her home to eat dinner, her sister, Mary, decided to sit at His feet and get some much-needed wisdom and spiritual guidance while He was teaching His disciples. Yes, Mary was in the midst of the male disciples when Jesus was instructing them. However, when Martha realized Mary was not in the kitchen, helping her prepare the evening meal, Martha confronted Jesus and requested that He make Mary come into the kitchen and help her. Martha was very frustrated that Mary had interpreted Jesus being at her home totally different than she had.

Maybe Martha was thinking like some of the churchmen of today; Mary's place was not in the pulpit with Jesus but in the kitchen with her (Luke 10:38–42). Jesus did not agree to Martha's request. Instead, He defended Mary's right to be at His feet with the male disciples. Jesus refused to allow the limited views of humanity prohibit His vision for the kingdom of God. If Jesus allowed women to come into His presence, are the preachers refusing to allow women into their pulpits saying their pulpits in local congregations are more sacred than the presence of Jesus? What are they saying to the masses and their congregations?

Jesus did not allow cultural traditions or societal norms to dictate who He allowed to minister in His kingdom. There are no biblical examples that Jesus discriminated based on the gender of a human vessel. Jesus never allowed Himself to get barred down or wasted time fighting over frivolous issues, like should women preach or enter the pulpits that were built by the sinful hands of men. Jesus is always more concerned about people's souls than where they are located in His presence.

When Jesus blessed and liberated people with His divine power and told them not to say anything, He knew it was a request that could not be kept. Jesus knew a blessing so awesome and a miracle so mind-boggling and spiritually liberating were impossible to keep shut in a human vault. Jesus knew the excitement was burning so contagiously human existence would not be able to hold such wonderful news about the goodness of God. Even today, when God does miraculous things in our lives, we cannot hold them. We have to tell someone, even if it is an animal or the wind. We let out a wonderful praise report in the form of a testimony.

Here is another scenario to consider as it relates to women in the ministry. John the disciple came to Jesus complaining and requesting permission to stop a certain man who was casting out devils in Jesus' name. John was under the false impression that because the man did not get approval from the disciples, he was operating outside God's will (Mark 9:38–40). Does this sound familiar to you yet? Many pastors and preachers have taken it upon themselves to think like John. If it does not line up with their theological perspectives, it is outside the will of God. John wanted the man to receive permission from the local ministerial alliance before he could perform the ministry of Jesus. John, like many male pastors, felt he had the right to tell Jesus what to do with His vineyard. John may have thought Jesus had given him more power, authority, or jurisdictional boundary than the other disciples. Or maybe John was just acting out of his selfish ambitions and wanted more authority than what God gave him.

However, King Jesus was of a different opinion from His disciples. The pastors were wrong; Jesus was right. Jesus told John and the other disciples to leave the man alone and not to hinder his work. Jesus said the man was doing a good work for the kingdom of God and should not be denied the opportunity to produce good fruit for the God's kingdom. Jesus shared a simple test that would prove the genuineness of a vessel in service. He informed His disciples the man was undoubtedly on heaven's team. According to Jesus, no one could have the power to cast out devils unless the Holy Ghost gave him or her the power.

Always remember Jesus will know things about people, things, conditions, circumstances, and situations that we do not know. That is why we should never jump the gun and think we have all the answers for heaven and earth. The best thing for us to do is go to God for guidance, directions, advice, clarification, and understanding. Jesus will never lead a person wrong or into confusion; He leads people out of confusion. Still, some refuse to follow Him to the land of peace.

I am convinced the passage is a wake-up call designed to inform everyone that no religious group, gender, ethnic persuasion, or nation will have a monopoly on what and whom God chooses to empower to do ministry in His kingdom. The disciples thought they were doing the right thing by opposing the man. However, their minds are never the mind of God. For this reason, we all can thank God for Jesus because He had to step in and stop the pastors of the local church from hindering a man on a mission from God (Luke 9:49–50). If people, including women, are doing great work in the name of Jesus, He says to leave them alone because "there are other sheep I have, which are not of this fold: them also I must bring, and they shall be one fold, and one shepherd" (John 10:16).

Instead of hindering women in ministry, why not help them help the kingdom of God win souls for Jesus? Yes, this is what we can do. Instead of fighting women ministers, start embracing them, and watch your stock in heaven rise. This is what happens when two or three gather in the name of Jesus for the glory of God. The Holy Ghost showers us with blessings from heaven (Matthew 18:19–20).

In John 1:1–13, the Holy Bible uses the masculine form of words to describe humanity. The writer never refers to man or woman, him or her, or male or female. It only uses pronouns that address men. We read phrases like, "and the life was the light of men" in verse 4. In verse 7, we read, "that all men through him might believe," and in verse 9, we read, "which lighteth every man that cometh into the world." We find in verse 12, "he gave them the power to become the sons of God, even to them that believed on his name." Finally, in verse 13, we read, "nor of the will of man, but of God." Does this insinuate God is saying Jesus came to save only men, or does it include women when He talks about man, men, them, and the "sons of God"? What is your answer?

If you say God is referring to women, it must apply to the call of the ministry and the preaching and teaching of the gospel. If you say He was only referring to men, it seems to cast a dark shadow on women in general as not having the opportunity to receive the marvelous light that came to change the world for the betterment of all humanity. John 3:16 says, "God gave his only begotten Son that whosoever believeth in him should not perish, but have eternal life." Yes, "whosoever" includes males and females. There is no gender delineation between male and female because the word is inclusive and does not imply a certain group of people. It specifies everybody that is willing, let him or her come to Jesus.

Furthermore, another example of Jesus demonstrating his gentlemen-like courtesy and politeness to women is when He shows respect and support for women while attending a marriage in Cana of Galilee (John 2:1–12). The host ran out of wine, and the request to produce wine by divine intervention was brought to Jesus by a woman of faith. This mother knew where to go to get the necessary help, and she knew who could help. Here is a woman who knew how to get her prayer request answered, while the men sat back, waiting in anticipation and delusional because they had run out of wine at a wedding celebration. Jesus had no intention of performing a miracle that particular day because He said His hour had not yet come. He wanted to wait before introducing His divine powers to the world. Jesus intended on serving us dessert, but He wanted us to wait until we had eaten the entrée.

However, because of the love and respect He had for the woman who requested His help, Jesus changed His mind and granted her request. The wedding host got a blessing on the prayers of a friend attending the wedding. The woman told the servants to do whatever Jesus told them, and they saw a miracle take place in the presence of their obedience to the mother of Jesus as she assisted Him in ministry. Mary carried the good news to the men, telling them to do whatever Jesus instructed them to do, knowing He was about to perform a supernatural miracle that would make the wedding the talk of the town and the surrounding areas.

After they left Cana of Galilee, Jesus, His disciples, His brothers, and His mother traveled together on the mission field. What do you think Mary, the mother of Jesus, did to promote Jesus' ministry during His earthly ministry and after He returned to heaven? Do you believe she went on a spiritual crusade to tell the world about her son, the Messiah? Or do you believe she kept quiet because of a male-dominated and chauvinistic culture? Do you believe Mary taught and told others about the life and ministry of Jesus? Just think. No other woman in the history of humanity or the world can ever claim to give birth to the greatest person to ever live and participated in one of the two greatest events that will ever take place on the earth—the birth of the Savior of the world!

9

The Holy Spirit Empowers Women in Ministry

According to Acts 1:9–15, there were women (including Mary, the mother of Jesus) in the upper room with the nearly 120 other disciples. Therefore, when the Holy Spirit fell upon the worshippers and God filled them with His Spirit, the women present received the same gift as the men, as the prophet Joel had prophesied through the Holy Spirit in the Old Testament (Acts 2:17; Joel 2:28). It is very interesting that God highlights the fact women were in the upper room with the men. Believe it or not, somewhere around the world, the Devil has convinced some people women were not exactly in the upper room. There is this belief or argument that believes maybe the women were somewhere in the house, but not in the upper room with the men on the day of Pentecost in Acts Chapter 2.

Earlier in the book I told you some men rejected women ministers because of the natural order of things. Well, some pastors do not believe the women were in the upper room simply because of the time of the month for some of the women. That would have been an issue for disciples some two thousand years ago. Some of the sick-minded rebels argue that even though the disciples of Jesus were Christians, they were culturally Hebrews, who did not abandon all their Jewish heritage and practices.

Preach My Sister Preach

While some pastors have silently tried putting women ministers in back rooms, it is ironic how God allowed them to be seated in the upper room with the apostles and the nearly 120 who would experience the blessing of the pouring out of God's Holy Spirit on those faithful saints there in the upper room. The women in the upper room experienced the same blessing as the men when the Spirit of God filled the room. Some men ministers want to see the Holy Bible operating only in parts when it applies to women preachers. The male ministers and pastors want to see the Holy Bible promoting them as preachers and ministers of the gospel of Jesus and not promoting the women in the same manner. They only want to read the parts of the Bible that reflects them as the leaders in the pulpit and not the women ministers as leaders in the realm of preaching the gospel of Christ.

For the most part, men have the tendency to exclude women until they get in trouble. Then men ask women for their opinions when it comes time to bail them out of trouble. God wants to make sure the writer points out women were in the upper room, so men could not use it as another opportunity to restrict women and leave them out of the kingdom-building process on earth. Although some men ministers will willfully disobey and disrespect God at His Word, they cannot ever say they did not know the truth when they stand before the Lord.

As I reflect over the awesome experience the disciples must have felt that day in the upper room, I wonder if the upper room could represent the pulpit area within local churches. Could the Holy Ghost experience for the women mean God's approval for them to proclaim His good news to the world from church pulpits? God had to be conveying some message to us about the role of women in the ministry. I am pondering the thought as to if God was sending us another message by having the women in the upper room with the men as they experienced the visitation from heaven (Acts 2:4). I believe God was letting His church know women in the gospel ministry had free range in the New Testament church as the men in the gospel ministry.

The fascinating thing about the Pentecostal day experience is not so much that God allowed the women to be in the same room with the men but that He allowed the women to experience the same baptism by fire as the men. Each woman in the room was filled with the Holy

Spirit and spoke in another tongue. Each woman, like each man, had to be in a place in her spiritual walk with God that met the Lord's approval. Each woman was able to emerge from the upper room with a testimony like that of their male counterparts. Do you think any person can have such a powerful experience with God and not talk about it? I do not believe anyone could hold back such a powerful miracle as the upper room experience, the day the Holy Spirit descended from heaven in the form of flames of fire and endowed people with power from God (Acts 2:1-4).

Here is a good shocker for the antiwomen ministers campaign. I tell you they will try and theologize this one with the eloquence and smoothness of the Serpent in the Garden of Eden. But God is true and every person a liar if he or she tries to deny or evade this truth. In Acts 8:1–4, we witness the church under great persecution by Saul. He has already murdered Stephen and was on a rampage to ethically cleanse Israel of the Jesus lovers. Saul wreaked havoc on the church and Christian community by entering the homes of the saints both males and females—and hauling them off to jail. In order to avoid the wrath of Saul, the Christians scattered and preached the Word everywhere they went. To a church on the run, prayer was always in order and a big part of the daily life of the saints of God.

To understand the full intent of this particular passage, one must go back to the crime scene, like CSI does, and piece the puzzle together with a play-by-play of what the author conveys to the reader. Saul was not only arresting the men of the community of faith, he was also arresting the women. Like the men, the women had to run for their lives. When the scattering took place, it pertained to everyone who believed in Jesus, including children.

So, the men and women of the households of faith went everywhere they could, preaching the Word of God. Keep in mind this is after the Pentecost day experience that left the women empowered with a special and divine anointing after they went through the experience with the 120 in the upper room. As the Holy Bible tells it, they all prophesied (spoke with other tongues as the Spirit gave them utterance). If there is any confusion about what Word they preached, read Romans 10:8–10. Please be very careful of those who will try to add something the text does not support by saying things like, "Well, it's talking about only men who scattered and went out preaching the Word," or, "Women were forbidden to preach during this era." Neither of these arguments has any validity in the text or Holy Scriptures.

Men have to be careful not to become lifted up with pride by attempting to proclaim God's glory. Although God has given men ministers great authority and placed them in significant leadership roles in His kingdom; but He has not turned over the entire kingdom to them. Also, God has not given them the authority or responsibility to become the superior judge, jury, and enforcer of His principles, commandments, standards, and so on. It is the duty of the Holy Spirit to ensure that things are in order for God. The Spirit of God has the responsibility of assigning missions, jobs and accountability to humanity and not humanity having the power of assigning these things to the Holy Spirit. When things are not in order as God would have it, the Spirit of God will act on the part of God to make things right for God. Although the Holy Spirit calls on humans to act on its behalf, one must never lose fact the Holy Spirit is always in charge (Matthew 28:18-20; John 1:12-13; John 3:3-21; John 14:16-18; Romans 8:5-17; 2 Corinthians 3:16; 1 Timothy 1:9-20).

Moreover, when men try to deprive women of the opportunity to serve God based on gender, it is an action that may be rooted in pride. When men start walking in the pride of their own greed, lust, and interpretation, and not follow after the compassion of the Spirit of God, destruction waits around the corner to greet you and escort you to a miserable ending. I encourage as many of my brothers in the gospel ministry as possible to open their hearts and hear the voice of God before saying no to allowing women to exercise their gifts as ministers/preachers in their pulpits.

I foresee some churches that refuse to open their doors to women ministers being sued. Depending on their flexibility, some will end up losing their tax-exempt status because of discrimination and violations of the U.S. Constitution, the highest law in the land. I pray to God you get the message within this message. Today, in the world that we live in, nothing is guaranteed but the Word of God. I know legal experts will tell you churches are protected by the separation of church and state clause in the constitution, but it does not actually exist. All it takes to desecrate religious protection in this country is for a few Supreme Court justices to hate the church or have a bad taste in their mouths for religious rights and freedoms.

There are so many things we thought were protected by the U.S. Constitution, but in 2010, we saw things like the traditional marriage laws being ruled unconstitutional and enemy combatants being given the same legal protections and rights as American citizens. Some of our sacred traditions, values, and standards are being diminished before our very eyes. At one time there was no issue or confusion about what constituted a family, even if the mother or father was absent. Today we need to make sure we clearly understand what we are talking about when we use the term "family," because it is no longer necessarily a husband and wife or one managed by a single parent.

Men have to be careful they do not end up walking after the likeness of Herod by sitting upon their own thrones and making personal orations that entice people to lift themselves up as gods, eventually seeing themselves as a god over God's inheritance. Like Herod, when we interfere with creation especially when it is designed to give God the glory and honor by the preaching of the gospel, we could be treading on dangerous ground (Acts 12:21–24). Male ministers refusing to accept female ministers could be rejecting God's plan by denying the move of God in the lives of His people.

Women, I challenge and encourage you never to allow any man or any spirit to forbid you from accomplishing what God has commissioned you to do. Whatever you do, be true to God, lest you, too, end up before the angels of God for not giving God His divine glory. God has your scorecard, and Jesus is the only one with the authority to write on it. Jesus is the only one who can pass or fail you. Jesus is the only one who can train and equip you for the mission and the ministry.

I am still amazed how God and the holy angel came to the women and gave them the words to give to Jesus' disciples. As asked earlier in the book, why would God give such a significant mission to women if He did not want them to deliver His Word? Why did Jesus stop the women after the angels gave them the message to deliver to the disciples? Why would Jesus give them such a powerful message if they were not allowed to deliver or preach His words?

The fact Jesus gave the resurrection message to women breaks the mode of bigotry in God's eyes. As stated earlier, this message was probably one of the most important messages delivered to humanity, past, present, and future (Matthew 28:1–10). If we truly mean God is no respecter of persons, why is there such a big issue when it comes to women ministers, or when it comes to women ministers in your church (Acts 10:34)? If the pulpit is the realm where God operates in the life of the "pulpiteer," why do some pastors try to stand in God's way?

The Holy Bible teaches us that women had a very vital role in God's kingdom while Jesus ministered on the earth. Their loyal presence can be seen even at the crucifixion of Jesus. The women in Jesus' ministry were willing to continue serving Him even at the tomb during His death (Matthew 28:1–10). If women can humble themselves and serve at the feet of Jesus while He ministered on the earth, surely they have enough faith and loyalty to serve Him in the local church pulpits across this land. How long will women have to endure second-class treatment from men and women who parade themselves as advocates for justice and equal rights for all, but refuse to allow women in their pulpits as ministers?

According to Mark 15:40–41, there were faithful and fearless women, like Mary Magdalene and Mary, the mother of James and Joseph, who observed the devastating agony of Jesus' crucifixion from a distance. They never lost sight of the significance of one of the most precious moments in the history of the world: the slaying of the most innocent man to ever live.

The Holy Spirit let us know that women played a vital, major role in the ministry of Jesus from the dusty roads of Galilee all the way to the great capital city of Jerusalem, where God established His great throne on earth. It is fitting and safe to say women followed Jesus from His birth to His death. Once these devoted sisters decided to follow Jesus, they never looked back or deviated from the course Jesus had established for His church. There was no turning back. Unlike male disciples, there is no information indicating any of the women who followed Jesus ever betrayed, rebuked, doubted, or denied Him. Although they had to flee for their lives like the rest of the disciples, women disciples were never caught in embarrassing situations, unlike male disciples.

The Holy Scriptures espouse the fact there were many other women who gave their lives in the service of ministering to Jesus. As a special footnote, when women made a commitment to follow Jesus, there seem to be only a few examples in the Holy Bible where you actually witness women committing diabolical acts of denial, betrayal, or rejection against Jesus and the presence of the Holy Ghost. The women who followed Jesus were very loyal to the cause and the Man who gave His life for the entire world. What an unselfish and awesome act of humility on the part of Jesus. There is no example known to humanity of a greater love than what Jesus did for humankind past, present, and future.

In Acts Chapter 5, we witness a husband and wife team (Ananias and Sapphira) paying the ultimate price of death for their betrayal of the truth concerning the Holy Spirit. The husband and wife made the foolish decision to operate in the realm of deception rather than let the truth become their eternal guide in life. The Holy Spirit held the wife to the same standard as her husband. It is important to know God made no distinction between male and female when it came to loyal and committed service in His kingdom. As the Holy Scripture says, "Righteousness exalts a Nation, but sin is a reproach to any people" (Proverbs 14:34).

When women put their hands to the gospel plow, they usually do not look back. While male disciples were probably hiding from the Pharisees, Sadducees, Scribes, and Roman government out of fear of being killed by the same terrorists who murdered Jesus, the women were on their way to Jesus' tomb, perhaps with the idea and hope of still being of service to Him. Even at Jesus' death, the women never stop serving Him. They quickly made way to the tomb of Jesus, possibly to see if God had performed a miracle, especially after the earthquake greeted the morning before the sun could give its salutations.

Although Holy Scripture never says why the women were at Jesus' gravesite so early, it is safe to say it was part of God's plan. It was not a coincidence for the women to be the first from the family of God to behold the awesome beauty of Jesus after His resurrection. How could women receive the good news we all preach about ahead of the men?

How could God allow women to deliver such a powerful message to the male leaders of the church? How could God use women who were not virgins to carry such a pure and wholesome message to His congregation? You can only begin to answer these questions and many more when you begin to see women as vessels God uses in majestic ways, like any other part of creation God decides to use for His glory.

Christian Discipleship Has No Gender

Would you agree discipleship has the mission of going out and making new disciples by spreading the love of Jesus to others? As a tool or mechanism for positive change, a disciple will have a personal story to share about his or her relationship with Jesus. Good recruiters for the kingdom of God have wonderful stories of triumph to share with people, especially people recruiters (disciples) who are trying to win over souls to Jesus. Keep in mind that every Christian had to be delivered from some type of sin. Regardless of the size or magnitude of sin, all sin is deadly and leads to the same deadly hole beneath the earth. Every Christian had to have his or her shackles broken by God's ax, which is the Holy Spirit. Every Christian has to make a personal profession of faith in Jesus to receive deliverance and liberation from sin. No matter how big or small the sin, the process for salvation remains the same.

Furthermore, disciples are trained in a particular doctrine, philosophy, and belief. Make no mistake; disciples are very loyal to their beliefs, teachers, missions, and comrades. Other than Jesus Christ, probably all other renowned teachers and religious and political scholars throughout the world and history started as someone else's disciple. Jesus never sat under the tutelage of another Bible scholar except his mother and Almighty Father. The term "disciple" explains God is more concerned about a person's soul than He is about a person's gender. God is more concerned about one's obedience to His commandments than his or her gender identification.

Moreover, under God's grace, gender has nothing to do with determining how or to what extent God will use a person in His kingdom. Under the law, gender was a discriminator. But under the period when God's grace reigns supreme, gender has no vote. Under the law, gender was used to isolate, but under grace, the gender card has no case in trying to stop you as a woman minister, with the zeal and desire to excel in ministry. Whether male or female, Jesus will give all His preachers of the gospel the opportunity to render a pleasing harvest to the great Savior of the world (Matthew 25:14–30).

In Acts Chapter 9, the Holy Scripture makes it every clear that a disciple named Tabitha was sick unto death. She had become bedridden and was in dire need of a miracle from God. It was Tabitha's faithful commitment to God and His saints that gave her favor with God and among the people in her community. God's favor supersedes the rituals and laws of humanity. It extends beyond personal boundaries and hidden agendas of humanity. God's favor is all you need to excel in life. Obedience to God is the beginning step in obtaining favor with God.

When Tabitha became ill, the local congregation sent for the chief apostle of the Christian movement to come and pray for Tabitha's healing. When the apostle Peter got word of how Tabitha committed her life to the service of the kingdom of God and the saints in the local congregation, Peter came to Tabitha's side. God's anointing met Peter with a blessing at the house where she lay. The moral to the story is Tabitha was miraculously healed, and the saints received a gift from God. Amen.

The Cost of Christian Discipleship

When we speak of the cost of Christian discipleship, we are attempting to forecast some of the things you may encounter on the battlefield as you serve as a warrior for King Jesus. As a disciple for the Lord, you must understand the kingdom of God is at war with the Evil One, who has a mission of dethroning God and elevating himself to the highest tower in the entire world, the throne of God. Although the Devil knows there is no possibility for him to defeat God or Jesus, he is foolish enough to try and fight against God's plan, like extremist terrorists fight to destroy the West, Israel, and Jews.

In the gospel as recorded in Matthew 10:24–42, the Holy Bible prepares Christians for battle by allowing the Holy Spirit to penetrate the hearts, minds, and souls of believers. When the words of God are obeyed and practiced during the Christian's daily walk with Jesus, he or she begins to walk in the favor of God. Reading and living out God's principles allows the true believer to personally experience a real-life scenario on the battlefield. The Holy Spirit lays out a vivid map with many of the obstacles Christians will encounter as disciples for Jesus.

In the previous passage, we must never forget the words of Jesus when He warned us that when a person surrenders and becomes His disciple, he or she needs to understand and prepare for war because although He is called the Prince of Peace, Jesus did not come to bring peace on earth. Instead he brought a sword, which represents war, struggle, and conflict. Although Jesus says He did not come to bring peace on earth, however, He did come to bring peace in our souls, spirits, and minds.

In the New Testament, the gospel as recorded in Luke 14:25–35, Jesus explains the serious commitment and hardship one will endure if he or she decides to become one of His true disciples. Jesus lays the foundation, so people will not have any doubt about His expectations for discipleship into the kingdom of God. It is a rigorous and dangerous journey that may require isolating or breaking off some relationships we deem valuable and necessary for our happiness, but could be a distraction or disruption for your entrance and service into the kingdom of God. As true disciples for Jesus, we need to decide in our minds and hearts what things in life are more important than the calling of Jesus. If Jesus is the most essential thing in life's journey, what is the cost of letting go of something that may distract you from listening to and obeying the Holy Spirit?

Believe me, God knows better than anyone what a person needs in his or her life to fulfill His divine mission. One of the hardest things for people to do while serving on the mission field for the Lord is to relinquish things you think you need or think are important to you. The quicker you understand some things and people in your life were not meant to go where God is leading you, the better off you will be for the Christian battlefield. Trust that God knows what is best for you.

Many people are willing to follow Jesus until He outlines the rules of discipleship. In Luke 14:25–35, Jesus is followed by a great multitude of people. Many in the crowd were sinners. As Jesus assessed the crowd and knew the things they were seeking, He turned to the crowd and shared with them the serious cost of Christian discipleship. As you read the text, please do not get lost in the word "hate," because Jesus is not telling you to hate anyone, because God is the God of love and not hate. The Holy Bible describes the attributes of God as love and goes as far to say God Himself is love (1 John 4:7–8).

Furthermore, in 1 John 3:18, the Holy Bible tells us to love each other in deeds and not only in word or what we speak with the tongue. We know God does not preach or teach hate, because the Holy Bible teaches that God so loved the world that He gave His only begotten Son to save the world from the destruction of sin and hate. Sin breeds hate, and love forces hate to dissipate. When you walk into an environment, you can nearly always determine if love or hate is center stage in the place. Love and hate are so powerful and so different that you never get them confused, unless they are disguised under a different umbrella. Sooner or later you will find out the true color of the umbrella and everything under it.

Think of what Jesus says to us in Luke 14:26 this way: "If a person comes as my disciple but is not willing to accept me over his father, mother, wife, children, brothers, and sisters, even over his or her own life, this person cannot be the disciple of Jesus." Jesus is letting us know He must rule as supreme ruler in our lives, and we cannot allow anyone to get in the way of our relationship with Him. Jesus is telling us when it comes down to serving God over the wishes and desires of those we love, God has to be our first love. Jesus is letting us know our love for Him supersedes our love for anyone or anything else. Jesus wants us to be clear about His expectations and the cost of Christian discipleship. It is like no other discipleship training because it is the way, the truth, and the life, and let us not forget about the light, which lead to Jesus, the only begotten Son of God.

Jesus reminds His disciples their journeys will involve persecution and hardship, and each of us must be willing to bear our cross. In the beginning, Christian discipleship can be a very difficult process. However, once someone makes up his or her mind that he or she is willing to die for the kingdom of God, the process is no longer about trying to please people who have no bearing on your life or the decisions you make. The entire process now becomes about our total commitment to Jesus, which includes the mission of proclaiming good news to the world. Whether people listen or not is not our duty; we are left with the task of preaching and teaching the good news. It is up to the hearers of the Word of God to receive the gospel of Jesus Christ.

Jesus demands we bear a cross, regardless of the difficulties that come along with it. Jesus demands we follow Him, regardless of where He leads us. Although life may throw you curveballs, Jesus wants you to be true to your commitment to follow Him. You will encounter some storms and setbacks in life, but do not allow anything to make you lose your anchor in Jesus. The glory and victory is worth following Jesus all the way to the end.

It is imperative we never lose sight of Jesus, even though we may get caught up in the various storms in life, He must always be our sure anchor. When we remain a true disciple of Jesus, God will come to our rescue, regardless of the situations we encounter while following Jesus. Christian discipleship means we must continue to trust and keep our eyes on Jesus, even if storms rage around us. A Christian disciple must always remember no storm has ever consumed Jesus. It is impossible for any storm to overwhelm God because He is the storm maker and storm dissipater, all at the same time.

If you continue to walk with Jesus, the battle has already been won. God is just waiting on you to shout for joy. Liberation in Jesus always calls for a moment of rejoicing and celebration, with vivid signs of outward expressions as the Spirit gives utterance (Acts 2:4). I charge you to stand boldly for the things that are right and just in the eyes of God and not for the approval rating of humanity. Christian churches should never allow the practice of discrimination to exist on the basis of a woman's gender. Where is the love of God when telling a female minister she could not become a preacher because of her sex?

Finally, women you have to, under the guidance of the Holy Spirit, push for change to come within churches across America and the world. You have to play a major role by letting church leaders know you will no longer sit silently and allow church leader to promote a caste system based on gender inequality within churches and denominations across America and the world. Women, if you do not speak out louder than anyone else in the world, then who will shout for you? The day is now and the time is ripe for women and women ministers to stand together and demand your seats as ministers of the gospel of Jesus Christ at the table of love. The Holy Spirit has already ordained it for you to stand boldly against the Devil's 'henchmen' and preach the gospel. So, my encouragement to you is to Preach, My Sister Preach until Jesus comes! Amen.

You Can't Make Me a Slave

You can steal me from my homeland against my will,
But you still can't make me a *slave*.

You can imprison me and lock me in your dark dungeons of despair,
But you still can't make me a *slave*.

You can treat me with hate and try to control my eternal fate,
But you can't make me a *slave*.

You can beat me, cheat me, and even kill me,
But you still can't make me a *slave*.

You can separate me from my family and sell us like animals,
But you still can't make me a *slave*.

You can take my rights and freedom with unjust laws,
But you still can't make me a *slave*.

You may try to poison my mind with your lies and deceit,
But I will never surrender to your defeat;
You can't ever make me a *slave*.

I will forever fight for truth and freedom;
You can't make me a *slave*.

Printed in the United States
By Bookmasters